Muslim Childhood

Muslim Childhood

Religious Nurture
in a European Context

Jonathan Scourfield, Sophie Gilliat-Ray,
Asma Khan, and Sameh Otri

OXFORD
UNIVERSITY PRESS

OXFORD
UNIVERSITY PRESS

Great Clarendon Street, Oxford, OX2 6DP,
United Kingdom

Oxford University Press is a department of the University of Oxford.
It furthers the University's objective of excellence in research, scholarship,
and education by publishing worldwide. Oxford is a registered trade mark of
Oxford University Press in the UK and in certain other countries

© Jonathan Scourfield, Sophie Gilliat-Ray, Asma Khan, and Sameh Otri 2013

The moral rights of the authors have been asserted

First Edition published in 2013

Impression: 1

Published in the United States of America by Oxford University Press
198 Madison Avenue, New York, NY 10016, United States of America

British Library Cataloguing in Publication Data
Data available

ISBN 978-0-19-960031-1

As printed and bound by
CPI Group (UK) Ltd, Croydon, CR0 4YY

Contents

List of Figures

List of Tables

Acknowledgements

Our thanks go first and foremost to the families who generously agreed to take part in the research and invited us into their homes. Thanks too to the Muslim organizations in Cardiff which have helped us conduct and disseminate the research. The project was funded by the Religion and Society programme, jointly sponsored by the Arts and Humanities Research Council and the Economic and Social Research Council (AH/F00897X/1). Thanks to Chris Taylor for Figure 3.1.

Some of the material in Chapters 2 and 3 has been revised from previously published papers:

Scourfield, J., Taylor, C., Moore, G., and Gilliat-Ray, S. (2012). The intergenerational transmission of Islam: evidence from the Citizenship Survey. *Sociology* 46(1): 91–108 (published by Sage).

Khan, A., Scourfield, J., Gilliat-Ray, S., and Otri, S. (2012). Reflections on qualitative research with Muslim families. *Fieldwork in Religion* 7(1): 48–69 (published by Equinox).

Glossary of Islamic Terms

Note on Glossary

There are places in the text where an Arabic word or phrase is used once only and a translation is provided, either in the text or in a footnote. These words and phrases do not appear in the glossary, which covers instead terms which are used more than once in the book.

Note on Transliteration from Arabic

The spelling used by Esposito (2003) has been employed. For simplicity, diacritics have been omitted, except in Qur'an, where the use of a diacritic is widely accepted. Italicization is used for common nouns in Arabic, except where these are now in common usage in contemporary UK English (hijab). We have followed conventional scholarly practice in not italicizing proper nouns (e.g. Qur'an and Eid).

adhan: ritual call to prayer

alim: religious scholar

Allah: God

aqiqah: birth ritual involving animal sacrifice and distribution of money to the poor

asr: third compulsory daily prayer, in the afternoon

Barelwi: sub-school of thought—probably the largest single group of UK Muslims and especially prevalent amongst South Asians.

dua: Supplicatory prayer

Deobandi: Indo-Pakistani reformist movement

Eid: generic term for religious festival in Islam

Eid al-Adha: festival celebrating the end of the annual pilgrimage to Mecca (Hajj)

Eid al-Fitr: festival celebrating the end of fasting (Ramadan)

fajr: first compulsory daily prayer, before sunrise

fard: compulsory

hadith: sayings of the Prophet Muhammad

hafiz: one who has memorized the Qur'an

Hajj: pilgrimage to Mecca

halal: Quranic term used to indicate what is lawful or permitted

haram: legal term for what is forbidden under Islamic law

hifz class: where one learns to become a *hafiz* (see above)

hijab: head, face or body covering for Muslim women

iqamah: summons to prayer

isha: last compulsory daily prayer, at night

inshallah: God willing (when speaking about future events)

Islamic Movement: a current of thought that aims toward the political and social mobilization of Muslims based on Islamic sources

jannah: paradise

jelbaab: long, loose-fitting garment

jinn: spirits

khitan: circumcision

madhhab (plural, *madhahib*): one of the schools of Sunni Islamic law

madrasah: institution for advanced religious learning

maktab: institution for elementary religious learning

mashallah: 'God has willed it'

namaz: ritual prayer (*salat*); term originally Persian but used in other Asian languages

Ramadan: month of fasting

Salafi: reformist movement calling for a return to the pure roots of Islam

salat: Arabic term for compulsory daily prayer, performed five times a day

Shaitan: Satan

shaykh: spiritual teacher

Shia: one of the two main Islamic sects. Shia Muslims believe Muhammad's religious authority was passed on to his descendants.

sirah: Narrative history of the Prophet Muhammad's life

sunnah: example of the Prophet Muhammad

Sunni: the largest of the two main Islamic sects worldwide (and in the UK)

surah: chapter of the Qur'an

tahnik: touching the lips of a newborn baby with a sweet substance

Ummah: worldwide Muslim community

wudu: ritual cleansing prior to worship

zuhr: second compulsory daily prayer of the day, at noon

1

Islam and Middle Childhood

To many people, a typical British child in the primary school years may spend her time, when not in school, playing computer games, watching television, playing with toys or playing outside (though not enough of that, many would think) but she does not read religious texts, or learn a classical language she is unlikely to ever converse in, and does not have a strong sense of the presence of God. We begin the book on this note, because this is probably the main reason why the religious upbringing of Muslim children should be of interest to non-Muslims. There is a risk that any idea of 'typical' childhood falls into stereotyping of course, but the idea of a child being socialized into a monotheistic world view from birth and then, when old enough, attending classes several times a week to learn to read the Qur'an in classical Arabic is certainly outside the mainstream of secular Western childhood.

Although it is about the specific topic of the religious upbringing of Muslim children, the book tackles some questions of wider interest. How do we learn to be religious? To make sense of this process should we emphasize the habitual reinforcement of bodily rituals or the active role of individuals in making decisions about faith at key moments? Or should we turn to cognitive science to explain the universal structures on which religiosity is built? And how does a relatively devout minority pass on religion in a generally secular Western context? What significance does religion have for family life in this situation? And how does a religious identity interact with other kinds of collective identification, for example with a nation, ethnic group or a locality?

Olivier Roy (2004: 8) has noted that there is a 'glaring need' for studies of ordinary Muslims because, as he puts it, 'the key question is not what the Qur'an says, but what Muslims say the Qur'an says' (Roy, 2004: 10). This book is about ordinary British Muslims' everyday religious socialization of children in early and middle childhood. It provides a detailed description of how Muslim families in a secular Western context attempt to pass on their faith to the next generation. Most of the book is rooted in detailed qualitative research with a relatively large sample (for a qualitative project) of 60 Muslim families in one British city. The families whose stories appear in the book are diverse in terms of ethnicity, language, social class and 'school of thought'.[1] There is therefore depth in the data but also breadth of social location. The book includes children's own perspectives, but also a considerable amount of data from parents as well. Our own analysis of survey data, presented in Chapter 2, suggests that Muslims in the UK more effectively pass on their faith to the next generation than other religious groups. This book is in part an attempt to explain why that might be.

After an explanation of how we understand 'everyday lived religion', this first chapter begins with an introduction to Islam in the UK, with material about the history of Muslims in Britain, the key demographics of the Muslim population and the cultural context of Islam in the UK in the 21st century. The second major section describes the wider social and cultural context of secularization and discusses the role of religious transmission in this context. The third section introduces theories which have explained how religion is learned, with particular mention of cognitive science, *habitus*, minority defence and the role of religious organizations. The fourth main section of the chapter introduces the study of childhood and the fifth explains some of the terminology used in connection with children's learning of religion. Finally, a sixth main section summarizes the traditions of religious nurture in Islam. Although primarily sociological, the book will be informed by inter-disciplinary debates and there will be reference from time to time to concepts from psychology and anthropology.

A Note on Everyday Lived Religion

In recent years, there has been a developing academic interest in everyday religion (Ammerman, 2007) and lived religion (McGuire, 2008). Attention to the place of religion in everyday life is, arguably, nothing new within anthropology, where the ethnographic method depends on the immersion of a researcher in the ordinary routines of a community.

[1] A broad definition is used in the book to capture different Islamic traditions in the UK, which is probably home to the world's most diverse Muslim population (Institute of Community Cohesion, 2008). Our use of the term refers both to formal Schools of Thought (*madhahib*) and also to movements within Islam.

However, within sociology there has perhaps been less research on what goes on outside of religious organizations (Cadge et al., 2011). We have attempted with the qualitative research featured in this book to encompass the mundane routines of everyday life, beyond the formal occasions of collective worship and religious festivals. Religious organizations are discussed (see Chapter 5), but the bulk of the research took place in the family home and not the mosque. It would be mistake, however, to separate out mundane, everyday, routine religious practice from what people believe and from the life of religious organizations, since these different domains depend on each other (Woodhead, 2012).

Therefore in the book we 'major' on the place of Islam in everyday childhood. In order to understand everyday religious nurture we need to look at family routines and family homes. We also need to consider the wider social context of children's lives in school and their social networks. We need to keep belief in mind as well as practice and part of what parents and children believe is what kind of collective identities are appropriate. This question includes the possible intersection of religious identity with nationality or ethnicity. And the role of religious organizations cannot be ignored. This is especially so for Islam when there are important traditions of formal learning via mosque schools or respected local teachers. The qualitative empirical chapters (4–8) therefore cover all these aspects.

Woodhead (2011) has recently written an impressive overview of the study of religion, identifying five different uses of the term 'religion' in the social sciences. Of the five concepts that Woodhead outlines, our approach comes closest to what she calls 'religion as practice', with an emphasis on ritual, embodiment and the quotidian. We return to Woodhead's paper in concluding the book, however, since we argue that multiple concepts are needed to understand religious nurture.

Muslim Communities in Britain

It is often assumed that the presence of Muslims in Britain is a relatively recent phenomenon, confined almost entirely to the post-Second World War period. This is far from the case; the British Isles have a long history of both temporary and more permanent settlement by Muslims (Gilliat-Ray, 2010). Although the decades after 1945 were certainly distinctive in terms of the *scale* of Muslim settlement in Britain, historical records indicate that Muslims have been coming to the British Isles as traders, students, seafarers, and explorers from as early as the 9th century (Ansari, 2004). However, many of these early Muslims coming to Britain were transient settlers, and they were usually unaccompanied single men who eventually returned to their countries of origin. It is questionable as to whether they would have regarded themselves as 'Muslims in Britain' in any meaningful sense, such was the temporary character of their residence in most cases. Furthermore, over the centuries there have been important changes in both the self-description and identity of Muslims in Britain, as well as changes in the way they have been perceived and described by others. For example, terms such as 'Mohammadans', 'Moors', 'Saracens' are now recognized as antiquated and disrespectful, while in the later decades of the 20th century, British Muslims themselves began to place less emphasis on their ethnic origins (e.g. as 'Pakistanis'), stressing instead their distinctive identity as 'Muslims'. These changes in ascribed and assumed identity sometimes mask the significance of a distinctive and well-established Muslim religious presence in the UK.

From the late 19th century, a distinct Anglo-Muslim community began to evolve in Britain, stimulated by Britain's colonial links, and especially those with the Indian sub-continent. The first registered mosque was established in Liverpool in 1887 and, later, the first purpose-built mosque was founded in 1889 in Woking, Surrey. The maritime port cities of South Shields, Cardiff and Liverpool were especially important at the turn of the 20th century. Muslim seafarers, especially from the Yemen, Somalia, and India, were recruited to work on colonial shipping routes. Having completed their passage on one ship, they would reside in dockland boarding houses, awaiting work on the next outbound vessel. But some of these seafarers became permanent residents in Britain, and the first embryonic 'British Muslim' communities were established in or near these port cities.

If the availability of employment was a determining factor influencing where these early Muslims settled in Britain in the 19th century, much the same can be said about the post-Second World War period also. With the need to re-develop towns and cities damaged by the War, and the expansion of manufacturing industries in the 1950s and 1960s, there was a demand for unskilled and semi-skilled factory workers. Britain looked to those countries with which it had colonial ties in order to meet the labour shortages. As a consequence, many relatively poor, uneducated migrant labourers came to Britain, especially from the Indian sub-continental countries of Pakistan, Bangladesh, and India. They were once again mainly single men and, like many of their earlier seafaring counterparts, they envisaged a time when they would return to their countries of origin. Having earned the social status and economic wealth associated with temporary migration to Britain, they looked forward to eventually returning home. This intention meant that relatively little was invested in a long-term future in Britain.

Being a Muslim in Britain at this time was therefore primarily a matter of belonging to a particular ethnic group or kinship network. Referring to this generation of South Asians, Anshuman Mondal has noted:

> ...for many Muslims of the older generation, the observance of Islam was less about piety and more to do with participation in communal life. Whether sincerely undertaken or not, the performance of rituals, the attendance at mosques and the undertaking of fasting during Ramadan were aspects of a social life which established a semblance of community for the older generation of South Asian migrants, and the dense network of relationships that such activities helped to sustain would provide them the stability and support they needed in an unfamiliar environment. It seems that this *collective* observance is what motivated the older generations in their adherence to Islam rather than any particular sense of personal religiosity. (Mondal, 2008: 4–5)

Important legislative changes in the 1960s and 1970s had a dramatic impact on the nature of Muslim settlement in Britain. The new legislation was designed to place strict limits on further large-scale immigration to Britain. This meant that among those Muslims already in the UK, the new policies were seen as obstacles to any possible reunification of families. In order to 'beat the ban' of the new immigration laws, many South Asian men in Britain sent for their wives and children from their villages and towns in the Indian sub-continent, to join them in the UK. Although permanent family settlement was not intended as a result of the arrival of women and children, it was an inevitable consequence. As children were born and educated in Britain, more time, energy and resources were invested in the development of community facilities, especially those that would support the religious identity and wellbeing of the new British-born generation. Some of the first institutions established by Muslims in the 1960s and 1970s were therefore independent schools, and mosques that incorporated religious instruction for children. With their construction came the 'myth of return' to homelands (Anwar, 1979), which meant that any serious intention to actually return became illusory. However, transnational links back to extended family members in countries of origin remained important for many British Muslims (and remain so today), and these ties are sustained through the continued practice of contracting marriages with relatives from 'back home', continuing to send financial remittances, holidays, and receiving visiting relatives and friends.

Alongside South Asian Muslim settlement in Britain, Muslims from other parts of the world have also made Britain their home. During the 1980s and 1990s, economic and political unrest in some parts of the world meant that Britain was an attractive destination for educated and professional Iranians, Arabs, Kurds, Turks, and those fleeing situations of persecution in Bosnia, Somalia, Uganda, and other African states. So during the later decades of the 20th century, the ethnic composition of British Muslims diversified considerably, and towns and cities with existing Muslim communities, especially London, provided obvious places to settle and to build new lives. These patterns of migration have influenced, and continue to influence today, the demography, the internal diversity, and the socio-economic circumstances of Muslim communities in Britain.

Adding to this diversity is the growing community of converts to Islam in Britain. Conversion to Islam by those of many different ethnic backgrounds (but mainly white British and African-Caribbean) is significant, not from a numerical perspective, but more because of the 'disproportionate contribution [they] can make to the indigenization of Islamic practice, thought and discourse in the West' (Zebiri, 2008: 1). It is difficult to estimate the number of converts to Islam in Britain today, but recent research puts the figure at around 100,000 (Brice, 2010). The reasons for conversion continue to fascinate journalists, research students, and to some extent 'born' Muslims themselves, who often take particular pride and delight in a new Muslim joining the worldwide Muslim community (the Ummah).

During the latter decades of the 20th century, statistical information about the number, ethnicity, or employment of Muslims in Britain was dependent upon speculation and intelligent guesswork. But in 2001 a question about 'religion' was included in the Census for the first time since 1851. The mere inclusion of this question was largely a consequence of lobbying by British Muslim organizations over many years, concerned that their religious identity should be regarded as a defining characteristic of their self-understanding, and a meaningful category of difference affecting their socio-economic situation (Sherif, 2011; Peach, 2006). As soon as the Census data were analysed and made public, it became clear that many British Muslims were seriously affected by a range of socio-economic disadvantages, each compounding the others. Compared to all other faith communities in Britain, the Census data revealed the vulnerable position of Muslims in relation to housing, education, employment, health, and so on (Hussain, 2008). The cumulative effect of these difficulties means that today, many British Muslims tend to reside in the most deprived areas of the UK, live in overcrowded homes of poor quality, and experience higher levels of ill-health compared to other faith communities. However, the basic statistical information gathered through the Census and subsequence government surveys has provided policy-makers with evidence that might provide strategies for alleviating this urban poverty in the longer term.

The very first 2011 census data on religion in England and Wales were published just as this book was going to press. However, Scottish census data have not yet been published, so for the British or UK Muslim population we need to turn to other sources. According to Labour Force Survey data gathered in 2009, there are approximately 2.4 million Muslims in Britain, and about two thirds are of South Asian (Pakistani, Bangladeshi, Indian) origin. Since 2009, the Pew report *The Future of the Global Muslim Population: Projections for 2010–2030* has been published, which places the number of Muslims in Britain at 2.8 million and 4.6% of the UK population (<http://features.pewforum.org/FutureGlobal-MuslimPopulation-WebPDF.pdf>; accessed 19 June 2012). This figure is regarded as slightly inflated by UK-based statisticians working on faith communities (<http://www.brin.ac.uk>), but it is clear that the Muslim population is increasing markedly, largely due to the higher rates of fertility within Muslim communities in Britain (approximately 3.0 children per Muslim woman in 2005–10 compared to 1.8 children per woman in the non-Muslim population). However, despite the population growth, Muslim fertility is in overall decline, and the gap with non-Muslims is narrowing. This is projected to continue to 2030.

What is notable, however, in the quantitative data regarding Muslim communities in Britain is the relative youthfulness of this population group. Approximately half of all Muslims in Britain are under the age of twenty-five and, by now, about half have been born in the UK itself. In contrast, only 5% of Muslims in Britain are over the age of sixty, compared to 20% in the rest of the population. This explains the greater rates of fertility; a disproportionately high number of Muslims are either in, or entering, the prime years for child-bearing. However, because of the migration patterns outlined above, Muslims have tended to be located in particular cities and neighbourhoods, and in some places they may constitute up to 36% of the local population (for example, in Tower Hamlets, East London). Thus, Muslim population growth is not evenly distributed around the UK. The average household size for Muslims in 2001 was 3.8, compared to the national average of 2.4, and about a third of Muslim homes contain five or more people (Hussain, 2008). The publication of detailed findings from the 2011 Census will obviously update these figures.

Many of the South Asian Muslims who came to Britain for work in the post-war period were from poor, rural areas and they had rarely received any formal education. Although this generalization masks important variations and exceptions, on the whole they arrived in Britain with relatively little social or material capital beyond their kinship networks. All this has had consequences for later generations. While some families have actively encouraged educational achievement as a means for improving their prosperity and social status in the future, it remains the case that not all families have had the knowledge or resources to enable this process to happen effectively. Therefore, educational underachievement remains a challenge within Muslim communities, and rates of economic inactivity remain higher, compared to all other faith groups (Hussain, 2008).

To some extent, however, higher levels of economic inactivity are due to the fact that compared to other faith groups, Muslim women are less likely to be in paid employment. This partly reflects the decision that many British Muslim women make that their primary role and responsibility is motherhood. Islam accords a high degree of respect to the status of mothers and numerous Quranic verses and *hadith* (sayings of the Prophet Muhammad) allude to the important role that mothers have as those who nurture and educate future generations. This does not mean that Muslim women who are mothers are confined to this role alone, however. Muslim communities in Britain still need female doctors and teachers, for example, and those who fulfil such roles are often doing so alongside their other domestic responsibilities. But still, the significance of motherhood is strongly affirmed within Islamic traditions, as we shall see in due course.

What becomes apparent from this brief overview of Muslim history, settlement, and demographics, is that it is difficult to speak about a 'Muslim community' in Britain. Instead, it is better to regard British Muslims as part of diverse linguistic, ethnic, racial, and geographically dispersed *communities* that retain strong transnational kinship links around the globe, as well as an abiding sense of identification with the worldwide Muslim population (the Ummah). Some have argued that Muslims living as minorities in the West are in fact uniquely placed to contribute to international debate about the meaning and significance of Islam in the contemporary world:

> Muslims living in the non-Islamic West face an unparalleled opportunity. Theirs is a promising exile: a freedom of thought, action, and inquiry unknown in the contemporary Muslim world...those who can break free from the inertial ties of national and ethnic personas will be the ones who will forge an Islamicity hitherto unexperienced. (Haider, 1996: 77)

Because of the relative youthfulness of Muslim communities in Britain (and other Western societies), they are well-placed to use and benefit from the growth of media technologies, used as part of these international debates. Reformist ideas originating in the Islamic world in the 19th and 20th centuries are being contested and evaluated in new circumstances and settings. Consequently and inevitably therefore, traditional forms of religious authority are now being challenged, re-imagined, re-framed, and democratized as Muslims seek 'authentic' ways of being Muslim that are meaningful and consonant with their new context (Cesari 2004). Above all, perhaps, Muslims living in the West have new opportunities to exercise individual choice regarding religious observance; the matter of religious upbringing and nurture is not necessarily taken for granted because Islam is not part of the dominant social norms of society. But being part of transnational networks comprising such things as missionary organizations, religious entrepreneurs, and mystical/Sufi movements, British Muslims have access to a wide range of resources from which to make choices about the place of Islam in the West, and the religious upbringing of their children.

Secularization and Religious Transmission

'God is dead', Bruce (2002) declares provocatively in the title of his overview of the secularization debate. The issue of whether or not we are experiencing increased secularization has been the staple diet for sociologists of religion for quite some time. Indeed the issue was a preoccupation for the earliest sociologists, as the recent review by Demerath (2007) demonstrates. The core idea of the classic statement about secularization, as expressed by Bryan Wilson, for example (see Davie, 2007) is of the decline in religion's significance for the social system. Various explanations have been given for this decline, including the pluralistic nature of modernity (Berger, 1967), individualism and rationality (Bruce, 1996).

It is a controversial field of study, with a range of positions being set out. In the UK, the main fault lines of recent secularization debates lie between those who emphasize decline in affiliation to formal religious organizations and those who point to the apparent continuing importance of some level of religious or spiritual belief and occasional use of religious ceremonies (Heelas and Woodhead, 2005). Davie (1994) is in the latter camp, having coined the phrase 'believing without belonging' to describe the continuing importance of religion in Britain despite the decline in attendance at worship. Voas and Crockett (2005) have taken issue with Davie and have robustly argued on the basis of data from the British Household Panel Survey and British Social Attitudes Survey that there is absolute decline in belief as well as practice over time and across generations.

Several authors have noted that patterns of secularization vary between countries. Martin (2005) emphasizes that there are different trajectories according to, for example, political regimes and the modes of the insertion of religion into the host society. Berger (1999) has used the term 'desecularization' to emphasize that in global terms religion is flourishing, arguing that with some exceptions (notably Europe), the world today 'is as furiously religious as it ever was, and in some places more so than ever' (p. 2). The evidence base for debates about secularization has its limitations. Chambers (2006) has argued that much of the secularization literature about Western countries only considers the majority population and is therefore focused on the decline in Christianity and does not consider whether or not there is secularization in minority religions.

If there is a process of secularization, this is in part due to the failure of the inter-generational transmission of religion. It is difficult to separate these two domains—secularization and transmission. To understand secularization we need to consider what is happening to religious transmission, and the rate and strength of religious transmission can only be properly understood in a historical context of social change (Hervieu-Léger, 1998).

It is usually assumed that the family environment is crucial for the passing on of religion. As Voas (2003: 94) puts it, '... people may come to religion at any age, but religious fertility is the most important component of growth in the long term' (by 'religious fertility', Voas means 'religious reproduction through initiation of children' [p. 94]). Much research in this field assumes the primacy of family socialization for the successful transmission of religion. There may be enquiry into the difference between the roles of fathers, mothers and grandparents or the impact of different kinds of parent–child relationship on the rate and strength of religious transmission but within these studies the primary importance of the family is not questioned (see, for example, Hayes and Pittelkow, 1993; Bengtson et al., 2009). Some researchers, however, have challenged any assumption that children are subject to passive socialization from parents, describing the transmission process as bi-directional or transactional rather than uni-directional (e.g. Pinquart and Silbereisen, 2004). Yet others have focused on the importance of peers or religious organizations to religious socialization, in addition to the family (Schwartz et al., 2006; Hoge et al., 1982).

10

Furthermore, some sociologists would emphasize the profound changes in the cultural climate of religious socialization in late modernity, noting the implications of these changes for our understanding of religious transmission. Woodhead (2010), for example, sees contemporary research on young people's religiosity as revealing the myriad influences they are subject to, including real and virtual social networks and a climate where 'the done thing is no longer the done thing' (p. 239). From these research insights she concludes it cannot be that children primarily learn religion from their parents. Guest (2009), however, argues that the process of religious transmission cannot be characterized by a crude conformity/rebellion dichotomy but rather it involves a complex interplay of tradition and individualization, with young people sometimes choosing conformity ('a "soft" individualism' [p. 663]) as seen in the work of Smith (2005).

Boyatzis et al. (2006), in a recent review of the field, have noted that the existing published research on inter-generational religious transmission tends to be based on largely white, Christian samples. Religious transmission in minority ethnic communities may be a very different phenomenon than in the ethnic majority population and understanding the process may require some distinctive theoretical insights. Martin (2005), for example, notes that just as globalization and increasing diversity can potentially lead to reactive re-assertion of religious identity amongst majority populations, so too can the experience of being in a minority lead to an affirmation of difference. Bruce (1996) robustly promotes the secularization thesis, but nonetheless acknowledges that when ethnic identity is threatened, for example, in the context of migration, religion can provide a resource for helping people to navigate this challenging situation. These authors are not the first to note the distinctive role that religion can play in relation to minority ethnicity. In his classic sociological study of religion in 1950s America, Will Herberg (1955: 30) cited Hansen's 'principle of third-generation interest'. This is the idea that religion can provide important answers to questions about identity and belonging for those twice-removed from the migration experience:

> What the son wishes to forget the grandson wishes to remember. But what he can remember is obviously not his grandfather's foreign culture; it is rather his grandfather's religion. (Herberg, 1955: 64)

More recent evidence has problematized Herberg's conclusions; Cadge and Ecklund (2007: 361) note that the relationship between religion and ethnicity is 'considerably more complex among immigrants in each generation'. Pluss (2009) argues that there are complex processes of migrants adapting religion to a host country whilst also maintaining common beliefs and practices with co-religionists in other locations. She notes that these processes have become more complex in an era of cultural and economic globalization. Despite this, Herberg's ideas remain interesting and relevant to minority religions in the context of migration.

When considering religious affiliation in contemporary Britain, Crockett and Voas (2006) observe that minority ethnic people are more religious than the white population. Despite this, they assert that the inter-generational decline in the religious practice of the minority ethnic population is broadly similar to that of the white majority. They base this claim on the Fourth National Survey of Ethnic Minorities (see Modood et al., 1997) and on data about attendance at a place of worship. They conclude that the effect of ethnic minorities on British religion 'may be to slow and delay decline but not reverse it, unless there is a very substantial increase in immigration' (p. 581). Although the data Crockett and Voas present do indeed show religious decline in all ethnic groups, their general thesis of generational decline across the board masks the variation between minority ethnic groups in patterns of religious transmission that their own analyses show. It is worth noting that they do acknowledge the possibility that since the Fourth National Survey of Ethnic Minorities was conducted in 1993–4 there may have been a return to religious practice amongst young Muslims. Most young British Muslims are of South Asian origin and their grandparents came to Britain in the 1960s and 1970s. A return to religiosity in this group would fit with Herberg's thesis.

Religiosity in late modernity is said to be changing in a number of ways. The authority of religious institutions is undoubtedly weakening in Western countries (Hervieu-Léger, 2000). This does not, however, mean we are experiencing a straightforward secularization. There is some evidence that spirituality and a subjectivist sense of personal well-being may be gaining in significance in the UK, for example (Heelas and Woodhead, 2005). Whilst this trend may well be emerging in the general (and mostly white) British population, the concept of individual spirituality is not traditionally associated with mainstream Islam— Sufism being the obvious exception—since faith and moral obedience, belief and behaviour, are intimately linked (Kemp, 1996). However, Roy (2004) has argued that in the West, in the context of a crisis in religious authority and a general climate of individualization, 'ordinary believers must find their own way to be more or less good Muslims' (p. 152). Whether practical Islam as played out in family interactions is individualized and encompassing subjectivist notions of spirituality in late modern Britain is a central issue addressed in the book.

The term 'individualization' refers to the process described most notably by Ulrich Beck and Anthony Giddens by which in late modernity we are expected to be choose our route through life; what Giddens (1991) terms 'reflexive life-planning'. Whereas in a more straightforward and less 'runaway' world (Giddens, 2002), people might have unquestioningly followed their parents and the teachings of religious institutions in terms of religious belief and practice, in late modern society, we have to critically reflect on what choices are open to us. As Beck puts it, 'the normal biography has become the "elective biography", the "reflexive biography", the "do-it-yourself biography"' (Beck and Beck-Gernsheim, 2001: 3). Olivier Roy's (2004) description of Islam in the West emphasizes the change that results from migration—moving from a country with Muslims in the majority to becoming a religious minority in a relatively secular one. He observes that cultural inheritance from Muslim countries of origin tends to be rejected by younger Muslims in favour of a supposedly purer original Islam. He makes the challenging argument that this tendency, although leading to a conservative version of Islam, should in fact be characterized as Westernization. Questioning of parental tradition should be understood in the context of the reflexivity and individualization of Beck and Giddens and it is therefore entirely bound up with Western late modernity.

Frank Peter's (2006) review of the recent literature on individualization in Islam notes that different authors have described different effects on Islamic belief and practice. Roy (2004) sees individualization as leading to a more conservative religiosity and Peter Mandaville (2001) in contrast describes a liberalizing tendency amongst young British Muslims, with travel and new media feeding into a critical questioning of some interpretations of Islam. Some research with young Muslims has suggested more of a middle way. Østberg (2006), for example, describes Muslim youth in Norway as having an 'integrated plural identity', so able to be reasonably at home with non-Muslim peers (and their Western youth culture) but also to maintain Muslim faith and practice. Østberg puts a theoretical emphasis on cultural flow as opposed to separate cultures existing alongside each other and separate from one another.

Learning Religion

In this section, we briefly review four theoretical perspectives which are relevant to our study and which surface at various points during the book. These are: firstly, theories about the universal cognitive processes that can be seen in religious transmission; secondly, an emphasis on embodiment and the development of *habitus*; thirdly the social significance for religious transmission of being in an identifiable and sometimes beleaguered minority; and fourthly the role of religious organizations in passing on religion.

Cognitive transmission

'Soft' social science has recently met the hard sciences in the merging of anthropological research with the cognitive science of religion. The idea here is that local manifestations of religious belief and practice are built on cognitive structures that are universal. Several different theories have been advanced within the field of the cognitive science of religion and it is beyond the scope of this predominantly sociological book to properly review them all. Useful reviews are provided by Barrett (2007, 2011). Instead, we focus on just one theory within the field that might have some purchase in explaining the especially successful transmission of Islam. This is the idea of modes of religiosity proposed by Whitehouse (2002, 2004).

Whitehouse is an anthropologist who has embraced the cognitive science approach. He identifies two modes of religious belief and practice into which religions can be categorized and which relate to different kinds of memory capacity. The imagistic mode involves intense and relatively rare events of high emotion. In contrast, the doctrinal mode involves frequent repetition of teaching and ritual. As Whitehouse explains:

> ... ritual action tends to be highly routinized, facilitating the storage of elaborate and conceptually complex religious teachings in semantic memory, but also activating implicit memory in the performance of most rituals. (Whitehouse, 2004: 65–6)

Mainstream Sunni Islam, with its five daily prayers and repeated recitation of the Qur'an, falls squarely into the doctrinal mode (Shankland, 2004). Although many other religious traditions also fall into the doctrinal mode—mainstream Catholic and Anglican Christianity, for example—our research shows the intensity with which Muslim children learn about Islam, in contrast to the approach of much Christian teaching (see Chapters 4 and 5 of this book).

Surprisingly, cognitive science theories have rarely been applied to Islam. Gibbon (2008) considers the relevance to Islam of the theory of Boyer (1994, 2000) that successful religions employ minimally counter-intuitive religious concepts. The only example we could find of applying Whitehouse's modes of religion theory to Islam is the essay by Shankland (2004), which considers the common ground between the work of Whitehouse and Gellner's (1981) anthropological work on Islam. Although Shankland (2004: 46) takes the view that the theories of Whitehouse are 'the most significant increase in our understanding of religious ideas since Durkheim', he also sees limitations in the modes of religiosity theory—he questions reducing religious influences to psychological causes and also questions why the analysis of modes should be confined to religion. There is considerable debate about the cognitive science of religion within social anthropology (see, for example, Berliner and Sarró, 2007a), as might be expected since it is effectively an attempt to bring scientific analysis to an interpretive branch of the humanities. Since this is only one of several theoretical angles we are drawing on in the book, however, it would not be appropriate to rehearse these debates here. Rather, we are taking the ideas of Whitehouse at face value and making an initial consideration of how they could apply to our topic. We cannot properly test them out without a fundamentally different research design, but we will reflect on their relevance in terms of interpreting our qualitative findings.

Embodiment and habitus

Another crucial process for the passing on of religiosity to children is micro-level socialization, both within the family and in interaction with peers. A key concept here is *habitus*. The term refers to our deeply rooted social inclinations, such as our values, tastes and bodily style. The term was used by Aristotle and Mauss (Mahmood, 2012 [2001]; Mellor and Shilling, 2010), but the best known use in the social sciences is that of Bourdieu (e.g. 1984). Bourdieu does not regard these inclinations as being consciously learned or developed through imitation. They are socially structured and are the means by which social conditions become naturalized. Mahmood (2012 [2001]) has used the idea of *habitus* in relation to Islamic practice. She takes issue with Bourdieu on the basis of his 'lack of attention to the pedagogical process by which a habitus is learned' (p. 130). We regard the concept of *habitus* as a very useful one for understanding how religion is learned, provided that a pedagogical dimension is included, as in the work of Mahmood.

Other scholars have also applied the idea of *habitus* to Islam. Winchester (2008) uses the concept of 'moral *habitus*' in relation to research with American Muslim converts. He argues that becoming a good Muslim is not just a process of taking on certain moral attitudes, but embodied religious practice is also crucial. He writes that moral selfhood and practice mutually constitute and influence each other, rather than there being a unidirectional process. In support of this he quotes a research participant Nina: 'It's like a feedback loop—[she chuckles] positive, hopefully... in that doing these things (religious practices) on a regular basis really instils and renews in you that sense of focus and obligation' (Winchester, 2008: 1755). Embodied practices such as fasting, ritual prayer and wearing an appropriate form of dress, help to produce the moral dispositions of a good Muslim, 'such as mindfulness, humility, discernment, moderation and modesty' (Winchester, 2008: 1755).

Oestergaard (2009) also applies the theory of *habitus* to Muslim converts, writing about the role of ritual and embodiment in converts proving themselves to be 'real' Muslims when some are suspicious of them. There are also echoes here of what Mellor and Shilling (2010) call 'body pedagogics' in religious socialization and what Orsi (2004: 74) terms the 'corporalization of the sacred'. All this adds up to the internalization of religious learning via a mutually constitutive relationship between morality and bodily practices. There is little or no room for agency in Bourdieu's concept of *habitus*, but Mahmood's (2012 [2001]) insistence on a pedagogical dimension does allow for some agency on the part of the religious learner.

Minority defence

In making sense of how children learn to be Muslims in a Western country, it is essential to keep in mind the social significance of being in a minority. The UK Muslim population is marked out from the non-Muslim population in several ways. Most Muslims are from a visible ethnic minority. Most have experience of migration, if not in their own lives then in the lives of parents or grandparents. Migration tends to be from countries of origin which are more religious than the host country (Voas and Fleischmann, 2012). The UK Muslim population is socially and economically disadvantaged (and especially Bangladeshis and Pakistanis) (Hussain, 2008).

The formation of minority identities is a complex process, with identity being both ascribed by others (and by the State) and also achieved by subjects. It can also be contingent and fluid. To some extent, collective identities are up for negotiation, but only within the limits of what is externally ascribed (Song, 2003). Despite the rise in primary identification with Islam rather than ethnicity which was mentioned earlier in this chapter, there is likely to be continuing overlap between ethnicity and religious identity for Muslims and perhaps especially Muslim children who have had less exposure to adult identity debates and may have a taken-for-granted Muslim identity on the basis of ethnicity. If families' main social networks are of other Muslims, often from the same ethnic group (Voas and Fleishmann, 2012), this is likely to reinforce children's identification with Islam.

Religion may remain stronger in the context of minority ethnic status than in the rest of the population as it has other work to do—helping to preserve the distinctive culture of an ethnic group which is outnumbered (Bruce, 1996) and perhaps helping to maintain social bonds in the face of discrimination and deprivation. There can be pride in minority status; what we might call a resistance identity (Castells, 1997). The idea of resistance identity may be especially pertinent in a post-9/11 climate, where the Muslim identity has become politicized. Connor's (2010) study of the European Social Survey in 2002, 2004 and 2006 found that on aggregate across Europe, immigrant Muslims were more religious than the host population. Connor's analysis further showed that where the host population was less receptive to immigration, Muslims' religiosity deepened. He hypothesized that this is a reactive response to an 'us and them' situation. Voas and Fleischmann (2012), in their comprehensive review of evidence on Islam in the West, take the view that the jury is out on this supposed association between experience of prejudice and increased religiosity and more evidence is needed.

Role of religious organizations

In any faith, religious organizations play a role in the socialization of children, although the character of organizations varies greatly, as does their involvement with religious nurture. There are particular traditions of religious education in Islam and some of these are alive and well in the UK. Over the centuries, Muslims have developed educational institutions which endeavour to support 'life-long learning'. These institutions are known by various names (e.g. *maktab, madrasah,* 'mosque school'), which are often used interchangeably within the British context (Mogra 2004: 22). Of particular importance to many parents is the reading of the Qur'an in Arabic and the teaching of the language to children so they can take part in this. In Islam there is no hierarchical and international organization comparable with some Christian churches, but rather there are looser networks, often relying on ethnic and linguistic traditions, with an important cultural status given to scholars who have interpreted Islam and laid down its traditions (see later in the chapter).

As well as formal supplementary education provided by religious organizations, another important source for learning religion is informal interaction with congregations. As Ammerman (2009) puts it:

> Congregations, in tandem with families, are the primary agents of religious socialization in places where religion has been institutionally separated from an integrated culture that carries religious meanings and practices in the warp and woof of everyone's everyday life. (Ammerman, 2009: 567)

In addition to families and friendship networks, congregations provide further opportunities for socialization into a religious *habitus*. They reinforce the idea that a child belongs to a community of believers and worshippers; a community which, for Muslims in Western countries, is often also marked by ethnicity (see above). They can also provide additional social activities for children outside of formal learning.

Childhood

Middle childhood

The particular focus of this book is children aged 12 and under (although the quantitative analysis in Chapter 2 is of data on children aged 11–15). Early and middle childhood are phases of the life course that have been relatively neglected in the study of Muslims. The same could be said of religious learning within the family. There are some studies which focus on the experiences of Muslim 'young people' (e.g. Jacobson, 1998) or on certain aspects of Muslim family life in specific ethnic groups (Shaw, 2000; Becher, 2008). There is very little sociological research which focuses on Muslim children in early and middle childhood, for whom some aspects of religious nurture are distinct from the experiences of older children (Husain, 2004). These are years when children, regardless of religious background, tend to be quite protected within families and spend considerable time in family homes rather than independently moving around in their communities (Borland et al., 1998). Greenlaw expresses this elegantly when writing about this phase of the life course in her memoir:

> My family held me. It was complicated but strong, a machine that made life happen so that I didn't have to. It protected me, too. Until I was eleven or so, I was not made to take on substance. (Greenlaw, 2007: 8)

In child psychology, a body of work on children's spirituality and religion has emerged in recent years, albeit on the margins of that discipline (see Roehlkepartain et al., 2006a). There is debate about the notion of *stages* of development (Fowler, 1981), both within this field and beyond. There is unease with the idea of a child's normal stage of development, on the basis that it tends to be overly deterministic, the evidence tends to be based on white Western children and there is an assumption that children's religiosity is less sophisticated than that of adults (Roehlkepartain et al., 2006b). There is certainly debate, but it needs to be acknowledged that in many respects younger children are indeed likely to have a simpler understanding of their faith than adults or older children, just as they have a simpler understanding of many issues. This is not necessarily a cognitive and biological approach, but it is an obvious sociological point that young children have not been exposed through social interaction to as many life experiences and as much knowledge as have adults. This does not mean their faith is in any sense of less worth, but it is not the same as faith in adulthood.

The criticisms of age-bound developmental 'stages' mentioned above have been strongly expressed in the sociology of childhood field in recent years (e.g. James and Prout, 1997; James, Jenks and Prout, 1998). Development psychology received particularly trenchant criticism within this literature for viewing children as pre-adult 'becomings' rather than 'beings' in their own right and seeing them as passive recipients of socialization by adults rather than as actively involved in constructing their own worlds. The nature–culture dichotomy in these disciplinary tensions has more recently been called into question by Prout (2005), who calls for a more inter-disciplinary approach to understanding childhood (as do Scourfield et al., 2006).

It is worth stating that we should not underestimate children's agency; the potential for them to make an impact on their own environment rather than simply be shaped by it. It is often implied in discussions of religion in childhood that children passively receive messages about faith. This is how Dawkins (2006) sees religious nurture and he rejects what he terms the religious indoctrination of children precisely because he sees children as passively accepting of what they are told. Many religious people would be concerned about the opposite scenario, with each generation becomingly increasingly secular and many children passively accepting the values of consumer culture. But time and again research shows us children not being passively socialized but doing their own thing with what they are given (within limits) and exerting their own influence on their immediate social environments. Having noted this, it is also important to keep in mind that agency is limited. We do not construct our own biographies under conditions of our own making. And it is especially true that in early and middle childhood, agency is limited by a child's very limited social horizons. It is limited, but not altogether removed.

There is relatively little research to date on how children negotiate religion and spirituality that is informed by the new sociology of childhood, allowing children to articulate their own perspectives through participatory methods, regarding children as significant social actors and understanding children's religion in relation to both micro- and macro-level social contexts. The situation has been changing somewhat in recent years (Hemming and Madge, 2011), but much of this recent research is on teenage children rather than those in early and middle childhood. The body of research closest to our approach is the impressive range of studies conducted by Nesbitt and colleagues at Warwick (e.g. Jackson and Nesbitt, 1993; Nesbitt, 2004; Nesbitt and Arweck, 2010), on Hindu, Sikh, Christian and mixed faith children.

Religious Nurture

There are gaps in terms of the more general picture of research on religious socialization in families. There is a literature on religious 'transmission', but as noted earlier, Boyatzis et al. (2006) have observed these studies tend to be American, solely quantitative and based on largely white, Christian samples. They also tend to be based on surveys of adults or (less often) young people in teenage years. Boyatzis et al. (2006), in their overview of research to date on the family context of the religious and spiritual development of children and young people, summarize the current gaps in research in this field. Our book fits into all but one of the categories they list, insofar as it is based on qualitative methods of inquiry, includes exploration of children's own perspectives on religious rituals and is focused on non-Christian families outside the USA.

At this point we consider the different terminology that can be applied to children's learning of religion. The term 'transmission' is especially used in connection with inter-generational patterns of religion in populations; that is, how successfully religious affiliation or religious practice are passed on across generations and over time within specific religious groups. Such research tends to be quantitative, often using aggregate statistics on whole populations. Unfortunately, the term 'transmission' is rather passive and does not capture the dynamic process of inter- and intra-generational negotiation of belief and morality. It is important to know about transmission. Inter-generational patterns of religiosity are crucial to debates about secularization and we focus on these in Chapter 2. However, there is also a lot that data on transmission do not tell us.

Socialization approaches have also been regarded by some commentators as overly passive, and especially with regard to children. Authors such as James and Prout (1997) and James et al. (1998) have placed a emphasis on children being social actors, in contrast to what they see as passive models of socialization from sociology and essentialist or mono-cultural approaches from developmental psychology. Our view is that the term 'socialization' is more open than 'transmission' to encompassing a dynamic process and an element of negotiation of religiosity, whilst also quite properly keeping a focus on social structural influences. However, we favour the term 'nurture', as it necessarily implies attention to micro-level social processes and a more detailed examination—probably via qualitative research—of the relationship between children and their carers. Arguably the term 'nurture' implies a positive construction on family life with the idea that adult–child relationships with regard to religion are necessarily nurturing. We need to acknowledge that the term 'nurture' has its limitations then, since some kinds of religious upbringing cannot be described as nurturing. If young people's wishes are consciously disregarded and over-ridden in the name of religion then we are looking at a process of religious coercion.

Our conclusion from this brief overview of terminology is to recommend as the way forward an approach which is the least controversial but probably the hardest to operationalize; namely to embrace theoretical and methodological pluralism. Both macro- and micro-level data are needed on both populations and individuals and we need therefore to employ both quantitative and qualitative methods. We need to study transmission (macro-level patterns across generations) and nurture (micro-level interactions between children and carers). Socialization is also a broad enough term to encompass much of what goes on where religion is learned in the family.

Traditions of Nurture and Education in Islam

According to Islamic teachings everyone is born a Muslim, and Islam is the 'natural' religion of humankind (*din al-fitra*). Whether this Muslim identity flourishes depends upon family upbringing, the wider social environment, and education. The centrality of the family in Islam is reflected in the complexity of jurisprudence relating to marriage and family life in Islamic law, and the extent to which Islamic scholars direct their scholarly endeavours towards interpretation and application of legal principles in this area. Islamic sources outline in detail the mutual obligations of parents and children towards one another, including the parental responsibility for the religious nurture and education of children. A saying of the Prophet Muhammad, often quoted by Muslims, reads: 'A father gives his child nothing better than a good education'.

Perhaps on account of this, and the numerous exhortations in the Qur'an to pursue knowledge (e.g. *Surah* 20: 114), Islam has a rich tradition of education that goes back well over a millennium. The Qur'an proclaims the superiority of those who have knowledge over those that do not (*Surah* 58: 11), and various Quranic verses stress the religious obligation to see knowledge and wisdom. Muslim scholars have agreed upon three Arabic words that outline the meaning and purpose of education, in an Islamic sense (Halstead, 2004). If we analyse these words in more depth, the full character and spirit of Islamic perspectives on education become apparent. The first word, *tarbiya*, derives from the Arabic root *raba* (which means to grow, or to increase) and it refers to the development of individual potential, and to the process of nurturing and guiding young people to maturity. The second term, *talim*, comes from the root *alima* (which means to know, or to be informed) and refers to the imparting and receiving of knowledge, usually through training, instruction, or another form of teaching. It is of course the basis for the word *alim* or the plural, *ulama*, which refers to the scholars of Islam. The third word is *tadib* and this derives from the root *aduba* (which conveys the sense of being refined, disciplined, or cultured) and from this word we also have the term *adab* meaning good manners and personal conduct. *Tadib* refers to the process of character development and learning the principles of social and moral behaviour within the community. It includes understanding and accepting the most basic social principles in Islam, such as justice.

In summary then, Islamic education covers individual development and God-consciousness, the transmission of knowledge, and the development of an understanding of society and its social and moral rules.[2] This comprehensive approach to education means that 'no aspect of a Muslim's life can remain untouched by religion' (Halstead, 2004: 522), and thus the acquisition of knowledge and education is, quite simply, a religious duty. Ultimately, education is necessary in order to 'attain success in this life and the next' (Association of Muslim Social Scientists/FAIR, 2004: 2).

---

[2] See also Parker-Jenkins (1995) for further consideration of Islam and education.

Teachers in schools and *madrasahs* have an important role to play in supporting the educational efforts of parents at home. Reflecting the comprehensive nature of education in Islam, a teacher is 'expected to exemplify in her/his life the content of that which is taught' (Hewer, 2001: 521). In other words, they are not simply transmitting knowledge and information, but are expected to act as guides and exemplars, in all aspects of personal conduct. The education and religious nurture that children receive at home is therefore ideally matched by teachers who reinforce and exemplify the values and teachings of Islam at school, thereby enabling children to understand the holistic and all-encompassing way of life that is intrinsic to Islam and a secure Muslim identity (Nielsen, 1981). As was noted earlier in the chapter, there is a strong tradition of supplementary schools for Muslim children, especially geared towards learning to read the Qur'an in Arabic.

Organization of the book

Chapter 2 presents the findings of secondary analysis of the 2003 Home Office Citizenship Survey. This dataset provides a rare opportunity to study the inter-generational transmission of religion in Britain and to compare different religious groups, since there was a boosted minority ethnic sample within the survey. This chapter considers national data and comparative data on different faith groups. The breadth provided by this dataset sets the context for the depth of focus in the rest of the book, which presents the findings of a local qualitative study (mostly interview-based) with Muslim families in one British city. Chapter 3 introduces the research project, the methodological challenges faced and how we sought to overcome them.

Chapter 4 provides something of an empirical overview to the whole qualitative study, summarizing the 'big picture' of Islamic nurture and mentioning some important issues which later chapters return to. However, it also focuses more specifically on family-based learning and how children are taught informally by parents and other family members. Chapter 5 then looks specifically at formal learning about Islam. Most of this material relates to religious organizations; mosques and Islamic studies schools. However, many children have formal lessons in teachers' homes, or teachers come to them, so the chapter also includes discussion of home-based formal religious education. Chapters 4 and 5 therefore form a pair of chapters which are focused on how children are explicitly taught about Islam. The remaining empirical chapters are less explicitly about the teaching of religion, but are concerned with how the social context of young Muslim children has an impact on religious nurture.

So Chapter 6 moves away from the family and the mosque to consider the wider social context of the children's lives. It deals with social relations in school, their local social networks and their contact with family members abroad. All of these are considered in so far as they affect religious nurture. Chapter 7 returns to the family, but with a wider consideration of family life and how religious nurture is implicated in particular family practices such as naming of children and birth rituals. There is also an overview of family structure. Chapter 8 is the final empirical chapter. It puts Muslim identities into the broader context of inter-generational collective identities, so also considering the significance of ethnicity and national identity. Chapter 9 then concludes the book by taking stock of what has been learned about the process of religious nurture, and also considers the implications for public services of how children are, in practice, brought up to be Muslims.

2

Inter-Generational Transmission of Islam: Evidence from the Citizenship Survey

(Chapter co-authored by Chris Taylor and Graham Moore)

Most of the book is concerned with rich description of the process of religious nurture in Muslim families, on the basis of our qualitative research. However, before we embarked on this qualitative study, in order to guide our research questions, we set out to undertake some quantitative secondary analysis of existing data. It was important to put our local research into a British context and also to conduct some comparative research to consider the relative success of religious transmission in different faith groups. The tone of this chapter is very different from that of the chapters which follow it. The data and the analysis are entirely quantitative, so the focus is statistical associations rather than the interpretation of qualitative data from observation, interviews and oral diaries. It is also the only empirical chapter which is not exclusively focused on Muslims (as it includes data on other religious groups), or on the city of Cardiff where the qualitative fieldwork took place (as the data are for England and Wales).

The source of existing data for the current chapter is the Home Office Citizenship Survey. O'Beirne (2004) has published some findings on religion from the 2001 survey. These include further evidence of social disadvantage for Muslims, evidence that religion is more important to self-identity for people from minority faith communities (including Muslims) than for Christians and more important to people from minority ethnic backgrounds than for those from the white majority. O'Beirne also notes that Muslims and Sikhs are more concerned about religious discrimination than people from other religions and that there are fewer Muslim respondents than the average for all respondents participating in social clubs/groups or in any kind of volunteering. However, there has been no analysis to date of Citizenship Survey data on religious transmission across generations and it is this issue that the current chapter focuses upon.

With regard to inter-generational transmission, Chapter 1 noted Crockett and Voas' (2006) finding that although minority ethnic groups are more religious than the majority, the rate of inter-generational decline in religion is broadly similar across ethnic groups. This issue warrants further exploration. There are some indications of possible differences between religions with regard to religious transmission across generations. For example, Becher's (2008) small-scale survey of parents recruited via primary schools found that Muslims were significantly more likely to cite religion as a 'very' or 'fairly' important influence on how they brought up their children than Christian parents.

The analysis presented in this chapter is structured in three parts. Firstly, by combining two linked surveys, we consider the inter-generational transmission of religion across three 'generations' from within the same families, comparing the incidence of successful transmission in different religious groups. Secondly, we explore the statistical associations between a number of different background factors and the incidence of religious transmission amongst the larger sample of adult respondents, with particular attention paid to Islam. Thirdly we consider indications of differences between faith groups in how teenaged children spend their non-school time, to lead us into the qualitative findings in subsequent chapters.

The analysis was exploratory rather than hypothesis-driven and was focused around the following primary research questions:

- In which religious groups is the inter-generational transmission of religion most successful?
- Which variables are associated with higher rates of religious transmission?

Methods

The Home Office Citizenship Survey (HOCS) and its accompanying Young People's Survey (YPS) provide a relatively rare example of individual-level and inter-generational British data on religious transmission, with indications of religious affiliation or practice across three generations. The findings presented in this chapter are based on analysis of the 2003 HOCS. This survey was completed by 14,057 adults[1] across England and Wales, with face-to-face interviews being conducted in participants' homes. The survey contains a Minority Ethnic Boost sample of 4571 respondents. Consequently, the 2003 HOCS contains responses from 1551 Muslims, for example; this provides the largest ethnic minority sample (including those with non-Christian religion) in any national survey[2] since the Fourth National Survey of Ethnic Minorities (Modood et al., 1997), which only considers ethnic minority groups and was conducted in 1993–4. Another benefit of the 2003 HOCS is that for that year there were additional children's (aged 8–10 years) and young people's (aged 11–15) versions of the survey. For the purposes of this chapter we only use data from the YPS. Although YPS respondents are in a different age group from those in our qualitative study, who are 12 and under, the YPS data proved the more fruitful for the study of religious transmission, as the HOCS children's survey did not ask about respondents' religious affiliation. The YPS was completed by 1666 young people and can be linked directly to the adult HOCS.[3]

Measures

Religion (HOCS and YPS). A number of items relating to past and current religion were included within the 2003 HOCS and YPS. In relation to past religion, HOCS adult respondents were asked, 'Thinking of your childhood, were you raised according to any particular religion?' Those who said yes were asked, 'Which religion was that?' Responses were coded as Christian, Buddhist, Hindu, Jewish, Muslim, Sikh or other. In relation to present religion, participants were then asked, 'Do you actively practise any religion now?', before again being asked, 'Which religion is that?' The potential utility and the limitations of these questions for secondary analysis are discussed below.

Three variables were derived from these HOCS items. These were 'religion (current)', 'religion (past)' and 'religious transmission'. Religious transmission was simply whether or not religion (current) was the same as religion (past). Due to the small numbers of participants

---

[1] Survey respondents are aged 16 years or over. Whilst 16–17 year olds are not usually regarded as adults, they comprise only 0.09% of the survey respondents (n = 12), so we use 'adults' as a shorthand description.

[2] 'National' for the HOCS/YPS means England and Wales, and not Scotland or Northern Ireland.

[3] The sample for the YPS was taken from the list of all eligible young people living in the household of the adults who completed the survey using a Kish Grid method (i.e. they had equal chance of being selected).

reporting other non-Christian non-Muslim religions, both past religion and currently practised religion were broken into a four-category variable: *Muslims, Christians*, people from other *non-Christian, non-Muslim* religions (such as Hindus and Jews), and those raised with or currently practising *no religion*. However, religious transmission was calculated using the expanded eight-category religion variables for current and past religion (including no religion) prior to collapsing these down to the four category variables used for analyses.

In the YPS the young people were asked, 'Do you have a religion?' Those who said yes were asked, 'Which religion is that?', and again their responses were coded in the same way as the adult survey. As with the HOCS, these responses were broken down into the same four-category variable.

Ethnicity (HOCS and YPS). Ethnicity was analysed as an eight category variable: white, mixed, black, Indian, Pakistani, Bangladeshi, other Asian, and other (with Chinese categorized as 'other' due to the small number of Chinese Muslims in the sample).

Country of birth (HOCS). A three category variable was created as follows: (i) UK and Ireland; (ii) Asian countries; and (iii) other.

Socioeconomic indicators (HOCS). Two indicators of socioeconomic position were used. Firstly, social class was based upon the National Statistics Socio Economic Classification (NSSEC), and divided into four categories (managerial, intermediate, routine/semi routine, or other). Secondly, respondents were asked to provide details of their own income, and if they were married or cohabiting, to also give their partner's income. Given that these are presented within the HOCS as ordinal variables with uneven distances between categories, summing own and partner's income was not possible. Therefore, the income of the participant was used if the respondent did not have a partner, or if the respondent earned more than or equal to their partner. For married or cohabiting individuals, the income of the partner was used if this was greater than that of the participant. This gave a fifteen category ordinal variable which was heavily skewed towards the lower end of the distribution. For this reason, this variable was broken down into three approximately equal groups.

Educational qualifications (HOCS). A categorical variable was derived, with participants categorized as having a degree or equivalent, a qualification above A-level but below degree, A-levels, GCSEs grade A–C or equivalent, GCSEs grade D–E or equivalent, foreign or other qualifications. Only participants aged 16–69 were included, with those aged 70 or over treated as a separate category and combined with those for whom qualifications were unknown.

Religious transmission across three generations

By combining the 2003 HOCS and YPS it is possible to examine religious transmission across three 'generations':

- First generation—based on the religion that the adult respondents to the HOCS were raised in.
- Second generation—based on the religion that the adult respondents to the HOCS currently practise.
- Third generation—based on the religion that the young people respondents to the YPS say they currently have.

Since the HOCS and YPS are linked by household and by parents (although this is a slightly smaller sample) we can see changes in religious activity across these three 'generations' within the same families. It is not necessarily the case that the adults who completed the HOCS are parents of the young people who completed the YPS, but some adult respondents were siblings or other relatives. Therefore, only parent–child pairs are used when YPS data are included in analyses.

There are two major caveats in examining religious transmission across these three generations. The first is that the young people are still living with their parents/adults, and are still at an age where they are less likely to have made independent decisions about their religious beliefs. Most had an adult present[4] and only 29% were alone. This may have some bearing on the responses made by the young people, and particularly on the sensitive questions asked in these surveys. The second main caveat to this analysis is that the questions asked for each generation were not the same. So, for example, the first generation is based on the religion 'raised in'. This may or may not have been actively practised and, also, 'raised in' could refer to influences beyond the family, such as community or school. Answering the question poses a challenge in relation to mixed-faith families, although this is likely to be more of an issue in future than it is now. The second generation is based on the active practising of a religion, and the final generation is based on whether the young people 'have a religion' or not. Given

---

[4] The proportions of YPS respondents with an adult present were as follows: 58% of Muslims, 61% of Christians, 66% of those with a non-Christian, non-Muslim religion and 65% of those with no religion.

these caveats, we would expect there to be some variation in the extent of religious transmission over time. However, our main interest here is to compare the transmission of different religions over time. There is no reason to expect that these two caveats should have a differential impact on the four-category religions we consider—if there is a stronger relationship between parents' and young people's reported religious activity for different religions then this is precisely what we are looking for.

Our analysis of inter-generational religious transmission is divided into two parts. First we consider religious transmission across all three 'generations'. Since this is based on combining the HOCS with the smaller YPS the sample size is relatively small—1278 parent–child matches. The second set of analyses presented is based exclusively on adult responses to the HOCS and therefore considers religious transmission from the first generation to the second generation (see above)— 13,988 adults who provided data on current religion. This greater sample size allows us to consider the statistical associations between religious transmission and other background factors.

For the second set of analyses, from the HOCS data only, the binary dependent variable was religious transmission (i.e. did or did not practice the same religion raised in). Independent variables were age, sex, past religion, ethnicity, country of birth, socioeconomic indicators (income and NSSEC), highest educational qualification and Government Office Region. For each independent variable, the incidence of successful religious transmission was examined, both for the group of all people raised in a religion and for the 'Muslim only' subgroup. Univariable logistic regression analyses were then conducted with each independent variable in turn before multivariable binary logistic regression models examined the extent to which variation between religions was independent of other demographic factors. Finally, univariable logistic regression analyses were repeated for the subgroup of respondents who reported being raised as Muslims. Analyses using the whole sample, or all participants raised in a religion, used weighting factors provided within the HOCS dataset to compensate for the overrepresentation of ethnic minority participants. However, as the 'Muslim-only' analyses focused almost exclusively on ethnic minority participants, these were not weighted.

Inter-Generational Transmission of Religion

The first thing to note from our analysis is the complex pattern of religious transmission over three generations, even though we are only using four religious categories. Clearly there is a lot of movement between and across the four different religious categories over time and within the same families (Table 2.1). This suggests that inter-generational religious transmission is not a simple process as it is often presented when using aggregated cohort data.

It is also evident from this presentation of religious transmission that although the number of people (or households) reporting no religious activity increases the most over the three generations, it is also the case that the number of Muslims and other non-Christian religious groups also actually *increases* over the three generations (Table 2.1). For example, in this sample the number of Muslims increased from 261 in the first generation to 277 by the third generation. The only religious group to show a decline in absolute numbers was the Christian group.

We see this process of decline amongst Christians again in Table 2.2, which illustrates the direct transmission (through related families/ households) of first generational religious groups to third generational religious groups. This shows that over a third of Christians (36.6%) in the first generation have 'no religion' by the third generation. However, a very different picture exists for other religious groups. The sustainabil-ity or even small growth of Islam and other non-Christian religious groups identified above is not only a result of a higher rate of transmis-sion of these religions over the three generations, i.e. a relatively high proportion of the sample continue to be Muslims over the three gener-ations, but it can also be explained by a number of third generation respondents now identifying as Muslim even though they are not from practising Muslim family backgrounds. These two processes are evident in Table 2.2. This shows that the children (third generation) of 97.7% of parent respondents brought up as Muslims (first generation) continue to be Muslim. Similarly, 88.9% of respondents from non-Christian non-Muslim religions ('other religions') have this same religious affiliation in the third generation. The transmission of Islam and 'other religions' is significantly more prevalent than the transmission of Christianity. It is

Table 2.1. Number of religious group members by generation

	First generation	Second generation	Third generation
Muslim	261	229	277
Christian	587	254	439
Other religions	135	113	150
No religion	256	637	412
Unknown	39	45	–

Based on 1278 parent–child matches between HOCS and YPS.

Table 2.2. Inter-generational transmission from first to third generation

| First 'generation' | Inter-generational transmission to third generation (as a percentage of related first generation religions) | | | |
	Muslim	Christian	Other religions	No religion
Muslim	97.7	0.8	0.4	1.1
Christian	0.5	61.7	1.2	36.6
Other religions	0.7	2.2	88.9	8.1
No religion	3.1	23.0	5.9	68.0
Unknown first generation religion	25.6	33.3	23.1	17.9

Based on 1278 parent–child matches between HOCS and YPS.

also apparently more prevalent than the transmission of no religion over the three generations. A word of caution is necessary here about what young people (in the YPS) mean when they say they have Christianity or Islam as their religion. In the light of the scepticism about the high proportion of the UK population who said they were Christian in the 2001 census (e.g. Voas and Bruce, 2004) it is important to note that there can be many reasons for this response, including exclusionary ethnic identification (against a Muslim other) and, as we noted earlier in the chapter, the possible tendency for young people to describe themselves not according to a thought-out belief but according to a perceived cultural tradition of their parents. There is also the possibility that YPS respondents attend a faith school and identify with a religion largely on this basis rather than because of what they themselves believe or practice. And there is the possibility that young people from relatively non-religious homes might identify as 'Muslim' mainly on the basis of minority ethnicity (rather than religiosity). Whilst acknowledging important caveats, it is none the less evident that there is movement between all the religious groups considered here, and it is not simply a process of secularization. Hence the number of Muslims and 'other' (non-Christian non-Muslim) religious groups can be seen to expand over generations.

This apparent movement of people between different religious categories over a number of generations is also a very good reason for not looking at the transmission of one particular religious group in isolation. For example, if each religious group were to be examined in isolation from one another it would seem that no religious group has been able to achieve complete transmission—i.e. no third generation religious groups have 100% of related first generation groups; there will always be some rate of attrition for inter-generational religious transmission. But the change in religious membership over time, albeit relatively small in many instances, has ensured that the number of people in Muslim and other non-Christian religious groups has been maintained (as illustrated in Table 2.1).

This overall complex pattern of religious transmission over time and generations is even more evident when we consider the transmission over each of the three generations—from the first generation to the second generation and then finally on to the third generation (Figure 2.1). It is worth repeating here that one of the main limitations of this analysis is that the way religious membership is derived over these three generations was collected differently. Hence it may be the case that any trends over time are largely a product of how membership is defined.

Again, Figure 2.1 demonstrates the high retention rate of Islam and other non-Christian religions over the three generations. For example,

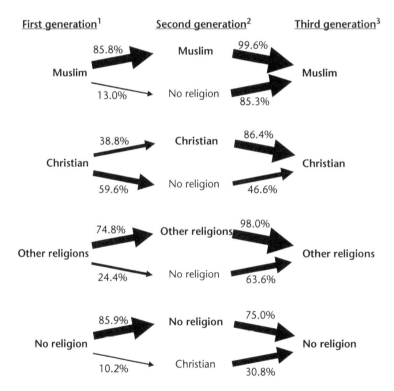

Figure 2.1. Religious transmission over three generations. Based on 1278 parent–child matches between HOCS and YPS. [1]Religion raised in; [2]religion practised (of adult respondents to 2003 HOCS); [3]religion held (of young respondents to 2003 YPS).

85.8% of first generation Muslims continue into the second generation, and 99.6% of second generation Muslims continue into the third generation. But Figure 2.1 also shows that large proportions of people in the third generation 'return' to the religion of their first generation ancestors. And importantly, this process of 'returning' is significant for all three of the religious groups considered here, even for Christian groups. Interestingly, Christians from the second generation who were raised with no religion are the least likely to see their children 'return' to having no religion. It is important to be aware of the possibility for young people to over-report religious affiliation, but the data are important to consider none the less, since these kinds of direct intergenerational data are relatively rare, at least in the UK. Also, the same problem of over-reporting could apply equally to all religious groups, so the especially high retention rate of Islam would seem to indicate differences between religions. At the very least it might indicate that Muslim youth are more likely to identify with the same religious label as their parents.

In Figure 2.1 it also appears that the successful transmission of the three main religion categories considered here is more prevalent between the second and third generation than it was between the first and second generation. The opposite is true for those in the 'no religion' category. This could potentially suggest that any process of secularization occurring over time is slowing down. However, such an interpretation would be open to challenge because of the different ways in which religious membership is defined over these three generations, particularly as the second generation religious membership is the only occurrence when religious *practice* is explicitly used. In which case, it is notable that the transmission of Islam is actually not that sensitive to the changing definitions of membership. Secondly, despite there being an apparent decline in the number of people *practising* Christianity, some religious affiliation to Christianity continues to exist well into the third generation.

Associations with Religious Transmission

The discussion above has demonstrated that religious transmission can be highly complex and that in order to fully appreciate and understand the process, comparisons between religious groups are very useful. We now begin to examine this process in more detail, looking at the key background characteristics of individuals alongside religious transmission.

Consequently, in this analysis we are particularly interested in identifying other possible reasons for religious transmission, which may or may not be shared across different religious groups. We do this by focusing only on the much larger sample of adult respondents in the 2003 HOCS according to the religion that they currently practise (i.e. from the second 'generation'). Table 2.3 presents the percentages of the whole sample of adult respondents, those raised according to a religion, and those raised as Muslims only, who reported practising a religion they were raised in, broken down by all independent variables of interest. For example, the rate of religious transmission for females is greater than it is for males, across all religious groups (38% of females compared with 25% of males) and for those raised as Muslims (80% of females compared with 75% of males). Table 2.4 presents odds ratios and 95% confidence intervals from binary logistic regression analyses examining the significance of these trends for all religious groups, and in a Muslim only subgroup.

We have already seen that membership of particular religious groups tends to be associated with the prevalence of religious transmission. Indeed, Table 2.3 clearly demonstrates that religious transmission amongst Muslims (77%) is more than twice as common as religious transmission amongst Christians (29%). After adjustment for ethnicity, age, country of birth, education and government office region, Muslims remained almost twice as likely as Christians to report practising the same religion they were raised in (see Table 2.4), though differences between Muslims and other non-Christian religions became non-significant. It is perhaps not surprising to see that there are significant associations between successful religious transmission and both ethnicity and country of birth, reflecting likely differences in the demographics of different religious groups in the UK. However, there are still some important differences by ethnicity and country of birth associated with the religious transmission of Islam. For example, respondents brought up as Muslims are more likely to continue to be practising Muslims if they were Indian (93%) as opposed to being Bangladeshi (84%), or if they were born in Asia (89%) as opposed to being born in the UK or Ireland (82%).

Age is another important factor associated with religious transmission. For all religious groups, respondents were less likely to be practising the religion they were brought up in the older they were (33% of 16–24 year olds compared with 29% of 45–64 year olds). The main exception to this trend was amongst the oldest age group, those aged 65 years or more. Indeed, this group was significantly more likely than any other age group of respondents to have the same religion as they

Table 2.3. Percentage of whole sample, all those raised within a religion, and all those raised as Muslims, who report practising the religion they were raised according to, broken down by past religion, sex, ethnicity, national statistics social class, income, country of birth, age, education, and region

		Percentage practising same religion as raised in		
		Whole sample	All those raised within a religion	Those raised as Muslims only
Religion (past)	Islam	77	77	77
	Christianity	29	29	–
	Non-Christian non-Muslim religion	65	65	–
	No religion	93	–	–
Sex	Male	45	25	75
	Female	55	38	80
Ethnicity	White	46	28	*
	Mixed	53	41	*
	Other Asian	71	73	75
	Black	66	65	74
	Chinese/other	66	57	59
	Indian	80	80	93
	Pakistani	85	86	87
	Bangladeshi	83	84	84
Social class	Managers	46	33	64
	Intermediate	46	30	72
	Routine/semi-routine	49	29	84
	Other	63	50	80
Income	<£10,000	51	36	80
	£10,000–24,999>	47	28	74
	£24,999	45	30	63
Country of birth	UK or Ireland	46	28	82
	Asia	84	85	89
	Other	59	54	57
Age	16–24	67	33	81
	25–44	53	31	76
	45–64	37	29	72
	65+	41	38	88
Level of education	Degree or equivalent	50	38	73
	Above A-level, below degree level	47	29	66
	GCE A level or equivalent	53	30	68
	GCSE Grades A–C or equivalent	47	25	88
	GSCE Grades D–E or equivalent	51	30	81

	Foreign and other qualifications	47	32	69
	No qualifications	47	26	86
	70+: qualifications not known	43	40	88
Government office region	North East	45	27	*
	North West	42	30	90
	Merseyside	45	30	*
	Yorkshire and Humberside	50	30	85
	East Midlands	48	31	76
	West Midlands	45	29	92
	Eastern	49	30	81
	London	52	42	72
	South East	47	29	55
	South West	51	35	*
	Wales	47	27	*

*n<30; percentages therefore not reported.

were brought up with (38%). This would suggest either that there is a 'return' to religion in old age or that there has been a generational shift in the overall rates of religious transmission over time. But, equally as important, this overall pattern of religious transmission by age is the same for Muslims only, albeit it at generally higher rates of religious transmission.

There are other socio-economic characteristics that also appear to be associated with religious transmission, including social class, income and educational qualifications. However, these factors appear to be related differently across the various religious groups examined. For all respondents raised within a religion, the likelihood of religious trans-mission increased with social class, though was highest amongst those of 'other' occupational status. Although those in managerial occupa-tions were more likely to be practising the religion they were brought up in (33%) than those in routine or semi-routine occupations (29%), those with low incomes (of less than £10,000) were more likely to have the same religion as they did during their childhood (36%) than those with higher incomes (30%). An equally mixed pattern was evident by level of educational qualifications, although notably respondents with the highest levels of educational qualifications were significantly more likely to still have the same religion as they were brought up with (38%). However, within the group of respondents brought up as Muslims there were more consistent associations between socio-economic characteristics and religious transmission. Those in more manual occupations, with relatively lower incomes and poorer

Table 2.4. Odds ratios and 95% confidence intervals from logistic regressions for associations of variables of interest with religious transmission amongst all those raised in a religion, and amongst those raised as Muslims only (significant associations highlighted in bold numerals)

	All those raised in a religion*		Muslims only
	Univariable estimates	Multivariate estimates	Univariable estimates
Religion (Muslim is reference category)			
Christian	0.12 (0.09–0.17)	0.58 (0.34–0.98)	
Non-Christian non-Muslim religion	0.54 (0.38–0.79)	0.92 (0.55–1.54)	
Sex (male is reference category)	1.82 (1.63–2.02)	2.01 (1.78–2.27)	1.46 (1.13–1.88)
Ethnicity†			
White	–	–	0.11 (0.04–0.30)
Mixed	1.71 (1.17–2.49)	1.56 (1.01–2.40)	0.37 (0.15–0.92)
Other Asian	7.00 (5.04–9.71)	3.89 (2.36–6.41)	0.47 (0.29–0.77)
Black	4.81 (4.09–5.67)	3.82 (2.91–5.02)	0.40 (0.26–0.61)
Chinese/other	3.34 (2.46–4.52)	2.08 (1.25–3.46)	0.31 (0.21–0.47)
Indian	10.29 (8.23–12.85)	5.56 (3.52–8.80)	1.98 (1.12–3.51)
Pakistani	16.69 (12.16–22.91)	9.51 (4.91–18.41)	–
Bangladeshi	13.04 (8.38–20.27)	6.44 (2.99–13.83)	0.91 (0.63–1.32)
Social class (routine/semi-routine is reference category)‡			
Manager	1.19 (1.04–1.36)		0.41 (0.27–0.61)
Intermediate	1.05 (0.91–1.21)		0.51 (0.35–0.74)
Other	2.38 (1.87–3.03)		0.93 (0.65–1.33)
Income (<£10,000 is reference category)			
£10,000–£24,999>	0.71 (0.63–0.81)		0.78 (0.58–1.04)
£24,999	0.78 (0.68–0.90)		0.34 (0.22–0.52)
Country of birth (UK or Ireland is reference category)			
Asia	14.64 (11.24–19.08)	2.53 (1.65–3.89)	2.06 (1.45–2.92)
Other	2.97 (2.49–3.54)	1.79 (1.37–2.33)	0.58 (0.41–0.81)

(continued)

Table 2.4. Continued

	All those raised in a religion*		Muslims only
	Univariable estimates	Multivariate estimates	Univariable estimates
Age (65+ is reference category)			
16–24	0.82 (0.65–1.03)	**0.60 (0.42–0.85)**	**0.51 (0.26–0.98)**
25–44	**0.73 (0.64–0.84)**	**0.62 (0.48–0.78)**	**0.47 (0.25–0.86)**
45–64	**0.67 (0.59–0.77)**	**0.77 (0.62–0.97)**	0.68 (0.34–1.35)
Highest qualification (no qualification is reference category)			
Degree or equivalent	**1.77 (1.48–2.11)**	**2.34 (1.90–2.89)**	**0.37 (0.25–0.93)**
Above A-level, below degree level	1.19 (0.97–1.45)	**1.65 (1.39–1.97)**	**0.47 (0.29–0.77)**
GCE A level or equivalent	1.20 (0.98–1.48)	**1.43 (1.12–1.84)**	0.68 (0.45–1.01)
GCSE Grades A–C or equivalent	0.95 (0.78–1.16)	1.24 (0.99–1.54)	0.74 (0.47–1.17)
GSCE Grades D–E or equivalent	1.23 (0.92–1.64)	**1.43 (1.03–1.97)**	0.89 (0.44–1.81)
Foreign & other qualifications	**1.34 (1.01–1.77)**	1.25 (0.90–1.73)	0.69 (0.42–1.13)
70 +:qualifications not known	**1.91 (1.62–2.25)**	**1.90 (1.49–2.44)**	1.39 (0.54–3.59)
Government Office Region (Wales is reference category)			
North East	1.00 (0.70–1.41)	1.06 (0.73–1.54)	
North West	1.17 (0.89–1.54)	1.11 (0.83–1.50)	
Merseyside	1.14 (0.75–1.74)	1.32 (0.86–2.04)	
Yorkshire & Humberside	1.14 (0.86–1.74)	1.14 (0.84–1.55)	
East Midlands	1.20 (0.90–1.61)	1.07 (0.79–1.45)	
West Midlands	1.10 (0.84–1.45)	0.93 (0.69–1.25)	
Eastern	1.16 (0.88–1.54)	1.12 (0.83–1.52)	
London	**1.90 (1.46–2.48)**	1.12 (0.83–1.52)	
South East	1.10 (0.84–1.45)	1.07 (0.80–1.41)	
South West	**1.42 (1.07–1.90)**	**1.51 (1.12–2.04)**	

*Weighted data with robust standard errors.
†For all those raised within a religion, whites are the reference category. For those raised as Muslims, Pakistanis are the reference category.
‡NSSEC and income were not entered into multivariate model, due to their strong association with education and the emergence of education as a stronger correlate of religious transmission in univariate analysis.

educational qualifications were significantly more likely to still be practising Muslims.

Finally, there were geographical variations in levels of religious transmission evident amongst the HOCS respondents. Although, overall, those respondents living in London were more likely to still be in the same religion as they were raised in (42%) than respondents in other regions, religious transmission amongst Muslims was more likely if they lived in the West Midlands (92%) and the North West (90%) than if they lived in other regions of the UK. Indeed, those brought up as Muslims who now live in the South East of England have a significantly lower rate of religious transmission (just 55%).

Further Evidence from the Young People's Survey about Religion in Childhood

We have already seen from Figure 2.1 that religious transmission appears to be stronger between the adults in the HOCS (second generation) and the young people in the YPS (third generation) than it was for the religious transmission to the adults (second generation) from their childhood (first generation). One obvious explanation for this is that children and young people are more likely to 'adopt' the chosen religion of their parents or guardians whilst still in the paternal home than when they become independent adults. But this would neglect the significant number and proportions who do not say they have the same religion as the religion their parents or guardians reported practising. For example, Figure 2.1 demonstrates that there is only a transmission rate of 86.4% between second generation and third generation Christians, and only a transmission rate of 75.0% between second generation and third generation non-believers. But these figures contrast quite markedly with the transmission rates of Muslims (99.6%) and non-Muslim non-Christian religious groups (98.0%). We already know that these religious groups are generally more likely to have stronger religious transmission over time. But why is it the case that nearly all children of Muslims and other non-Christian religious groups adopt their parents' religion? Furthermore, what are the consequences of such relatively strong religious transmission on their childhoods?

It is difficult to fully answer either these questions simply by analysing the HOCS and YPS. But the YPS does provide the opportunity to begin to speculate about differences in the childhood experiences of young people from different religious backgrounds that may extend our understanding of religious transmission. For example, Table 2.5 illustrates the

Table 2.5. Participation in out-of-school clubs

| | Religious group (percentage) | | | | |
	Muslims	Christians	Other religions	No religion	Total
School holiday playschemes	10.2	11.0	11.3	9.5	10.1
Environmental clubs/groups	2.2	3.1	0.7	1.9	2.2
Sports clubs/teams	31.6	42.6	30.0	40.9	38.5
Political clubs/groups	0.7	0.3	0.0	0.6	0.6
Debating clubs/groups	0.4	0.6	0.7	1.1	0.9
Computer clubs/groups	11.6	5.0	6.7	5.8	6.8
Art, drama, dance or music clubs/groups	7.3	23.2	17.3	16.6	16.8
Human rights groups	0.7	0.6	0.0	0.1	0.3
Religious groups or organizations	23.6	12.9	17.3	3.0	10.0
Youth clubs	17.5	27.3	14.0	25.2	23.1
Animal (welfare) groups	1.8	4.1	2.0	2.1	2.5
Voluntary groups helping people	2.9	1.9	4.7	1.6	2.2
Safety, First Aid groups	2.2	1.9	1.3	2.9	2.5
Local community or neighbourhood groups	2.5	4.1	3.3	2.2	3.0
Other clubs/groups	5.1	7.8	2.7	7.9	6.8
None of these	46.5	27.0	39.3	29.5	32.8

participation of young people in out-of-school clubs by religious group. This shows quite marked differences in the kind of out-of-school experiences young people from different religious groups may have—just under half of young Muslims do not participate in any kind of out-of-school clubs compared with just over a quarter of Christian young people. But on the other hand young Muslims are approximately twice as likely as any other religious group to participate in out-of-school religious groups or organizations. Given that young people might think Qurancic or Islamic studies classes are too serious an activity to be put in the category of an 'out-of-school club' the 23.6% of Muslim children attending religious groups or organizations might well be an underestimate.

Another important difference between young respondents was in their peer group relationships. For example, only 77.5% of young Muslims said that they ever had friends come round to their home to spend time there compared with 85.0% of young Christians. Similar proportions said that they visited friends in their homes or met with them outside either home (Table 2.6).

Table 2.6. Peer-group socialization by religious group

	Religious group (percentage)	
	Muslims	Christians
Friends come round to home	77.5	85.0
Visit friends in their homes	77.5	89.3
Meet friends outside home	76.2	89.0

Table 2.7. Barriers to participating in (more) clubs

	Religious group (percentage)				
	Muslims	Christians	Other religions	No religion	Total
I have no way of getting to the clubs or groups	10.2	10.7	12.0	13.2	11.9
There are no good groups or clubs locally	16.4	17.6	18.7	24.4	21.1
I can't afford to join clubs	6.2	5.3	3.3	5.1	5.1
I wouldn't feel safe travelling to and from clubs	12.0	6.0	7.3	5.0	6.8
There are no clubs or groups that I'm interested in	18.9	11.0	18.7	17.2	16.3
I'm too busy	22.2	16.6	19.3	18.5	19.1
I don't want to	19.3	11.6	13.3	15.0	14.9
I don't have time after my homework	26.5	17.2	28.0	16.4	19.4
I am not allowed	12.7	3.4	4.7	4.6	6.0
Other reasons	5.5	7.8	5.3	5.0	5.7
None of these	30.9	31.0	28.7	28.3	29.3

The YPS also asked the young people to indicate what were the main barriers to doing things (or more things) in groups (Table 2.7). This shows that young Muslims were much more likely to report not having the time to participate in (more) clubs or groups after they have finished their school homework. But it also shows that young Muslims are three to four times more likely than other religious groups to say that they are not allowed to participate in (more) such activities.

Conclusion

In concluding the chapter, the limitations of the secondary analysis should be restated. Slightly different questions were asked about each of the different generations of religiosity. There are also difficulties with the conflation of religion and ethnicity for both Christians and Muslims. These ambiguities pose a challenge for any interpretation of the data, of course. However, our main aim was to compare religious transmission in different religious groups, and the limitations noted apply equally across the religious categories. A further limitation was that data from respondents with non-Muslim, non-Christian religions were collapsed into one category for analytical purposes. There are, however, at the very least some issues that our analyses highlight for further exploration. There are broadly speaking two themes here—one about secularization in general and the other about Islam more specifically.

The first set of issues relates to the complexities of the inter-generational transmission of religion. Our analyses of the HOCS and YPS suggest that there may be more movement in and out of religiosity than many discussions of secularization allow. Generational shifts to no religion might in fact be reversible within families. Even if young people's choosing of Christian or Muslim labels for themselves is nominal and not really indicative of belief or practice, the fact that in a secular age the children of non-practising parents have even chosen to say they have a religion might at least be worthy of further study. Furthermore, the apparently much higher rates of inter-generational transmission in Muslims and members of other non-Christian non-Muslim religions are again certainly worthy of further exploration and may in fact pose a challenge to blanket judgements about the decline of British religion. Given that most people in these faith groups are from minority ethnic backgrounds, these higher rates might suggest support for the theory that for minority ethnic populations, religion can be an important resource in bolstering a sense of cultural distinctiveness (Martin, 2005) and the theory that religion can help people manage the difficult process of migration (Bruce, 1996), especially if we see adjustment to migration as a process that might span a few generations.

The second set of issues relates to Islam specifically. On the basis of the HOCS, Islam could be seen to be distinctive in some respects. According to the multivariate regression analysis, even after controlling for ethnicity, country of birth and income, Muslims remained almost twice as likely as Christians to report practising the same religion they were raised in. A central purpose of this book is to attempt to explore via our qualitative research why this might be.

The univariable logistic regressions suggested that Muslims in lower social classes pass on religion more successfully than those in higher social classes. Similarly, Muslims with lower educational qualifications were apparently more successful at passing on religion than those with higher qualifications. In both cases, Muslims were different from the other religious groups in our analysis. These findings are certainly worthy of exploration in further research. They suggest that the responses of families to the place of Islam in late modern Western societies might vary according to social class and education. Our own study is unlikely to be able to answer these questions. Although we worked hard to achieve a diverse sample (see Chapter 3) which was reasonably representative of the Muslim population, many of the sub-groups were too small to allow comparison and anyway a qualitative study poses challenges for robust comparison. We therefore make some tentative comments on differences between Muslims according to class, education and ethnicity, but cannot claim any definitive findings in this regard.

The YPS indicates more involvement of Muslim young people in religious organizations and less involvement in other out-of-school clubs, as well as young Muslims being less likely to have friends round to their houses. All this argues the need for some detailed qualitative research, to illuminate the process of religious transmission in Muslim families. It is to our qualitative research that we now turn. Our study was of children aged 12 and under, so a rather different stage of the life course from the 11–15 years olds who completed the YPS. The next chapter explains the research setting and methods used, focusing on some interesting methodological challenged in conducting research with Muslim families.

3

Qualitative Research on Islamic Nurture

This chapter introduces the qualitative study which forms the main empirical basis of the book. It also includes reflection on some of the methodologically interesting issues involved in researching Muslim families, which are of wider relevance beyond our own study. Although there has been a relative proliferation of studies into Muslims in Britain (and other Western countries) in recent years, there have been very few substantial discussions of the methodological issues involved in researching Muslim communities. Methodological commentary is often buried deep within papers, books and doctoral theses and there is relatively little open discussion of how research methods work out in practice. There is a lack of academic publications based on actual fieldwork experiences which critically reflect on the *process* of research with Muslims in the UK. We try to go some way towards addressing this issue here.

In order to initiate such a dialogue we will offer some critical reflections on our use of a range of qualitative research strategies and methods. We begin with a brief review of the current methodological literature on conducting research with families and research with British Muslims. We then move on to give a summary outline of our own research project and describe the setting—the city of Cardiff. The rest of the chapter is then taken up with a critical discussion of some of the strategies and methods we employed.

Relative Lack of Methodological Reflection in Research on Muslims in the West

In recent years (and perhaps especially in the aftermath of 9/11 and 7/7) there has been a certain flourishing of research projects and resulting academic literature which have aimed to understand and explain the experiences of Muslims in Britain, Western Europe and the US with a focus on issues of identity and citizenship (e.g. Jacobson, 1998; Østberg, 2006; Hopkins, 2007; Seddon, 2010). Although these academic endeavours have added substantive knowledge about the lives and identities of Western Muslims, there has tended to be a lack of thorough discussion of the methodological frameworks the researchers have employed. This gap in the existing literature became evident to us at an early stage in our own qualitative research project, when searching the existing literature for guidance on methods.

As Bolognani (2007) notes, within the existing social science literature on Muslims, discussions of methods have been mostly confined to issues of access and discussions of insider–outsider status (e.g. McLoughlin, 2000; Gilliat-Ray, 2005; Sanghera and Thapar-Bjorkert, 2008). Where there may be a detailed description of aspects of research design and process, for example sampling strategy, there tends not to be much discussion about interactions between researcher and researchers (e.g. Becher, 2008). Given the diversity of Muslim communities and the diverse backgrounds of researchers of these Muslim communities, we would suggest that a fuller discussion of methodological issues is useful and relevant reading for teams undertaking this work in future.

Undoubtedly it is a challenging time to be conducting research with British Muslims. Bolognani (2007: 282) notes that research which 'exponentially developed among minority communities in the 1990s seemed to have created the idea of researchers as "predators" or "sojourners"'. She notes that the climate of Islamophobia post-2001 had a further impact, with a more general sense of mistrust having developed towards researchers studying British Muslims (Bolognani, 2007: 281, Gilliat-Ray, 2006).

To consider the issue of insider and outsider status in fieldwork with Muslims, advantages and disadvantages of both kinds of status have been noted by various commentators. Omar (2009), who was known as an *alim* (scholar) found some people unwilling to be interviewed by him because of his status, perhaps because they felt aspects of their lives were less than perfectly Islamic and they were self-conscious about this. In a contrasting example, Breen (2009) found no problem with access to Muslim primary schools, despite his prior expectations that his male gender would be problematic. In fact it seemed easier for him as a non-Muslim to get access to the school for fieldwork than it might have been for a Muslim man. Hall (2004) has argued that during her research into women of South Asian origin and the legal processes of citizenship, her whiteness signified neutrality to her participants. However, there are also accounts in the literature of Muslim identity or shared ethnic identity facilitating research with British Muslims (Phillips, 2009; Phillipson et al., 2003)

While we note the general lack of writing about methodological issues, there have been some recent important contributions to the literature which need to be highlighted. For example, Tahir Abbas considers the power and knowledge dynamics and implications of research conducted by Muslims, about other British Muslims (Abbas, 2010). Likewise, there have been reflective articles about the use of *particular* qualitative methods in relation to British Muslims (such as 'shadowing') (Gilliat-Ray, 2011), and the methodological consequences that arise from an understanding of fieldwork with British Muslims as an especially *embodied* process (Gilliat-Ray 2010). These developments suggest that researchers are developing a more reflexive approach to their methodological strategies, and problematizing the data-gathering process. This chapter seeks to build upon this emerging trend.

Our Research with Muslim families

The qualitative study involved recruiting sixty Muslim families from Cardiff with children of primary school age to take part in semi structured interviews (in total, interviews with 99 parents and 120 children). In addition to interviews, children from 24 families took part in a second phase of fieldwork, which involved keeping a digitally recorded audio diary and taking some photographs which were then used to inform a second interview. Both audio diaries and photographs were meant to be about a typical week of learning to be a Muslim. We also carried out observation of formal Islamic education in a number of different settings.

Spalek (2005) argues that the diversity within the Muslim population means research results are not generalizable. Whilst agreeing that caution is needed, we would advocate that it is possible to more closely examine differences between and within Muslim communities using a combination of qualitative methods and a large enough sample to capture diversity. Our sample was diverse in terms of ethnicity, social class and school of thought. The families also lived in a range of different districts of the city with different density of Muslim population. Table 3.1 below gives a summary of the diversity in our sample of sixty families and Table 3.2 lists each family and study participant. Table 3.2 is provided for readers to refer back to when reading data excerpts in Chapters 4–8. As can be seen from this table, culturally appropriate

Table 3.1. Sample description (number of families in each category out of a sample of sixty)

Ethnic backgrounds	Social class (NS-SEC 3-class version)	Islamic school of thought (researcher inferred)	Density of Muslim population in local area (3.7% is city average)
20 Pakistani	15 managerial and professional occupations	17 Islamic movement	23 living in a ward with 10 % Muslims or more
10 Bangladeshi		11 Barelwi	
5 Indian		10 Salafi	18 living in a ward with 4–9 % Muslims
5 Somali	24 intermediate occupations	9 Deobandi	
9 Middle Eastern	18 routine and managerial occupations, never worked and long-term unemployed	4 Shia	19 living in a ward with the city average proportion of Muslims or less
7 Mixed ethnicity couples		3 Tablighi Jamaat	
		1 Sufi	
4 Others		5 not known	
	3 unclassified (students and asylum seekers)		

pseudonyms were selected by the research team for family name and children's given names. Parents are simply identified as Mr and Mrs + family name.

Families' social class status was allocated on the basis of the parent with the highest social class occupation in the family, this being matched against the three class version of the National Statistics Socio-Economic Classification (ONS, 2005: 15). This was a simple enough strategy but it did also have its problems. A good number of families fell into the middle category on the basis of self-employment, even though their income—for example from the father's taxi driving—might have been low. Ethnicity was defined by the research team, although this was on the basis of discussion with parents. It is common for research participants to self-define their ethnicity and indeed we are very interested in self-identity (see Chapter 8). However, we decided it was important both to ensure our sample was ethnically diverse and also to ensure it reflected to some extent the balance of different groups in the population. This was not a simple matter, as we had both the UK Muslim population in mind (very largely made up of South Asians) and also the particular history of Cardiff, with relatively high proportions of Yemenis and Somalis. Therefore we set ourselves recruitment targets for different ethnic groups and social classes and hence did our own categorization of family ethnicity. We did this of course on the basis of initial discussion with parents about their ethnic background.

Table 3.2. List of all families participating in study

Family pseudonym	Interviewees, with child pseudonyms (sex/age)	Density of Muslim population*	Ethnicity§	Researcher inferred school of thought	Primary schools (state school unless noted)	Social class†
Abdul-Rahman	Father	High	Somali	Salafi	Not known	3
Adam	Mother and children: Sahra (f/10), Fathia (f/8), Awa (f/6)	High	Somali	Islamic Movement	Private	2
Ahmed	Mother, father, and child: Sana (f/7)	High	Pakistani	Tablighi Jamaat	English-medium	2
Ahmet	Mother, father, and children: Isra (f/8), Metin (m/5)	Low	Other	Barelwi	English-medium	1
Akbir	Mother, father, and children: Sadeka (f/12), Ahmed (m/9), Taj (m/4)	Medium	Bangladeshi	Islamic Movement	English-medium	2
Akhtar	Mother and children: Farid (m/17), Litan (m/14), Haseeb (m/12), Habib (m/4)	Medium	Bangladeshi	Barelwi	English-medium	3
Akras	Mother, father, and children: Nadia (f/8), Samiah (f/4)	Medium	Middle Eastern	Deobandi	English-medium	2
Altaf	Mother, father, and child: Haris (m/3)	Low	Pakistani	Deobandi	N/A (too young)	2
Anwar	Mother, father, and children: Genwa (f/12), Arwa (f/11), Salmaa (f/7)	Medium	Pakistani	Islamic Movement	English-medium	U
Arshad	Mother, father, and child: Yasmine (f/4)	High	Mixed family	Islamic Movement	Muslim private	1
Asaad	Father and child: Hamza (m/10)	Low	Mixed family	Salafi	Muslim private	2
Ashraf	Mother, father, and children: Aabida (f/10)	High	Pakistani	Islamic Movement	Muslim private	3
Ayub	Mother, father, and child: Iza (f/7)	Low	Pakistani	Islamic Movement	English-medium	2
Azzad	Mother, father, and children: Karimul (m/11), Kamarul (m/9)	High	Other	Islamic Movement	English-medium	3
Barakah	Mother and children: Fadi (m/12), Badr (m/11), Manal (f/8)	High	Middle Eastern	Not known	English-medium	3
Chowdary	Mother, father, and child: Rihana (f/4)	Low	Bangladeshi	Not known	English-medium	2

(Continued)

Table 3.2. Continued

Family pseudonym	Interviewees, with child pseudonyms (sex/age)	Density of Muslim population*	Ethnicity§	Researcher inferred school of thought	Primary schools (state school unless noted)	Social class†
Fathullah	Mother, father, and children: Ayaa (f/10), Khadija (f/8), Ilyas (m/5)	High	Mixed Family	Salafi	Muslim private	2
Faysal	Mother and children: Daniyal (m/10), Ehlenoor (f/8)	Low	Middle Eastern	Shia	English-medium	3
Hamid	Mother, father, grandfather, and child: Hashim (m/10)	Medium	Pakistani	Barelwi	English-medium	2
Hashim	Mother, father, and children: AbdulAzim (m/4), Ismaeal (m/7), Rabiea (f/8).	Medium	Pakistani	Salafi	English-medium	3
Hassan	Mother, father, and child: Zubir (m/11)	Medium	Pakistani	Deobandi	English-medium	2
Hooshmand	Mother, father, and child: Neda (f/10)	Low	Middle Eastern	Shia	English-medium	1
Hussain	Mother, father, and children: Ilyas(m/ 12), Aman (f/ 8), Abbas (m/ 5), Latif (m/ 3)	Medium	Pakistani	Barelwi	English-medium	1
Ibrahim	Mother, father, and child: Farid (m/10)	High	Other	Islamic Movement	English-medium	U
Ishmael	Mother, father, and child: Jasmine (f/5)	Low	Other	Not known	English-medium	3
Islam	Mother, father, and children: Ayaan (m/11), Saniya (f/6)	Low	Bangladeshi	Salafi	English-medium	1
Jamil	Mother, father, and children: Habib (m/11), Asad (m/8), Amani (f/6)	High	Bangladeshi	Barelwi	English-medium	3
Jawad	Mother, father, and children: Khansa (f/ 10), Sana (f/ 8), Mohammed (m/ 7), Khalid (m/4)	Medium	Pakistani	Deobandi	Muslim private	1
Karmo	Mother, father, and children: Aram (m/15), Omar (m/12), Nada (f/10), Azim (m/9)	Low	Middle Eastern	Islamic Movement	English-medium	2
Kennedy-Shah	Mother, father, and child: Daniyal (m/4)	Low	Indian	Shia	English-medium	1
Khalid		High	Somali	Salafi	English-medium	3

(Continued)

Family pseudonym	Interviewees, with child pseudonyms (sex/age)	Density of Muslim population*	Ethnicity§	Researcher inferred school of thought	Primary schools (state school unless noted)	Social class†
Khaliq	Mother, father, and children: Kauthar (f/10), Kaleem (m/8), Kinan (m/5)	Low	Pakistani	Deobandi	English-medium	3
Khatun	Children only: Saima (f/13), Akbar (m/11)	Medium	Bangladeshi	Barelwi	English-medium	2
Mabrouk	Mother and children: Mahmood (m/9), Asiya (f/5). Mother, father, and child: Asiya (f/8)	Medium	Mixed family	Salafi	English-medium	1
Mahfouz	Father and children: Layla (f/13), Tahirah (f/11), Nur (f/4)	High	Middle Eastern	Islamic Movement	Welsh-medium	1
Mahmood	Mother, father, and children: Fariha (f/12), Madiha (f/10), Zainab (f/5)	High	Pakistani	Deobandi	Welsh-medium	1
Miller	Mother, father, and children: Aamira (f/11), Musa (m/5)	Low	Mixed Family	Islamic Movement	Welsh-medium	2
Mir	Mother, father, and children: Haider (m/9) Yusuf (m/8), Ibrahim (m/6)	Medium	Pakistani	Islamic Movement	English-medium	2
Morris	Mother, father, and children: Huda (f/6), Hajer (f/9)	Low	Indian	Sufi	Alternative private	1
Mubashir	Mother, father, and child Nurul (m/7)	High	Bangladeshi	Deobandi	English-medium	2
Mughal	Mother, father, and child: Azim (m/5)	Low	Indian	Salafi	English-medium	1
Mustafa	Father and children: Balqees (f/7), Hafsa (f/10)	Low	Mixed Family	Tablighi Jamaat	English-medium	2
Omar	Mother, father, and child: Adam (m/11)	High	Somali	Salafi	English-medium	2
Rafique	Mother, father, and child: Fateh (m/10)	Medium	Bangladeshi	Islamic Movement	English-medium	3
Rahman	Mother, father, and children: Asad (m/11) Nadifa (f/8), Aziza (f/6).	High	Somali	Islamic Movement	English-medium	2
Rana	Mother and children: Sabah (f/8), Aneesa (f/10), Sofia (f/5)	Medium	Pakistani	Islamic Movement	English-medium	3
Rasheed	Mother and children: Fatima (f/12) Muhammad (m/10)	Medium	Mixed Family	Islamic Movement	Alternative private	3

(Continued)

Table 3.2. Continued

Family pseudonym	Interviewees, with child pseudonyms (sex/age)	Density of Muslim population*	Ethnicity§	Researcher inferred school of thought	Primary schools (state school unless noted)	Social class†
Saad	Father only	High	Middle Eastern	Not known	English-medium	3
Sajaad	Mother and children: Nabeel (m/9), Ayman (f/6)	High	Pakistani	Deobandi	English-medium	2
Salah	Mother, father, and child: Zeenat (f/9)	Low	Indian	Tablighi Jamaat	English-medium	1
Shahzad	Mother and children: Sami (m/6), Umar (m/4)	Medium	Pakistani	Islamic Movement	English-medium	2
Shiraz	Mother, father, and children: Naveed (m/11), Faraz (m/8), Omar and Abdullah (m/twins/6)	Medium	Pakistani	Barelwi	English-medium	2
Shirazi	Mother, father, and child: Zarrin (f/8).	High	Middle Eastern	Shia	Muslim private	1
Sohail	Mother, father, and child: Husna (f/6)	High	Pakistani	Barelwi	English-medium	U
Tahir	Mother, father, and children: Faiza (f/7), Hassan (m/4)	High	Pakistani	Deobandi	English-medium	2
Tawfeeq	Father and child: Musa (m/10)	High	Middle Eastern	Salafi	English-medium	3
Tufail	Mother and children: Ali (m/3), Najeeb (m/4), Umaira (f/9)	Low	Indian	Not Known	English-medium	1
Uddin	Mother and child: Fakhir (m/10)	Low	Bangladeshi	Barelwi	English-medium	3
Yaqub	Mother, father, and children: Usmaan (m/14) Naima (f/12yrs), Sajid (m/10), Abdullah (m/8)	Medium	Pakistani	Barelwi	English-medium	3
Zaid	Father only	High	Bangladeshi	Barelwi	English-medium	2

*This column refers to 2001 Census data on electoral wards in the city. High = living in a district with >10% Muslim population; medium = living in a district with 4–9% Muslim population; low = living in a district with <3.7% (Cardiff average) Muslim population.

†Relates to the three class version of the National Statistics Socio-Economic Classification (ONS, 2005: 15). 1 = managerial and professional occupations; 2 = intermediate occupations; 3 = routine and manual occupations, never worked and long-term unemployed; U = unclassified because a current student or asylum seeker (and therefore not allowed to work).

§ 'Other' in the ethnicity column is used to anonymise an ethnic group which has a small population in Cardiff. Naming the ethnic group would have risked identifying the family.

Categorizing families according to school of thought proved to be very difficult and rather unsatisfactory. Identifying the different religious traditions of the British Muslim population is a complex process (see Institute of Community Cohesion, 2008). It was explained in a footnote on the first page of the book that we are employing a broad definition of 'school of thought', to include both formal Schools of Thought (*madhahib*) and also movements within Islam (e.g. Deobandis, Salafis, Islamic movement). We are using the term 'school of thought' as shorthand for a more complex range of different traditions. One difficulty for categorizing families was that very few people explicitly identified a school of thought. A large majority simply declared themselves to be 'Sunni, only Sunni'. The clearest differences of belief and forms of worship were indeed between Sunni and Shia Muslims in our sample. This reluctance on the part of parents to identify which tradition within Sunni Islam they came from was interesting in itself. In some cases it may have hidden a lack of knowledge of the different traditions. For most people, however, regardless of their Islamic knowledge, we would interpret this declaration of 'only Sunni' as suggesting an impatience with divisions that exist between Muslims. One way in which decisions about categorization could be complex was where there was a mismatch (in just a few families) between a parent's own religious traditions they had grown up with and those of their mosque. Some people attended a particular mosque because it was the most local option and not because they consciously preferred its interpretation of Islam. However, for those families who did not give any other indications of which school of thought or tradition they favoured, we had to use what we knew about the mosque they attended to categorize them. Because of the decisions we had to make in the research team, sometimes on the basis of little knowledge, in Tables 3.1 and 3.2 the relevant column is headed 'researcher-inferred' school of thought.

Thematic analysis of the qualitative data was facilitated by Nivo 8 software. The initial coding frame was carefully developed by the whole research team after reading a subset of interviews. It went through several drafts before the final version was agreed upon. Most of the themes in the coding frame reflected the original research questions and the interview schedule, but some were added because they arose inductively from the process of data collection or from reading the initial subset of interviews. The two researchers (Asma Khan and Sameh Otri) were responsible for the coding of transcripts. This coding was checked for consistency by Jonathan Scourfield. The thematic codes were inevitably fairly broad and given the large size of the data set some included a very large amount of data. Further thematic coding took place within codes as first drafts of book chapters were being developed. Much of this more detailed coding was practically managed in Microsoft Word via the copying and pasting of data excerpts.

As is now fairly standard in childhood studies research, we used relatively child-friendly techniques within the interviews, in an attempt to make the children feel reasonably at ease. So we offered the options of individual or sibling group interviews and used various engaging activities that will be described later in the chapter. We used a wide range of activities during the fieldwork and it is not possible to discuss every aspect here. Instead we will focus on some key issues which we believe will be of interest to others working in this field—both researchers and perhaps practitioners working with children. The rest of the chapter is structured into five main subsections:

- The Context of Islam in Cardiff
- Mixed-faith and mixed-ethnicity research team
- Recruitment of research participants
- Fieldwork conduct and rapport
- Child-centred methods

The Context of Islam in Cardiff

Cardiff is the capital city of Wales, a stateless nation within the United Kingdom with a population of just over 3 million people, of which approximately 350,000 live in the capital itself. Cardiff acquired City status in 1905, and what had been a small town of a few thousand inhabitants in 1800 was by 1900 the largest coal exporting port in the world and home to over 150,000 people. Cardiff is today the social, economic, political and cultural hub of Wales, and is enriched by its long history of ethnic, linguistic, and racial diversity.

According to the 2011 Census, Muslims account for 1.5% of the total Welsh population (49,950 people), and yet in Cardiff, they constitute 6.8% of the City's inhabitants (23,656 people). The Welsh and Cardiff Muslim populations more than doubled between 2001 and 2011. Data at a more local level were not yet released at the time this book was going to press, so constituency- and ward-level data here are from the 2001 Census. Muslims have a significant presence in areas such as Butetown, Grangetown and Riverside, with Butetown as the most deprived ward in Cardiff according to the Welsh Index of Multiple Deprivation (Welsh Assembly Government, 2008). Cardiff has an overall ethnic minority population, according to the 2011 Census, of 68,292 (20%) so Muslims

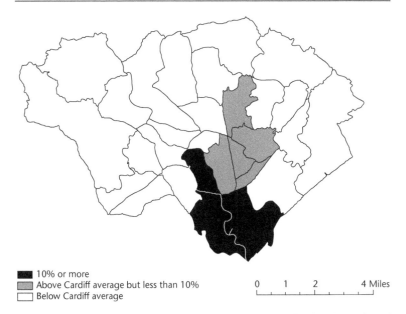

10% or more
Above Cardiff average but less than 10%
Below Cardiff average

0 1 2 4 Miles

Figure 3.1. Proportion of population stating religion as Muslim by electoral ward in Cardiff (2001 UK Census).

constitute 35% of the 'ethnic minority' population of Cardiff. (We acknowledge that of course not all Muslims are from minority ethnic backgrounds). Figure 3.1 shows the density of Muslim population by electoral ward in Cardiff, based on the 2001 Census, with wards grouped into three bands, as also used in Tables 3.1 and 3.2.

Despite the long history and well-established character of the Yemeni and Somali communities, most Muslims in Wales are from Asian backgrounds. Compared to the Muslim community in England, there is a slightly lower percentage of Pakistani and Indian Muslims, and a higher percentage of Bangladeshis. Compared to the overall number of British Muslims born in the UK, a lower percentage of Muslims in Wales were born within its borders in 2001 (36.6% compared to 46%), suggesting that there is a higher rate of new Muslim immigration into Wales, compared to other parts of the UK. Again, 2011 detailed Census data, when released, will indicate whether there has been a change in the intervening decade.

The City of Cardiff provided a particularly interesting location for our research, largely on account of the longevity of Muslim settlement, and the diversity within its Muslim population. As noted in Chapter 1, maritime cities such as Cardiff have particularly well-established Muslim communities, largely due to the number of Muslims who settled here from the late 19th century onwards (Gilliat-Ray and Mellor 2010). Most of the early migrants to Cardiff were seafarers, recruited to work on the maritime routes of the colonial empire. Hence, Muslims from Yemen, Somalia, and the Indian subcontinent found their way to Cardiff which, at the turn of the 20th century, was an important centre for commercial shipping. Having completed their passage on one ship, they would reside in boarding houses in dockland areas until new employment could be found on an outbound vessel. Over time, an increasing number of boarding houses were owned and managed by Muslims, and these provided a physical, social, religious, and economic base for these transient male seafarers. Boarding houses also began to provide the foundations for the emergence of a more settled community, and in particular the establishment of worship facilities. Later in the 20th century, Muslims based in, or travelling through, Cardiff contributed essential labour to the First and Second World War efforts. During the 1930s and 1940s, Muslims in Cardiff began to establish religious institutions in the City, including a mosque, a school for the religious education of children, and social facilities centred on alcohol-free cafes and shops serving 'ethnic' products. The most substantial growth in the Muslim population in Cardiff occurred after the Second World War, when large numbers of economic migrants from the Indian subcontinent came to the UK to boost the post-war economy. Again many were single male workers, who intended to stay for a relatively short period of time. However, a number of political, legislative, and economic factors saw a change from temporary male residence to more permanent family settlement, largely due to the arrival of women and children. This created the conditions for the growth of further religious facilities and institutions.

The question of exactly 'what counts' as a mosque is of course debatable, but based on publicly accessible information about the location of religious institutions in Cardiff, there are currently ten mosques in the City that serve the interests of Muslims from a range of 'schools of thought'. There are two Muslim primary schools, and a range of high-street organizations that serve Muslim needs and interests, such as Islamic charity shops, halal butchers, and Islamic bookshops. Muslims in Cardiff have also established an Islamic Scouts association (Mills, 2009), and supplementary schools that offer Islamic education to children after school, as well as at weekends. In recent years, there have been particular efforts to establish pastoral and welfare services for Muslims, including a network for 'new Muslims' (converts) as well as an Islamic social support service to provide counselling and advice for Muslims from an Islamic perspective. The 'Muslim Council of Wales'(MCW) is an umbrella body that aims to represent the interests of Muslims in Wales, particularly in terms of engagement with civic and political leaders. It has been a catalyst for the establishment of a range of welfare, leadership, and youth projects in recent years, and provides responses and comments to current affairs in the media that pertain to Islam.

Despite the size and historical significance of early (if transient) Muslim settlement in Cardiff, relatively little research has been conducted about the religious lives of Muslims in the city. The paucity of evidence is also compounded by an emphasis on race, employment, and labour relations in the research that does exist (Sherwood, 1988, Evans 1985). Muslims in Cardiff are discussed through these particular analytical frames, and their religious activities are often only mentioned incidentally in accounts which otherwise tend to focus upon their migration or socio-economic conditions, especially in the 20th century. In many ways this is not surprising. After all, Muslim settlement in the city has been directly related to economics in terms of maritime trade, and the demand for additional labour during and after time of war. In recent years, researchers at Cardiff University have undertaken a range of studies to explore the religious history and identity of Muslims in Cardiff more explicitly (Gilliat-Ray and Mellor 2010). Our research on the religious nurture of Muslim children contributes to this growing body of qualitative work.

Mixed-Faith and Mixed-Ethnicity Research Team

It was noted above that there can potentially be advantages and disadvantages of both insider and outsider status in fieldwork. There is, therefore, no easy answer to the question of which researchers are best to approach potential research participants. In our project we had a mixed identity research team, with three Muslim researchers, one of whom is British Pakistani and another Syrian, and gender composition of two women and two men. Two Muslims—a man and a woman (Sameh Otri and Asma Khan)—were appointed as the main fieldworkers. The person specification for the post included 'knowledge of Islam' as an essential criterion and knowledge of one or more community languages as desirable. These criteria need not have necessarily have led to the appointment of Muslim researchers, but they did make it more likely. The advertisement specified that at least one woman would be appointed, in the light of the difficulty that a male researcher might have going into Muslim family homes with only the mother present.

Some researchers studying the practice of Islam and the lives of Muslims in the UK have had to spend a great deal of time with managing the outsider–insider relationships within their fields of study (Bolognani 2007, for example). Whilst not wanting to suggest that insider status is always straightforwardly beneficial (see Omar, 2009), the fact that some of the researchers on the project were Muslim and had lived and worked with Cardiff's Muslim community over a number of years meant that issues of access were perhaps easier for us because of this. However community-level access or acceptance of a research project or a project team is a very different issue from family level access. This requires explanation of confidentiality, flexibility about practicalities of times and locations, and also a degree of intuition on the part of the researcher about family members' expectations. For Asma Khan this meant some identity management to ensure her self-presentation met those expectations in terms of dress, use of a particular language and behaviour. Often there was a need for on-the-spot decision making as to how far she should go in meeting those expectations.

Our fieldwork experiences lead us to conclude that the involvement of a female researcher in fieldwork with Muslim families is fairly essential. The female researchers on the project were able to conduct interviews with both Muslim fathers and mothers, together and separately without this being an issue for research participants and their families. However, the male interviewers carried out individual interviews with fathers only. The option of a male interviewer was not presented to the mothers, but the reason for it not being offered was that it did not seem appropriate. Where male researchers interviewed couples, this may have affected the data collected, in so far as the mothers interviewed seemed less likely to answer questions fully and seemed more likely to agree with the answers given by their husbands, in contrast to interviews conducted by the female Muslim researchers which sometimes led to interesting three-way dialogue, with both male and female adult participants feeling comfortable enough to disagree or debate certain points.

Interview questions were based on the potentially sensitive and in some ways very personal and intimate subject matter of the lived experiences of families and the option of allowing interviewees the choice of being interviewed by a male or female researcher was an essential requirement of conducting the research project within the current context of this city. Interviews conducted with mothers by Asma Khan often covered subjects such as childbirth, circumcision and pregnancy.

It is almost certainly the case that these topics would never have been covered in such depth and ease with a male researcher.

The Muslim fieldworkers were able to use aspects of their identities (ethnicity, gender and religion), knowledge (Islamic and languages) and experiences (parenthood, discrimination, racism) to redress some aspects of the researcher–researched power imbalance and to build and develop trust and rapport with the families—both with parents and with children. In some situations, displaying sound knowledge of Islam was helpful. In others, it was perhaps more important to display knowledge of popular culture, especially for children, such as being familiar with the characters from High School Musical and or the footballer Cristiano Ronaldo. In other situations, ethnic background was important for rapport, such as Asma Khan's encounter with Mr Hamid, a grandfather with whom she spoke Urdu and made connections in terms of families they knew in common both in Cardiff and Pakistan.

Sophie Gilliat-Ray had relatively little engagement in data collection. Where she did take part in interviews, she may not have been known personally to families, but the Centre for the Study of Islam in the UK she leads in Cardiff is well known and generally respected by local Muslim organizations. The Centre is perhaps known for having a particular ethos and empathic approach to the study of Muslims in Britain, which is focused as far as possible upon grassroots community engagement, and partnership. However, the fact that the Centre is well known for collaboration with the Muslim Council of Wales, might have been seen negatively by some families in the study, who might have had a critical or sceptical view of this particular organization or indeed of British universities more generally.

Sameh Otri is a well-known figure in Cardiff's Muslim organizations, having taken part in teaching Qur'an, Islamic Studies and Arabic, as well as being a regular attendee at one of the most popular mosques. His social networks of local Muslims were very helpful for recruitment. We might speculate that some people would be put off from taking part in the project because they see it as associated with a devout local Muslim or might have held back some of their views for this same reason. Sameh Otri's interviews seemed to generate a range of responses, however, and overall his status as a respected active local Muslim seemed to enhance the rapport with families.

Jonathan Scourfield came to the project with relatively little prior knowledge about Islam. He was aware of his limitations as an interviewer, for example in not knowing children's own (ethnic) terms for things—e.g. younger Pakistani children looking blank when he asked about fasting and they themselves would use the Urdu term *rosa*. Where his relative lack of prior exposure to Islam could arguably be an advantage in fieldwork was in the interpretation of data. There is a certain sense in which a relative outsider can see the wood for the trees. This approach as an outsider to Islam was useful for making sense of our data and a helpful balance to the insider knowledge of other team members.

Some community languages were spoken by members of the research team (Urdu, Punjabi and Arabic), but not all. There were language barriers with some families and this could cause initial difficulties with informed consent. One family seemed to think that when Sameh went to their home to interview them he was in fact coming to discuss teaching Qur'an to their children. In another case, a mother wanted to discuss the possibilities of her getting a job in the university and it was not quite clear that she had agreed to take part in a research project. We did have a project leaflet with basic information about the research in multiple languages. However, as many social researchers find, this was not always read and the research team had to explain carefully before any interviewing began what was expected of research participants. In the two cases of possible confusion mentioned here, the project was fully explained and both sets of parents agreed to take part.

The main fieldworkers' familiarity with some of the local Muslim communities provided something of a shortcut to accessing families. As a research team it did not seem as though we were thought to be from 'an ivory tower' (Bolognani, 2007), because of some established links with Muslim communities. Insider knowledge proved invaluable throughout the research process, from designing leaflets to analysing the data, with discussions in weekly team meetings for checking any potential over-familiarity. Also, given the diversity of the sample in terms of ethnicity and language and practice of Islam there were plenty of opportunities within team meetings to ask what certain phrases meant for the individuals who expressed them. No researcher can be expected to know everything in the field and sometimes admitting ignorance can lead to a more clear explanation and definition of what a certain practice means to a research participant.

Local knowledge of mosques, leading community figures and Islamic schools was also important in building a rapport. This knowledge was in part enhanced and legitimated by having representatives from key local Muslim organizations as members of a project advisory group. We were able to share useful information about the locations and presence of Muslim organizations that participating families expressed an interest in. This was especially useful for those families who were isolated from Muslim communities because of where they lived or a lack of knowledge about services available to them.

The Muslim researchers on the team carried out the majority of fieldwork interviews and there were plenty of shared experiences, rapport building and empathy. Women were more likely to express that they enjoyed the interview experience and found it empowering and positive, though some fathers expressed that it had made them think more about their parenting and teaching and that this reflection made them want to act. In referring to shared experiences, we are of course departing from a model of social science as requiring detachment to ensure objectivity. The idea that qualitative fieldwork should be in some respects reciprocal has become increasingly mainstream since early contributions on feminist methodology (Oakley, 1981), just as the importance of reflexivity in the qualitative research process (Coffey, 1999) is increasingly accepted. It is this tradition of reflexive, reciprocal field relations that this chapter draws on.

Recruitment of Research Participants

The project advisory group was helpful to the project in terms of useful advice, contacts, insights, direct help with access and lending credibility to the project through their support of the research aims. Taking the advice of this group and our own initiative, we 'took the project out' to a number of events in the city. This included holding information stalls about the project or distributing leaflets at key Islamic events (e.g. Eid parties), a South Asian cultural festival (mela), Muslim schools, children's activity centres and state primary schools. It is interesting to note that all of the families living in non-conventional Muslim family structures (e.g. divorced) were recruited at non-Islamic activities and locations. Face-to-face and direct forms of recruitment were on the whole most positive. We were able to compile a database of potential research participants and were able to choose which families to interview according to the needs of our sample, for example to achieve a balance across the sample in terms of ethnic origin and social class.

Most parents we spoke to were positive about the aims of the project. Some said a straightforward 'no' to participation and others said it was a busy time for the family, due to the birth of a new baby or a family wedding, and some allowed us to keep their details to use at a later date. Negative responses to the research and its aims mostly seemed to be to do with suspicions about the team spying for the government or MI5; this was a surprisingly gendered response, with only men asking such questions and only the male Muslim researcher (Sameh) being asked the questions. This may be because men are more concerned about government strategies which are more likely to target the behaviour and actions of Muslim men. However, it may also have been influenced by the researcher's own Arabic origin or his position within the community. It may also be to do with spaces where certain concerns can be raised; Sameh was much more likely to recruit families at a mosque than Asma and this is to do with the gendered character of mosque attendance in the city.

Recruitment was very successful and we were able to select the most appropriate sample rather than having to take everyone who we could get, which is probably a more typical scenario for qualitative studies. The extent and breadth of successful recruitment was largely due to making the research project accessible by attending a large variety of activities and events for the local Muslim community rather than a reliance on word of mouth recruitment (snowballing) or an expectation that potential participants would contact us in response to a distributed leaflet or poster. All those who agreed to be contacted were sent a written response to acknowledge their interest and were informed whether they had been selected to be interviewed immediately, or that their details had been retained for use in the future or (in some cases) that they could not be included in the sample because they did not live in the study catchment area.

As well as letters on official university headed paper, modes of communication with families included text messaging, Facebook, email and phone. We found that text messages were a very effective means for communicating with families in order to confirm details for times and locations of interviews as compared to phone and email. Texting allowed research participants time to respond (so they could liaise with other family members if required) and it was also a fairly unobtrusive method for those at work or busy with children. They could reply when they had time and also most parents of young children keep their phone to hand so we could be sure that they had got the message.

The results of our secondary analysis of the Citizenship Survey (see Chapter 2) showed Muslims to be relatively more successful at the intergenerational transmission of religion than other religious groups in the UK. This headline finding was useful as a positive introduction to the research project for families and also allowed us to emphasise that we were approaching Islamic nurture positively and were not out to criticise families.

It is only ever possible to be a partial insider with a diverse population. The research team was successful in engaging the diversity of families as set out in our original sampling frame. However, we did find recruitment of some groups within our sample, namely Bangladeshi, Shia and Indian families, harder than others. In order to ensure we captured some Shia families within the ethnically diverse sample we had a recruitment target for this religious position. For Indian and Shia families the main difficulty with recruitment was simply the small number of these families in Cardiff. We succeeded in recruiting Indian and Shia families through perseverance and full use of our social networks and contacts. There was some snowballing, with research participants suggesting friends or contacts. There is no established Shia mosque in Cardiff, but only small venues with weekly worship, making them less visible. However, once we had located these communities it was not a problem to find families willing to be interviewed.

The difficulty in recruiting Bangladeshi families was more surprising, given that they are fairly numerous in the city. Our impression of the Bangladeshi community was of a certain reluctance to take part in the project. One Bangladeshi community worker suggested that this may be due to research fatigue, with Bangladeshis being over-researched, not necessarily by academics but by policy researchers working with local or national government, and with these organizations also being more likely to make incentives available. We had decided at the outset not to offer financial incentives for participation. Another factor to note is that we did not in the research team have any ethnic or linguistic connection with Bangladeshis, nor any established social networks with this ethnic group. Despite these issues, the study included the number of Bangladeshi families we had initially hoped to engage. We wanted to ensure that our sample of families were representative of other social characteristics of their ethnic groups such as social class and area of residence within the city. It would have been somewhat easier to recruit Bangladeshi families from higher social classes. However, we decided to persevere to attain our target sample. A specific practical difficulty with recruitment of this ethnic group was that the Bangladeshi fathers often worked in shift patterns which involved night time work, for example in restaurants. This made recruitment of families via fathers and male spaces such as mosques more difficult and also made the practical arrangements for interviews with mothers and children more difficult to negotiate.

Fieldwork Conduct and Rapport

We selected families from our database of contacts with our sampling strategy in mind. In particular we needed to work hard to ensure a diverse sample, attempting to meet target numbers we had set for recruitment of ethnic groups and participants from a range of social class backgrounds. After initially meeting parents via one of the routes mentioned above, contact was made by phone to check whether they were still happy to take part and to arrange a time for interview. During this conversation we offered the families a number of alternatives for the interview process. These included conducting the interviews at a place of the research participant's choice; having both a male and female researcher come to the house to conduct all the family interviews at a time of their choice; or a staggered fieldwork process wherein the researchers could carry out the interviews separately with adults and children at different times and locations. Most people chose to be interviewed at home, although a small number of interviews took place in alternative locations such as the project office at the university, workplaces and on one occasion an interviewee felt that the best available location would be in his car. With a combination of Qur'an classes, after school activities and leisure activities, the busy lives of the children meant that the researchers had to be extremely flexible in terms of diary planning and many interviews were conducted in the evenings and at weekends. Particular times of the year, especially Ramadan, proved to be very quiet fieldwork phases with entire families occupied with the religious requirements of the holy month.

Another important point to note about making interview arrangements is that although the option for the whole family to be interviewed in the space of one fieldwork session was seen to be more convenient by a number of families, we realized early on that this might not be the best arrangement for data collection. When the whole family was present in the family home the male researcher and the father in a given family would normally be shown into the 'front room'—a space traditionally reserved for non-*mahram* visitors to a Muslim family home. *Mahram* refers to a man that a woman can never marry because of closeness of relationship, such as a father, brother, uncle or son. A woman's husband is also her *mahram*. A non-*mahram* is therefore any other man outside these categories. Therefore the female researcher would interview in the family room or kitchen, the children would inevitably end up here during their mother's interview with requests for food and drink or other similar requests and the interviews were often rushed or became stressful for the mothers. We then made a conscious effort to always suggest to mothers that they might prefer to be interviewed at a time when their children/child were at school or nursery and even during the nap times of very young children, and this resulted in a richer interview and a far more rewarding interview experience for both the interviewer and interviewees.

Despite a plea we have heard from health and social care practitioners for a list of 'DOs and DON'Ts' for the behaviour of guests in Muslim family homes, it is impossible to produce such a list and, arguably, attempting to do so may actually assist the process of 'othering' Muslim families and marginalizing families who fall outside the scope of any given list. As with the expectations of any good guest, it is important to be mindful of any social cues and religious teachings. For example, during an interview with a Muslim family where we guessed that the parents had separated and the mother had agreed for us to interview only herself and her children, we decided it was best for the female researcher to conduct the interview on her own. In hindsight this was probably the best decision due to this particular family's circumstances. A good host might insist that the researcher does not take their shoes off at the door. However, if a shoe stand is positioned by the door and all the family members are wearing slippers or no footwear, it is probably a good idea to remove your shoes, as there is symbolic importance to these small acts of respect. An Islamic greeting can also be appropriate, although there are those who would only expect such a greeting to be given by Muslims and would only return the greeting to other Muslims.

A self-conscious building of rapport could be seen as treating Muslim families as 'Other'. Rather, a more natural sharing of common experiences, such as parenting or the knowledge of the area where the family live, can work well. Sharing of information about one's self—what Bolognani (2007) refers to as 'reciprocal exposure'—can be effective in rapport-building, although at times it can be experienced as intrusive or challenging by the researcher. For example, the grandfather mentioned earlier in the chapter asked Asma Khan some questions in Urdu which might be considered rather rude and too personal for most polite English conversation, such as her caste, where her family lived in Pakistan, the name of her father, grandfather and father-in-law. However, this would be fairly standard introductory conversation for many older Pakistani people as they are keen to establish links with people from back home. This exchange led to a very strong rapport with this family member and helped the researcher's 'respectability'. It could of course have been a rather difficult situation if the answers from a different researcher had not met with approval and social acceptance.

We had not expected at the onset of the project that interpretation would be needed in many cases, primarily because most parents of primary school age children are either first language speakers of English or are able to converse fluently in English and also because the researchers were able to converse in Punjabi, Urdu and Arabic. A number of parents were interviewed in community languages. These were carried

out by the researchers themselves where possible or by family interpreters. An external interpreter was used only once throughout the research
project although the choice was always made available where required.
There were in fact two interviews where older children translated the
interview questions and their mothers' responses. Here, professional
interpretation was offered, but the interviewees preferred asking help
of their own children. For another interview, a community Arabic
teacher, known to both interviewer and interviewee, was asked to interpret. Although the use of non-professional interpreters may have added
to the comfort and confidence of the interviewees, the relationship with
the interpreter did have an impact on the data gathered from these
interviews. The Arabic interpreter was open about her own views
about some of the questions although she did appear to translate the
responses directly into English. During an interview with one Bangladeshi mother where her 15 year old daughter was translating it became
evident that the daughter was not giving her mother's responses but
her own version of what she decided the correct response should be.
This was evident from the difference in the length of the responses that
her mother gave to the daughter and the ones the daughter interpreted
and because of some of the similarities between Urdu and Bangla. Also it
was clear that negotiations were taking place (in Bangla) between
mother and daughter and it seemed as though the mother's version
was not quite being conveyed. Asma Khan regularly reminded the
daughter that she would really like to hear what her mother had
to say. She had to take care to ensure the daughter felt that her point
of view was valuable but also that she wanted to hear the mother's
point of view as well. This meant that the interview took longer than
it normally would have done but provided valuable data on the family
and inter-generational differences within the same family.

Although a large proportion of the parents and children were interviewed in English and for many English was their first or preferred
language, religious practices, occasions and spaces were often referred
to by interviewees in community languages. For many people, being
able to use the cultural or ethnic references to which they were accus-
tomed rather than an English interpretation, which may or may not
have conveyed the essence or true relevance of that practice, event or
place to them, meant that conversations flowed without interruption to
their narrative accounts. Children were also apt to use cultural references for religious practices and were often unable to provide an accurate interpretation of that reference in English. By making the possibility
of being interviewed in some community languages relatively unproblematic it was possible to engage some individuals or families for

whom language barriers may have made participation in such a research project complicated or discomforting.

Child-Friendly Techniques

Interviews with younger children and the use of activities

We put no bottom age limit on our recruitment although in practice the youngest children we interviewed were aged four. Generally children over the age of five were able to talk about religion and learning and where there were siblings of primary school age to be interviewed with, this increased the child's confidence and their ability to dip in and out of the interview as they wished to, adding to the comments of elder siblings, playing with toys or leaving the room. This meant that the interview was not a testing experience for them. However, where children around the age of five were interviewed on their own for one reason or another, this was more challenging for them. Fifteen of our sibling group interviews (a quarter of the families in our sample) involved children aged five or under.

In designing an interview schedule for children we ran a number of focus groups with children from the local Muslim Scouts Groups, in order to better understand the language children use to articulate their religious belief and practice. We also conducted pilot interviews with a small number of families to ensure that the interview schedules were effective. The use of activities and 'props' during interviews is well established in social research with children (see, for example, Hill, 1997). We used a card-sorting exercise to prompt discussion of identities (as in Scourfield et al., 2006) and a pots and pasta exercise (Thomas and O'Kane, 1999, as adapted by Holland and O'Neill, 2006), for children to indicate the relative importance of different kinds of behaviour that might be expected of Muslim children. The exercise involved allocating a separate pot for each of a list of behaviours (see p. 97). Children were then asked to put as much pasta as they wanted into each pot to indicate the importance of that behaviour for being a good Muslim. So, for example, very high importance might mean filling a pot to the brim and very low importance might mean only one or two pieces of pasta in a pot. Adults were also asked about both these issues (i.e. identities and behaviour), with card prompts but no pasta. In addition to activities within the children's interview, we took books, toys and colouring activities with us and allowed the children to choose what to look at or do. Some of this material had an explicitly religious theme and some was taken from popular culture (e.g. children's television programmes). Some of the religiously-themed material (e.g. images from Islamic books for children) was useful as a prompt for children who were initially unresponsive to direct questions. It was important to be informed by parents about the health and well-being of their children. It was useful for interview planning to know about learning difficulties or health problems which may lead to a child feeling tired or frustrated during an interview. The interviews with children were very flexible to allow for such circumstances, as well as variation in children's understanding of the process.

There was a lot of variation between families in terms of the level of supervision by parents. Some parents remained with their children throughout the interview and others left but popped in and out of the room, mainly whilst undertaking domestic tasks such as cooking a family meal, whilst others left and came back when the interview had concluded. In all cases where parents (usually mothers) came and went, they remained more or less within earshot. The presence of parents is unavoidable and to be expected. Although not necessarily problematic it does influence the data collected and this has to be acknowledged. There are some situations where the involvement of parents in their child's interview can be problematic as it can cause the child to feel uncomfortable but this can vary from family to family. Even within families, the presence of a parent can have different effects on different children. A parent directly commenting on a child's interview—for example 'she should know this' when a child seems to be struggling to articulate some knowledge of Islam—can be a difficult situation to negotiate, as the researcher can assert that it is good to hear a child explain in his/her own words but it is also important not to seem to be telling a parent how to speak to their child. It is impossible to predict the way in which a parent will deal with the interview situation and the difficulties inherent in being a 'good guest' (Yee and Andrews, 2006) have to be dealt with flexibly and sensitively by researchers on a case-by-case basis.

Multimedia research: voice diaries and photo diaries

Multimedia approaches have been used before in the study of children's religion. For example the work of Nesbitt and colleagues at Warwick on religious nurture in Hindu, Sikh, Christian and mixed faith families has involved photography, diary-keeping and on-line 'cyber ethnography' (Nesbitt, 1999; Nesbitt and Arweck, 2010). The use of multimedia and multimodal methods in this field is in its infancy, however, and in global terms the study of children's religion is dominated by quantitative methods (see Roehlkepartain et al., 2006a). The use of photographic and oral diaries is an original approach with regard to researching Muslim children and families.

We asked our sample of sixty families if they would like to take part in the second phase of our fieldwork which involved the children in keeping a voice diary to record some aspects of their lives as Muslim using a digital voice recorder and to take some photographs of significant objects, places and people using a digital camera, with a view to discussing these photographs in a further interview. In thirty-four families, parents said no to the children taking part. Some parents thought their children were too young. Other parents said no because they were wary that the children would damage the 'expensive' equipment, although we took pains to say that we had purchased robust equipment and we were fully expecting wear and tear. Other parents said no because of the lack of time they had themselves. In these cases the parents obviously thought that parental direction or supervision was necessary—this view was common across the sample as there were instances where parental influence was evident in the photos or the voice diaries.

Cameras were not used quite as we might have hoped. Pictures were mostly taken inside the home, often of Islamic images such as framed Quranic verses and *surahs*, the name of Allah or the Prophet Muhammad. The limited use of cameras could perhaps reflect the limited freedom of these children. It may be that compared with their non-Muslim peers, Muslim children have more limitations on their movement and are more home-based. Possibly they are not allowed out as much, have busy lives with attending mosque classes, and parents are concerned about bad influences and hanging round on the streets (see Chapter 6). (It should also be noted that in the primary school years most children, regardless of religion, are restricted in their mobility and spend large amounts of time in the family home [O'Brien et al., 2000]). It is also quite possible that there was some parental control over the use of the camera and the images they presented to us of themselves and their lives. We had the impression in some families that some images had been deleted before we arrived to discuss them. Other researchers have used disposable cameras (Clarke, 2004) in photo elicitation research with young children; this would eliminate parental concerns about damage to equipment as well as editing of children's photographs; however the inability to edit might have inhibited parents from giving permission for their children to take part in the phase of the research.

Although cameras were not used quite in the way we might have hoped, the images were none the less interesting in their own right and the discussions of photographs generated some rich data. This was the second time we interviewed these children. In most cases they looked forward to our return and were often waiting on doorsteps or in windows for us to arrive. Children were comfortable and talkative and said some things that they perhaps would not have said in the first interview when the researchers were strangers (e.g. 'My mum, she shouts at us'). This was perhaps more a feature of familiarity than it was to do with any effect of discussing the photographs. There were also instances where additional data were more directly connected to photo elicitation. For example Asiya showed pictures of her bedroom—her private 'space' within the home—where she displayed her integrated plural identity (Østberg, 2006), with her Qur'an and hijab alongside her Nintendo and jewellery stand. Discussion of photographs taken over the period of a week or longer led to children talking more about their social networks than they had done in initial interviews. These data reveal a picture of Muslim childhood that is quite directed and structured by parents in terms of social and educational activities (Islamic and non-Islamic) and social networks are those which are controlled and influenced by parents. It is also true that in middle childhood the social horizons of most British children, regardless of religion, are set by parents to a great extent (Scourfield et al. 2006). However, as explained in Chapter 2, our analysis of the Young People's Survey which accompanies the Home Office Citizenship Survey suggests there are different trends in Muslim and non-Muslim childhoods, with Muslim young people more likely to be involved in religious organizations, less likely to be involved in other out-of-school clubs and less likely to have friends round to their houses than young people from other religious groups.

The use of oral diaries, made with a voice recorder, is very much in line with the current fashion in social science research for multiple methods using diverse media. It seemed a potentially fun way of gathering data on children's lives outside of interviews, perhaps allowing something of an insight into some more private thoughts. In practice the use of diaries varied enormously, from very rich stories to very brief summaries of the main activities the child had taken part in that day. There tended to be a lot of detail about what the children had done as opposed to why. This may have been in some respects a methodological artefact, but in the context of other data this could also be taken to indicate the emphasis on learning practical aspects of Islam, with understanding developed later.

To be more sceptical, diary keeping could be criticised as being something of a white middle class habit, which may perhaps be rather outdated. A cutting-edge 21st century version might be the use of Twitter, but this would not have been particularly relevant for children aged 12 and under. We did at least use technology so children were not required to write and we allowed children to play with the recorders. Another critical perspective on diaries would be that socially desirable responses are no less likely than in interviews, if it is known that someone will be listening to the recording. Asma Khan remembers being asked to write a diary in primary school and being too embarrassed to admit to what she had really done outside school as this was so different from her friends' activities. So ice skating was made up for the diary's benefit and beans on toast were eaten for tea, rather than chicken curry and chapattis. Hopefully some of these racialized cultural expectations would have been at least partially removed from our research process, however, by having Muslim researchers from Pakistani and Syrian backgrounds introduce the idea of the diaries.

Conclusion

The chapter's aims have been, firstly to introduce the qualitative study on which most of the book is based and, secondly, to describe our field relations and reflect on them, in the hope this will be of use to those conducting research with Muslim families in future. In terms of lessons learned, we would suggest that an ideal research team will be ethnically diverse, but certainly including Muslims; have both men and women; and have local knowledge and credibility. Multi-level acceptance and recognition of the project from Muslim organizations, families and individuals is necessary. If possible, a large and diverse sample will give a more rounded view of diverse Muslim perspectives and experiences than a sample which is homogenous in terms of class, ethnicity and school of thought. Mixing methods is important, to develop a more complex picture of Muslim family life. No one method should be seen as the answer to everything and, in particular, the use of technology, whilst well worth exploring, will be no panacea and will bring particular challenges of its own.

As with any research, this project had time and budgetary constraints. The research had to be completed within a given time frame and having some minority ethnic Muslim members of the research team meant that issues of access, language, negotiation were perhaps easier because of a level of 'insider' or community knowledge. We would certainly not want to say that non-Muslim researchers or those not from minority ethnic backgrounds cannot conduct meaningful and insightful research into Muslim communities. It is possible to acquire the language, behaviour, contacts and networks required to conduct such research, but this in itself may constitute a lengthy and complex process. Our own research team was mixed in terms of religious and ethnic background and, arguably, the particular complementary mix of knowledge and experience enhanced the research process. However, the essential requirements for rigorous and ethical qualitative research are to prioritize sensitive and user-friendly research methods, to keep in mind the researchers' responsibility to the researched community and to have a credible sampling frame.

4

Learning Islam in the Home

This is the first chapter to discuss findings from the qualitative research and its focus is the teaching and learning of religion in Muslim homes. It forms an introduction to all the other empirical chapters in two different ways. Firstly, it includes an overview of the 'big picture' of Islamic nurture (not just in the home) in the first main section. Secondly, it covers the general issue of children's learning in the home and then later chapters pick up specific aspects of this general theme for more in-depth consideration. Chapters 5 and 6 are focused on domains other than the home: religious organizations (Chapter 5) and the wider community context of Cardiff and beyond (Chapter 6). However, Chapter 7 returns to the home with a discussion of family structure and specific family practices. Chapter 8, in dealing with issues of identity, is also in large part about inter-generational transmission within families.

The chapter begins with how parents see their own upbringing and the influence this has had on how they want their own children to learn about Islam. This is followed by a brief overview of the issue of tradition and innovation in religious nurture and then some discussion of which adults take responsibility for religious nurture and how this process works. The question of commonality and diversity amongst the study families is then picked up for discussion. After this, there are three separate sections on belief, religious practice and appropriate behaviour. In the section on practice we explicitly consider how exactly this teaching makes children into Muslims, although this question is also hovering throughout the chapter.

Family Regimes of Religious Nurture

Parents' own religious upbringing

Before discussing how contemporary Muslim children are brought up, it is important to begin by considering parents' faith and in particular their learning about Islam. All parents were, after all, once children themselves.

When referring to their childhoods, there was fairly frequent reference within the parents' interviews to the distinction between religion and culture. When contrasting these two, culture almost always comes out as the loser—it refers to backward-looking non-Islamic practices from countries of origin, including majority Muslim countries. Sometimes these are the interviewees' own countries of origin and sometimes those of their parents. This is in keeping with what Olivier Roy (2004) describes in his analysis of globalized Islam. Roy writes of a process of deculturation wherein Western Muslims distance themselves from the ethnic cultures of their parents in favour or a 'pure' Islam. Mrs Morris, for example, who was brought up in a wealthy educated Indian family, said religion was 'always there' in her childhood but 'it kind of came out when the need was there, you know, like a beautiful dish that everyone gets out and then put away'. Several adult interviewees spoke of their parents as not being able to explain aspects of Islam (Mirza, 1989), perhaps because they themselves had little knowledge. Mrs Adam told us she would ask 'why?' questions, for example about wearing hijab, only to be told by her (Somali) parents, 'No, you just got to do it—it's the faith, that's it'. Mrs Ashraf was unusual in speaking very positively about her religious upbringing in Pakistan as she considered herself well taught at home by scholars, but none the less saw her country of origin as not 'very Muslim' and she thought her own children would learn more about Islam from growing up in Cardiff.

Parents' decisions of faith were sometimes described in individualized terms as a positive choice, with an explicit contrast being drawn with any notion of cultural or social obligation. Mr Mahfouz told us he found himself 'reverting to a more, not a hard line, but, to try to be much more Islamic than I ever was before!' and again distinguished this from the kind of Islamic practice he had grown up with in Cardiff. For him this was about making his own decision.

> 'You reach a certain age where you want to make your own decisions. I suppose I didn't want, I wanted to make my own decisions and not be influenced by the community because I'd always kept asking questions, you know, like is that religious or is that cultural? I suppose, through your own learning you can make your own distinction.' (Interview with Mr Mahfouz)

Mrs Adam used the Christian term 'born again' in relation to her decision as a young adult to properly embrace Islam, having been influenced by some Muslim women friends who took her to Regent's Park mosque when she was living in London:

'These sisters, what they were teaching me was better than what my parents taught me and I was going regularly, every week, to *halaqas* and talks and Islamic events and then next thing I'm going into work with my hijab on and there was a lot of things I stopped doing, like not going down to the pub with friends and stuff like that, things like that I used to do with my work colleagues like now I would not do at all. And so all those, just stopping things basically that wasn't, that was really forbidden for me to do which totally relegates my Islamic values so as I was learning more, I became more, I would say more spiritual.' (Interview with Mrs Adam)

This last statement raises the separate issue of 'spirituality' and the question of whether or not it might mean something rather different to Muslim families from the highly flexible individualized conception we come across both in popular usage and in academic analyses. We return to this issue later in the chapter.

Not everyone rejected their upbringing. Mrs Chowdary, in this next excerpt, wants her children's religious learning to be like her own, in contrast to what she sees as the 'extremism' they might otherwise be exposed to. What is interesting here in relation to individualization is that although she is talking of the importance of *maintaining* her own family tradition, it is none the less clearly a conscious choice. And in fact, in taking a different stance on the religion–culture distinction referred to above, she is going against the grain of contemporary British Muslim culture. She has critically reflected on the available options and made the decision to teach the children herself.

'Yes, I don't know, there's a lot of things about getting extremist, I'm worried that—I don't want her to get mixed up with the wrong crowd. So, I rather teach her because I believe that my husband and I can teach her just as well as anyone else, with the religion, you know and how you practise it. So, that's why I'd rather bring her up the way that I was brought up.' (Interview with Mrs Chowdary)

There is quite a bit of critical discussion of regimes of religious learning in the parents' own childhood learning. Some negative views are expressed, for example about coercion from parents, harsh treatment from teachers and rote learning of the sound of *surahs* from the Qur'an (in Arabic) without any explanation of their meaning.

'Well, we just went to the mosque on an evening, to learn Arabic, but even then it was the Qur'an, but, even then it was, you were just learning this, what you didn't understand and you'd just parrot fashion, just saying it to yourself and learning all of this but we never knew what it was.' (Interview with Mrs Mir)

'...later on we got more aware, because we moved to this part of Cardiff, there is more Muslims, I guess I didn't like it, I didn't think, I thought my religion was very cruel, because we used to get hit a lot [*laughs*], we used to get hit a lot, whether we liked it or not. I didn't like it much because you know it's too hard, and there was no enjoyment.' (Interview with Mrs Akbir)

These issues are well known in many British Muslim communities, and efforts have been made to reconsider the role and delivery of Islamic teaching (Mogra 2004, 2005).

It is equally the case, however, that several parents reflected on their own childhood learning in positive terms, even whilst recognizing its rather old-fashioned style. Mr Tahir experienced various punishments, such as being struck with a stick and being told to hold his ears from under his legs. He would say this worked for him. When asked how that informed the way that he practised Islam he said,

'It makes me more strict. It scares you as well, cos you gotta learn it then and then he made you read all the namazes at the time as well so it has prepared me, it made me more toward Islam.' (Interview with Mr Tahir)

Mrs Uddin remembered how she hated being forced to learn by her mother, with the television switched off for recitation of *surahs*, but said 'I'm glad she did now because I do remember them a lot better'.

It is worth noting that where parents distanced themselves from their own experience of religious nurture it was generally confined to style of teaching or failure to properly explain the faith. If they were critical of their parents' religiosity, this tended to be in a more conservative direction. It was unusual for parents we interviewed to reject the dogma of their own parents' Islam in favour of more liberal interpretations of what it means to be a Muslim.

The wood and the trees

To sum up what we have presented so far, there is certainly evidence from parents of critical reflexivity about their childhood experiences. There is a certain debate about how to teach children to be Muslims. Islam is often seen as something which needs to be 'embraced' rather than simply being taken for granted, except perhaps by the youngest children. However, when we consider the big picture of Islamic nurture and the ways in which contemporary children are brought up to be Muslims, we would question how useful it is to emphasize individualization when what is more striking about religious nurture in Muslim families is continuity in regimes of learning; conformity to collective traditions; and fairly conservative belief, if not also practice.

Both Mrs Chowdary's 'choice' to conform to family traditions of religious learning and the commoner stance of parents which was 'choosing' to reject ethnic cultures in favour of a pure Islam could be described as a 'soft individualism' (Guest, 2009), in so far as these reflexive life choices lead to conformity to a religious pattern rather than to a creative post-modern diversity.

The most striking aspect of Islam in the UK is not really the individual faith decision. Arguably, to emphasise individualization in Islam is to fail to see the wood for the trees. When we consider religious nurture, more striking is collective practice and continuity of tradition. With few exceptions, the families we have spoken to arrange for their children to learn to read the Qur'an in Arabic ('the language they use in Heaven', as one of the children told us). The importance of this, even when the children's functional Arabic language may be very limited, is not fundamentally questioned. There is a certain acceptance that the classes will not result in an in-depth understanding for many children. Some parents choose to send children to Islamic Studies classes, in addition to Quranic learning, or may themselves endeavour to explain key beliefs in the language the children best understand, but the importance of reading the Qur'an in Arabic remains (Gent, 2011). The religion the children are being taught is therefore fundamentally a traditional Islam. That does not mean there is no diversity amongst the families we have spoken to. Later in the chapter we discuss some of the diversity we heard about. But it is important to keep in mind that there is more that unites the families than separates them. The 'outliers' are those families with no teaching of Islam at all. Such families are rare in our sample. We would have to acknowledge they would be much less likely to agree to take part in our research than more families to whom Islam is meaningful. We cannot generalize in any quasi-quantitative way about the level of Islamic practice amongst all British Muslim families because of this sampling issue. Where we can perhaps claim 'moderatum generalization' (Williams, 2000) is in relation to dominant discourse about what matters in Islamic nurture.

The practice of sending children to religious education classes was almost universal amongst the families in our study and many Muslim parents saw this as an important way of fulfilling their parental responsibilities (Gilliat-Ray, 2010). The age at which this process began varied, but some children attended classes from as young as five years of age. In close to half the families in our study this meant classes at least three (but often five) days a week, typically in a 5–7 pm slot. For the select few who aspired to memorize the Qur'an and become a *hafiz*, the classes would be 4.30–8.30 pm six days a week (Gent, 2006). This more intense learning is relatively rare and is comparable with children training for elite sport, but going to mosque (as children would term it) every evening during the week was a fairly mainstream experience in our sample (see Gent, 2011). Other children had less intensive teaching, perhaps as little as one class a week, but they would none the less be expected to recite the Qur'an on the basis of thorough teaching. As Becher (2008) notes, the structure of Muslim children's time tends to be heavily influenced by religion and particularly formal learning. The range of classes attended by the children in our sample included at least three different kinds. Some children attended more than one kind of class.

1. Primarily Arabic language tuition, with some Islamic input—these classes would especially be used by the children with at least one Arab parent and may meet only once a week, but for a session lasting several hours (five of the families in our sample).

2. Learning to read the Qur'an in Arabic, preceded by a basic intro-duction to the Arabic language. This is the commonest type of class and can take place in a variety of settings—mosque, child's home, teacher's home, on-line. In our sample, children from 27 families attended home-based classes and children in 24 families attended mosque-based classes. Home-based classes were usually taken by specialist teachers but in 11 families, these classes were taught by a parent. Two children did all their Quranic learning in a Muslim primary school. This total of 53 added up to all but one of the families who had children clearly old enough to attend, as six of the families we interviewed only had children aged five and under.

3. Islamic studies classes, which are focused on the main teachings of the Qur'an and *hadith*, and typically meet only once a week (eight of the families in our sample).

In Chapter 5 we introduce Islamic supplementary education more thor-oughly and consider parents' and children's views of these kinds of classes.

There is plenty of nuance revealed in our study about how parents and children understand the practice of Islam in the context of their lives in a largely non-Muslim and largely secular city. This understanding does involve negotiation and not simply straightforward acceptance and application of a detailed set of rules. The rest of this chapter and other later chapters will attempt to convey some of this diversity. None the less, the 'big picture' is of religious teaching which is more marked by tradition than it is by innovation. There is diversity but the families we have interviewed are arguably more marked by what unites them than what divides them.

Who is responsible for religious nurture and how is it done?

The theme of gender is developed more fully in Chapter 7. At this point, we simply note the overall picture of gendered patterns in religious nurture. Mothers are, in general, much more heavily involved in child care than fathers. This means that it is mothers who in practice tend to be the main guardians of appropriate behaviour for Muslims and mothers who are most involved in teaching children about belief and practice in Islam (in families where this happens), or in making sure children get to classes to read the Qur'an or learn about their faith. The extent to which fathers are involved varies, but many are fairly uninvolved in religious nurture and this is often connected to working hours. This pattern is very occupationally based as well as gendered. As noted in Chapter 3, categorizing Muslim families according to social class can potentially be misleading unless definitions are kept carefully in mind. It is important to distinguish occupational status and income, because of the high proportion of men in our sample who are self-employed but none the less living in relative poverty. What is most important to note in relation to gendered patterns of religious nurture is the impact of particular racialized occupations on family life. Fathers who work in restaurants tend to be out at work at the crucial hours between the end of school and bedtime, so even if they were inclined to contribute to religious nurture, have little opportunity to do so, except perhaps at the weekend (Birt, 2008). These families would also tend to be poorer, although the picture varies according to whether fathers own the restaurants or simply provide their labour, and they would also most likely be Bangladeshi, given that most UK 'Indian' restaurants are run by Bangladeshis (Tackey et al., 2006). We were told by one mother (Mrs Jamil) that 'Bangladeshi dads, they don't really interact' with the family. She put this down to her culture, but economic factors would also seem to be very important. Obviously caution is needed here and no blanket judgements should be made about variation according to ethnicity without more robust quantitative evidence. There are, however, some stark differences in occupations according to ethnic group and these can potentially have implications for family life. For example, many Pakistani men drive taxis (Kalra, 2000) and men who work only late shifts, when there is greatest demand for taxis, can in theory spend quite a lot of time with their children at certain times of day, although of course actual practice will vary between families.

The theme of extended families is also discussed in Chapter 6. At this point it is simply important to note that family members other than parents do often have a role in religious nurture, when they are available for children (i.e. when they live nearby). This might mean a grandparent having regular care of the children and teaching them about appropriate ways to behave as a Muslim or making sure that formal religious learning takes place. It might be that older siblings are an important influence, especially where they are fairly devout and interested in their faith. In some families, siblings were highlighted as especially important role models.

Although we emphasis the common core of belief amongst the families in our sample and the agreement that children should be formally taught to read the Qur'an in Arabic, there is none the less considerable variation in terms of how to bring up children to be Muslims. One key distinction is between families who see Islamic nurture as holistic and influencing all aspects of life and those who instead seem to it more narrowly as learning to pray and read the Qur'an. Some families in the latter group seemed to see their main duty as Muslim parents being to ensure children attended classes at the mosque. Some of these perhaps did not feel qualified themselves to teach children about Islam. This could be a form of self-deprecation and bowing to scholars with expertise or it might suggest an actual deficit in understanding. Other parents may feel more confident in their own abilities to teach children but feel too busy to do this properly themselves. The other group of families was those who made a point of introducing Islam to children more holistically from a very young age. This might involve teaching children basic aspects of belief well before they are old enough for formal Quranic learning. It might involve encouraging children to copy the motions of prayer. It might also involve encouraging more formal learning, such as reading verses from the Qur'an, in the course of the daily routine. The Sajaad family provide an example here. The mother got the children to play 'mosque-mosque':

MRS SAJAAD: 'Basically Ayman wears her scarf and Nabeel comes in with topi and stuff and it's just about sitting them down and teaching them about Islam. We make it into a game, so, they bring their books and stuff out and then Ayman wants to read a story to everybody, so she can pick her own story so she reads her story and they have to go and read a *surat* so they both have to learn a *surat* and look up the meaning and stuff. Obviously they've got this book which is at my dad's house, it's got like the *surat* in and the translation in English but in different colours so they like looking at it. Then if they don't want to read a *surat* cos they obviously read Qur'an every single day so they go and learn a *dua*, so they're learning all their *duas* now and then sometimes they even want to act plays and stuff: "Oh someone's fallen over I'm going to pick them I'm going to pick them because in Islam we're supposed to help". So they learn all of that, we actually pretend it's like a school.'

ASMA (researcher): 'Are you the teacher?'

MRS SAJAAD: 'Well, I'm supposed to be the teacher but they take over most of the time.'

'Mosque-mosque' took place every weekend (with children aged 9 and 6). Mrs Sajaad told us 'sometimes it lasts for hours and sometimes it lasts half an hour; depends what mood they're in'. This is certainly not a typical family, in that Nabeel, the 9 year old, was taking a *hifz* class to learn the Qur'an by heart. But this example is indicative of a family where an effort was made to incorporate Islamic learning into normal family routines within the home, rather than it being something that only took place when attending classes. Whilst the more holistic approach might seem more intensive, it should be noted that for a minority of families in our sample, sending children to classes involved attendance on three or more days a week, so this approach to Islamic nurture can also be fairly intensive.

As Pinquart and Silbereisen (2004), amongst others, have noted, religious nurture is not a one-way process. There is a certain amount of give-and-take in families' religious learning. Islamic birth rituals (see Chapter 7) were something that many parents had to find out about at the time of a first pregnancy. More generally, for many parents, parenthood was the point at which they found out in earnest about Islam and perhaps decided where they stood in terms of school of thought, if they consciously had one. The Akbir family were an interesting example of generational give and take, as the 9 year old son reminded his father to pray; the children nagged the father about selling alcohol in his restaurant; and there were debates within this family about religious issues, such as whether it is right to celebrate the Prophet Muhammad's birthday or go to the cinema. Becher (2008: 139) describes some Muslim children 'acting as re-instaters of tradition' and she notes that 'generational transmission can also occur "upwards"'. Different families took different views on children expressing opinions and asking questions. In the Rahman family, the parents spoke about learning themselves about Islam so as to answer the children's questions. Mrs Barakah, however, said that when asked questions by the children when they were very young she did not know how to answer so would not respond.

Learning about Islam is inevitably a multi-media experience, to some extent. Although classes such as those we observed in Islamic

81

studies or Qur'an reading tended to be mainly based on the use of books and spoken interactions between teacher and students, we also observed a role-play of the Hajj, with the different stages of the pilgrimage recreated in various different rooms of the mosque. Perhaps more use was made of modern technology in home-based learning, with some parents showing children DVDs and Islamic television channels and websites. One family used a karaoke machine for children to practice *nasheeds* (devotional songs) and prayers. One girl was taught Qur'an in a one-to-one web-based video conference with a teacher. Some of the technology was associated with leisure though, of course, hence it was a source of tension for some children who were tempted to watch their favourite secular TV programmes or to play computer games (see the quotation from Daniyaal Faysal in Chapter 6).

Commonality and Diversity

Is not possible from our sample to make robust comparisons between any categories of family—for example, variation according to class, ethnic group or school of thought. Whilst we ensured the participation of a diverse range of families, probability sampling was not used so we could be sure that any difference between subgroups was not caused by our sampling strategy. Also, the numbers of families from some ethnic groups and schools of thought were too small to make comparison very meaningful. In this section we simply give an overview of some possible indicators of variation we noticed in our qualitative research that would be worth studying in future research with a different design from our own.

The commonality of belief and regimes of formal religious education has already been noted. What is probably most striking in terms of the diversity of religious nurture is that there could be as much variation within the most obvious subgroups (by class, ethnicity, school of thought or density of Muslim population) or social categories as between them. There were diverse family formations. Some parents had divorced or separated. This could have implications for religious nurture (see Chapter 7), with different parents taking different views on what is an appropriate Muslim upbringing and this sometimes being the cause of tension between parents or between parents and children. In one family we interviewed, two of the three children were living separately from their parents, with their uncle. This was apparently due to the parents being in the country illegally, having over-stayed on their visitors' visas. There were also implications for religious nurture, as the uncle's family were said to be more observant Muslims.

Parents had a diverse range of migration histories, from those whose families had long history in Cardiff to those who had only arrived from abroad in the last few years. We spoke to some families who were seeking asylum or had been granted refugee status. We spoke to converts as well as those brought up as Muslims. There was a range of views about religion and place. An example of the different stances taken on the extent to which different countries are Islamic can be seen in an exchange between Mr and Mrs Mahmood. Mrs Mahmood was brought up in Pakistan and sees no religion–culture conflict. She, like many other parents who grew up in Muslim countries, tended to compare the UK negatively with her country of origin as a context to bring up Muslim children. To her, Pakistani culture and Islam seemed to merge, up to a point. Mr Mahmood, however, who had never lived in Pakistan, although he has visited relatives there, disagreed and they had a lively and good-humoured exchange in the interview. Mr Mahmood argued against the conventional wisdom, saying that he thought Muslim countries were 'more decadent'. He went on to assert that 'children from here know more about Islam than Pakistani children about what religion means, its purpose, or the stories, the *hadith*'.

It seemed as though the parents with more experience of education were able to engage in more discussion with their children about the meaning of Islamic belief and practice. Some had gained this education in Muslim countries and others in the UK (usually in adulthood). Although education and social class often map onto each other (see, e.g. Whitty, 2001), the picture could be complex for families in our study. For example, Mr Zaid is a taxi driver—not a job which requires any particular academic learning—but is highly educated about Islam. There were only two families in our study which could be described as 'liberal' in their religious belief and practice. Both these were professional middle class families with educational backgrounds in secular disciplines.

Different schools of thought in Islam were connected to differences in Islamic practice, as noted in some of the other chapters of this book, but did not map on to many noticeable differences in religious nurture. When directly asked about this variation, no families believed that school of thought affected anything. There was a general tendency for them to dismiss the possibility of differences between schools of thought and to assert the commonality between Muslims (see King, 1997). One difference that could be observed, however, was a tendency for those in the Hanafi tradition to believe that girls from age eleven should not go to mosque. Other than this point, we did not find marked differences in the expectations of boys' and girls' learning. That is not to say that eventual differences according to gender were not expected. Adult men and women were generally seen to have very different roles. But in middle childhood, there was no particular issue about segregation and the regimes of learning were similar for boys and girls.

Although caution is needed in the light of the small samples of each subgroup within our study, it was noticeable that we found the more holistic style of Islamic nurture to be most prominent in the mixed ethnicity families we spoke to. This is most obviously explained by all these families containing one parent who is a convert, meaning that this parent at least has had to learn themselves as an adult, and quite possibly from scratch, what Islam is all about. It is also perhaps explained by these families having relatively smaller family networks of other Muslims, meaning they are slightly more isolated from established local traditions of religious nurture. In contrast to this, it was in the largest ethnic groups, namely Pakistanis and Bangladeshis, that learning about Islam was most likely to be seen primarily as about going to classes to read the Qur'an. This is perhaps explainable by these being the most numerous ethnic groups, so that ethnic traditions of religious learning are more likely to build up over time. An example of a family where we can see ethnic religious learning traditions in play is the Mubashir family. The seven year old boy seemed in the interview to have a very limited understanding of his faith. Interviews with the parents suggested their idea of bringing him up to be a Muslim did not extend beyond checking his progress with learning the Qur'an. Despite this they spoke of wanting him to go to an Islamic boarding school in Leicester with a view to becoming a hafiz and an Imam. The practice of sending him to classes to learn to read the Qur'an could perhaps be seen as primarily an ethnic tradition. That is not to say that the family were not sincere in their desire for him to memorize the Qur'an, but only to note that there seemed to be something of a gap between this aspiration and the current reality of his Islamic knowledge.

To memorize the Qur'an was not a strong tradition amongst the small number of Arab families in our sample. These families seemed at ease with their faith which did seem to be integrated with everyday routines, perhaps because knowledge of Arabic makes the understanding of religious texts so much easier. In contrast to the larger ethnic groups in our study, some of the ethnic groups that are smallest in the city of Cardiff understandably put a lot of emphasis on learning community languages. For example, the one Kurdish family we interviewed tended to emphasize the children's learning of the Kurdish language over their learning about Islam.

Some advantages of class could be seen amongst the families in our study. The Akbir family, for example, owned a restaurant and their interview revealed some of the financial investment of religious nurture. They used books, television programmes (e.g. Shaykh Zaki Nayek on Peace TV) and Islamic DVDs. The twelve year old daughter was sent abroad for one year to learn Arabic and Islamic studies. A teacher came to the home to teach Qur'an and the children attended Islamic studies classes. It was noticeable that the children who attended the weekly classes of organizations such as 'Islamic Studies for Children' tended to be from middle class backgrounds.

A range of experiences were reported according to where in the city families lived. Being an isolated Muslim child in a mostly non-Muslim area could bring its challenges. Mr Ayub explains in this next excerpt that this experience had led them to look for options to live in a Muslim country abroad:

'In Iza's class, Iza is the only Muslim child. And that's how sometimes she gets influenced by, um, by the peer group, if you like. Most importantly, when she goes to the parties, she comes back, she's crying that my friends, like X,Y and Z, she mentions their names, and they are eating sausages so why am I not allowed to do that? Things like that. So that's a very delicate thing. I mean, I have to explain to her that it is something which we just don't know. And to be honest, I myself don't know, I mean in a great depth, about why Muslims are not allowed to eat ham. I mean, we just know that we don't and we follow that. We never actually tried to go into it, what was the reason that we are not. So if I don't know, I can't explain to her. And then I give her examples of other Muslim children, and that's basically the main reason that we have decided to move out of the country, basically.' (Interview with Mr Ayub)

The picture can be more complicated than this of course. There is a range of possible responses to living in an area with very many or very few other Muslims. For example, in previous research in the South Wales valleys (Scourfield et al., 2005), a virtually all-white post-industrial area with a very small Muslim population, one Muslim teenager explained that her father thought it was easier to be a good Muslim when not socially contaminated by living near bad Muslims.

Belief

In the next three sections, we distinguish belief, practice and behaviour. Inevitably, any such distinction can be rather artificial as these domains can be very bound up with each other. Although they often overlap, it can also provide useful insights to consider separately children's learning about the core principles underpinning faith; everyday religious activities (such as prayer and fasting); and appropriate behaviour for young Muslims. In this section on belief we place particular emphasis on children's perspectives on belief as Muslims.

To start with the views of parents, however, it has already been noted at various points during the chapter that there is a shared common core of belief, and some aspects of religious nurture are almost non-negotiable (reading the Qur'an in Arabic) but there is considerable variety in what kind of Islamic practice is expected of children. It is notable that parents did not criticize Islam itself. They might be self-critical or critical of mosques or groups of Muslims, but not critical of the faith itself. There was a general view that a true Islam is beyond reproach and any problems that are caused by Muslims are due to people straying from the true faith or confusing religion with culture.

'Values' were only explicitly mentioned by a few families (liberals and converts), but implicit ideas about Islamic values came across in many of the interviews and we discuss this theme in the 'behaviour' section below. Reference to spirituality also came mostly from the mixed ethnicity families which included converts. These families cannot fall back on culture from Muslim countries in the same way as single ethnicity families where both parents were brought up as Muslim, so, as noted earlier in the chapter, they have to much more consciously construct their own Muslim parenthood. The language of 'spirituality' does not sit very easily with Islam. There is perhaps an assumption of an individualized religiosity, which is more in line with a liberal Western discourse of self-development. Although there are traditions within Islam which emphasize a spiritual dimension, most notably Sufism, Islam's fundamentally collective body of belief and practice does not easily lend itself to the individualized conception of spirituality which is conjured up by most contemporary uses of the term (Gilliat-Ray, 2003).

Although the core beliefs of Islam were generally not questioned, we did see variation in the ideas about the kind of relationship Muslims can have with Allah. The range of ideas can be illustrated by two contrasting mothers. Mrs Morris was brought up in an Indian Muslim family but says she takes her faith much more seriously in adulthood than her own parents did when she was a child. Her husband is a white Welsh convert to Islam. She bemoaned the lack of attention paid to 'spiritual parenting' and herself taught classes on this topic to Muslims and non-Muslims alike. She emphasized the spiritual common ground between different religions and for her own children, prioritized the meaning of prayer rather than the act. She seemed to encourage in her children a more personal connection with Allah. In contrast to this, Mrs Altaf taught her son Haris that Allah lived in the frame on the wall containing Quranic verses.

> 'When I want to tell him off I say "Allah will hit you". I tell him that Allah lives in this picture here. So whenever he does something wrong he looks up here and says, "Sorry Allah Ji, I won't do it again.'" (Interview with Mrs Altaf)

It should be noted that Haris was only three years old and the idea of Allah in the frame was seen by Mrs Altaf as age appropriate. But Allah was a rather more judging presence for Mrs Altaf than for Mrs Morris and being a good Muslim in this home seemed to be more about *what* was done than *why*. Themes of punishment and reward were far from confined to the Altaf family, but were also spoken about by many of the children as important aspects of Islam, as we will see.

The children seemed to know what religion they had from a very young age. Hassan was only four and knew he was a Muslim (and not an alien, which is what his big sister told us he used to say he was). In fact a religious identity seemed to be made a priority in this family from a very young age. Hassan said he was told he was a Muslim 'every time'. We tended to get fairly conventional messages about the children's faith—answers that good Muslim children would expect to give. This was in part an artefact of the way we conducted the research. Most children have enough social awareness to have an idea of what they think they are supposed to say to adults. In this case they were being asked about their religion mostly by Muslim adults, so of course there was a strong element of social acceptability in their answers.

The children tended to describe a process of gradually learning a set of facts and rules. So it was, in fact, impossible to separate belief and practice for most of the children. Sahra (11) when asked, 'Why is it important to read the Qur'an if you're a Muslim?' replied, 'So then you know why you're a Muslim and you know your faith and then you know what Allah has told you to do and you can obey those rules and then you can find if he will give you a reward or something.' The children's relationship with Allah was nothing abstract. It was not really captured by an individualized notion of 'spirituality'. It was very much about a set of prescriptions for living your life.

> ASMA: 'What do they teach and when do they teach you about Islam?'
> ADAM: 'They teach me like the right stuff and like good stuff and bad stuff.'
> ASMA: 'What's good stuff and what's bad stuff? Maybe you can give me an example?'
> ADAM: 'Bad stuff is like when you don't pray and you don't read the Qur'an and good stuffs when you read the Qur'an and when you pray.'
> (Interview with Adam Omar, age 11)

Adam saw the world in fairly simple terms and not all the children were like this, but he described a more general tendency to see learning Islam as about learning the rules about what is good and what is bad. In working all this out, children asked questions of their parents of course. As Mr Mustafa put it, 'They ask many, many questions like, you know, who Allah is, why we are here, why are we all a different colour?' Examples mentioned by other parents included, 'Can you telephone Allah?' and, 'Does Allah have a moustache?'

We saw examples in the data set of children taking for granted their Muslim identity as something they just had, rather than something they chose to embrace. This taken-for-granted Muslim identity may well be more to do with ethnic and racial identity than religion. The idea of minority defence might help us understand the comparative strength of inter-generational transmission in Islam. This approach would argue that religion is stronger for social minorities as it has other work to do, such as helping to preserve the distinctive culture of an ethnic group which is outnumbered and perhaps helping to maintain social bonds in the context of discrimination and deprivation (see Chapter 3). We saw this process at work when children took a Muslim identity for granted, perhaps being especially aware of the identity because of the way they looked or spoke (clothes, skin colour, language). We see different versions of being a Muslim here from Sahra and Fathia. Sahra, who was a couple of years older, spoke of Islam as a faith decision, whereas for Fathia it was a received identity:

ASMA: 'OK so you don't think that it's good to force people to be Muslim, you think that we should choose?'
SAHRA: 'I think it's good for, I think if somebody wants to force them I don't think they should force them I think they should teach them into Islam and then, and then they get a choice, so.'
FATHIA: 'But we're already Muslims.'
(Interview with Sahra, age 10, and Fathia Adam, age 8)

Becher (2008) also describes some Muslim children conflating religion and ethnic culture. For example, one boy in her study saw his mother as more religious than his father because she spoke Urdu with him. She suggests (Becher, 2008: 71) he found it 'difficult to distinguish' between 'cultural and religious symbols of expression'.

The youngest children did make mistakes with the facts of Islam. That is, they misunderstood some things, as we might expect them to at their stage of development. Here is an example:

ASMA: 'When do they do that? Do they do that at special time of day? After they pray? Yeah? Do you ever do that? When do you do it? Do you do it when you're praying with your daddy? Okay. And what do you say when you do that with your hands?'

RIHANA: 'And you wish.'

ASMA: 'You wish? What do you wish?'

RIHANA: 'Um. Do you know the fairy takes my teeth and her saw a flower on my, and it was shining and, and a fairy give it to me, and he gave me money and it has been really shiny.'

(Interview with Rihana Chowdary, age 4)

This does not seem to be an Islamic tooth fairy, but what was interesting here was that Rihana was making a connection between prayer and a sense of enchantment and an unseen world (*ghayb* in Arabic) beyond the material one. A four year old is perhaps less self-conscious than an older child would be to talk in these unconventional (for Islam) terms.

It is certainly evident from our data that the stories children repeated were the ones with the more shocking elements. Isra was asked what kind of stories he liked best and he said, 'the parts where it is kind of scary and that'. Ibrahim, when asked what he liked about a particular story, told us boldly that the best bit was the 'killing'. Asiya told us she had learned about fasting at her Islamic Studies class. When asked what she had learned she told us, 'pregnant women can't fast because of their babies, they can die in their stomach'. It is often these vivid shocking details that children mentioned when discussing their learning about Islam.

We were occasionally reminded that religious experiences with meaning for adults did not necessarily strike children in the same way. Asiya (again), who was eight years old, has been to *Umrah*, which for many Muslim adults would be a very powerful experience. However there did not seem to be the same spiritual connection for her:

ASMA: 'Did you enjoy it? What was our favourite place to see in Umrah?'

ASIYA: 'Seeing the black stone.'

ASMA: 'Do you think it's important to go to Umrah? Why?'

ASIYA: 'Because, I'm not sure.'

ASMA: 'You liked it? Did it make you feel special in any way?'

ASIYA: 'Not really.'

(Interview with Asiya Mabrouk, age 8)

Sometimes what seemed on the face of it to be idiosyncratic beliefs in younger children turned out to be more mainstream than they first seemed. Daniyal Kennedy-Shah, aged 4, showed his interviewer a picture in the kitchen of the Aga Khan (Imam for Ismailis). He said that

'Mowla Bapa' was 'dead now but he is all around us—I went to see him in hospital when I was a baby'. There was some confusion in this statement. The 'dead but all around us' comment might possibly be a reference to Christian theology learned at his church primary school, but the latter statement did in fact relate to him going to see the Aga Khan in London the year before ('when I was a baby' in four year old terms) and the mention of the hospital related to some ill people having been brought to see him on stretchers.

Religious Practice

Variation in Islamic practice is perhaps inevitable. In our study there were families where parents prayed five times a day and children joined in when present. There were other families who only prayed in the mosque. Not all attended mosque regularly. There were debates about what is and is not Islamic. There was a certain amount of negotiation about religious practice. For example there were examples of different views about when children should really start to pray. These excerpts below show the variation:

ASMA: 'Do you pray five times a day?'
FATHIA: 'Not all the time.'
SAHRA: 'If we're in school, when we, when we reach puberty my mum says we have to.'
(Interview with Fathia, age 8, and Sahra Adam, age 11)

MOHAMMAD: 'I'm practising to pray.'
SAMEH: 'How many times?'
MOHAMMAD: 'Because I'm nearly seven I gonna need to practise and do it good, I need to do it all the time in seven.'
(Interview with Mohammad Jawad, age 6)

ASAD: 'Yeah. And the um, the age that you've got to like pray compulsively, you've got to pray and to fast and everything is 15.'
ASMA: 'Is 15?'
ASAD: 'Yeah.'
ASMA: 'So before then you can practise?'
ASAD: 'Yeah, you can practise. It's better to practise um, because if you practise at fasting when you are younger, you won't struggle when you are older.'
(Interview with Asad Rahman, age 11)

Predictably, we saw some variation according to school of thought. One example relevant to children was birthdays. Nesbitt (2004) describes the spectrum of different approaches to children's birthdays amongst adherents of other religions where there is no tradition like the secular Western birthday celebration. Some Muslim families in our study thought it wrong to celebrate a birthday as such, although they might think some kind of gathering is acceptable. Others happily celebrated a birthday. The point of difference between the two rests upon the idea of birthday celebrations as possibly 'innovative' and therefore a deviation from the Islamic path as exemplified by the Prophet. In the Mir family, the two separated parents took a different view on this issue so the boys were allowed to decide for themselves. Some families were open to children's questions about Islamic practice, seeing the value of discussion, while others took the view that questioning was best avoided. A certain amount of agency was expected in some families. For example, we came across a couple of examples of parents or children explicitly saying interpretation of Islam (and associated practices) was something children could choose as they get older.

At the liberal end of the spectrum, Mr Kennedy-Shah emphasized values rather than practice. He echoed Mrs Morris (earlier in the chapter) in saying that for Ismailis, 'it's about developing a relationship with Allah Himself, so it's very meditative and it's internal, so the ceremonies are secondary, so it doesn't matter about covering your head or things like that'. With reference to his son Daniyal he said, 'I would imagine if you ask him what being a Muslim means he'll talk about the values rather than saying his prayers.' The two liberal families in our study were notably different from the other 58. Across most of our families there was a certain agreement about children's learning of Islamic practice. From age one to five there was an expectation of basic belief in Allah and a certain awareness of *haram* and *halal*, especially in relation to food. From age five to ten there would be some trying out ('practice') of prayer and initial learning of Arabic for reading the Qur'an, with children probably starting to be part of a collective activity. From around age eight onwards children might be expected to have built up a social life surrounding the mosque or Islamic Studies classes.

For many of the children, religion came across in interviews as fairly instrumental. That is, the motivation was reward in the afterlife rather than, for example, doing something because Allah wants you to or because it is fair to other people or for any other altruistic motivation. So prayer makes you feel happy, Fadi told us, because you have 'done something good and then we might go to *Jannah* (paradise)'. Nabeel was learning to be a *hafiz* and said that success 'would mean that I've done loads of good deeds and I'm not scared to die or something because I know I'm going to go to *Jannah*'. Asiya told us *Jannah* was 'a big place where you can have whatever you want, if there's a flower on the floor, if you wanted a lollipop, you just think and then it's there'.

How does teaching religious practice make Muslims?

Firstly, we consider how the cognitive science of religion can aid our understanding of the particular strength of the transmission of Islam in a broadly secular context. As Chapter 3 explained, Sunni Islam, with its five daily prayers and repeated recitation of the Qur'an, can be seen to fit with what Whitehouse (2002, 2004) terms the doctrinal mode of religiosity, a form of religion which is predominantly characterized by frequent repetition of low intensity ritual and teaching. As we have already noted, most children attend Qur'an classes at least once a week and often at least three times a week (typically after school, e.g. 5–7 pm). Even more routine is the repetition of Islamic phrases at key points throughout the day for some children. Here is an example from Asad's voice diary:

'I did my homework then I got ready then I left the house and to go to a Eid party with my sisters and my mum before I left the house before we leave the house we say *"Bismillaahi, tawakkaltu alallahi, wa la haula wala quwwata illa billah,"* which means in the name of Allah I depend on Allah there is no ability above us except by the relief of Allah and then I got in the transport and when you enter any transport or car you say *"allahu akbar, allahu akbar, allahu akbar, Subhaanal ladhi sakh-khara lana haadha wa ma kunna lahu muqrineen. Wa inna ila Rabbina lamun qaliboon"*, which means glory to him who subjected these to our use for we could never have accomplish this for ourselves and to our lord surely we will be returning.' (Voice diary by Asad Rahman, age 11)

The doctrinal mode involves the learning of complex teaching via semantic memory. This is a form of explicit memory which concerns general knowledge about the world; knowledge whose specific source we usually cannot identify. Learning of the Qur'an for non-Arabic speakers might perhaps be more difficult to reconcile with this aspect of the doctrinal mode, if the meaning of the verses is not properly understood so there is in fact no complex teaching. Most of the children we interviewed did, however, seem to have learned many Islamic teachings, from parents (as with Asad in the excerpt above) or from what meanings they did manage to pick up in classes.

The doctrinal mode also involves the repetition of rituals activating implicit memory, that is, what we know without being aware of it. This aspect of cognitive science theories is arguably quite close to Bourdieu's

(1984) unconsciously-learned (and sociological) version of *habitus*. One of the fathers in our study seemed to hint at his son's unconscious absorption of Islamic practice in this excerpt:

> 'I don't think it was a thing of introducing Islam to him because actually it was just part of our culture, you know, the praying, you know, the getting up for *Fajr*, you know, the fasting, you know. Even the way we conducted ourselves in trying to bring him up. So I don't think it was a thing of introducing Islam to him. I think it was something he just came into.'
> (Interview with Mr Assad)

However, as explained in Chapter 3, acknowledgement of an overtly pedagogical dimension is also required to make sense of learning to be Muslim. The words of Aamira below convey the idea of gradually copying adults. This has happened in such a natural way that it did not particular seem like teaching and learning at all, but it was imitative and therefore fits more with the version of *habitus* in the work of Mahmood (2012 [2001]) than it does with that of Bourdieu.

> ASMA: 'So you learned how to pray because you watched your mum and you joined in?'
> AAMIRA: 'It's just weird, it's just, all of a sudden I just knew. Probably because you know your *surahs* because you do your Qur'an cos I know a few off by heart, they're like some of the back ones and they're not that long and once you know *surahs* and the main bits like when you go down, when you're like when you put your hands your knees, stand up, when you're kind of bending yeah? You just learn because you do it for every single day basically of a year yeah? Well most of the year. And like you're just never going to forget it.'
> (Aamira Miller, age 11)

Figure 4.1 shows a photograph taken by one of the children in the study of a child praying at home. Learning ritual prayer (*salat*), even if the ritual is not strictly observed five times a day in families, is a core aspect of the embodied learning of Muslim habitus (Mellor and Shilling, 2010; Mahmood, 2012 [2001]). As Mellor and Shilling note, *salat* constitutes a physical enactment of submission to Allah (the meaning of the term 'Islam').

There is a pedagogical process—you learn by participation—but this is not being thrown in the deep end. It is gradual socialization into particular ways of thinking and doing. And the doing is very much embodied. You will never forget it, as Aamira put it in the excerpt above. In cognitive science terms, it enters your implicit memory or, from a sociological perspective, it becomes part of your *habitus*. Nadia in

Figure 4.1. A child praying at home—photograph taken by child research participant.

this next passage described what an embodied religious experience—feeling at peace through prayer. She was no doubt repeating what she had heard adults tell her. But that does not make it any less real. She had taken on this embodied experience of the process of prayer:

ASMA: 'And, um, if I ask you a question, it might sound a bit strange, but why do you pray? How does it make you feel?'

NADIA:*[laughter]* 'Like before that I do some *wudu* and then I feel really, really, really like, I don't know, like annoyed and tired. Then when I pray, it just all sort of goes out of me.'

(Interview with Nadia Akras, age 8)

The next excerpt involved Hassan who was only four years old. This early socialization seemed to be fairly unforced. His siblings had clearly tried to teach him what to recite but were amused when he was not quite ready for it. This is another example of how Islamic nurture works. It is not that all families are starting to teach children quite as young as this necessarily, but many of the families in the study did start to induct children into ritual practice before perhaps they were old enough to fully understand the process.

ASMA: 'Does your brother let you pray with him? Read *namaz* with him?'
FAIZA: 'Yeah. He lets anybodys (. . .)'
ASMA: 'Does he show you how to do it? Does he tell all the words as well?'
FAIZA: 'He telled me already. Hassan just goes *'Bismillah*[1], *Bismillah, Bismillah, Bismillah*, I'm done!'
HASSAN: 'I only know the *Bismillah Irraham Niraheem*[2]; oh I've forgotten, say it again.
ASMA: *'La illaha.'*
HASSAN: *'La illaha illalla Muhammad ur Rasul Allah.*[3]'
ASMA: 'Well done! That was lovely! And who taught you those special words?'
HASSAN: 'No one.'
FAIZA: 'My Mum. I told him, no my Mum did, it's hard to teach him.'
ASMA: 'Why is it hard to teach him?'
FAIZA: 'Because he keeps saying the wrong words and you have to say it again and again and again.'
(Interview with Hassan Tahir, age 4, and Faiza Tahir, age 7)

Children's Behaviour

It was mentioned earlier that 'values' were only spoken about explicitly by the two liberal families in our study and by the families that included converts ('reverts' as they tended to call themselves). By noting this, we do not mean to suggest that other families did not have any values. It is simply that explicit use of the term 'values' did not occur in most of the families. There was plenty of implicit mention of values from both adults and children, usually with reference to what is appropriate behaviour for good Muslims. There was a sense of audience being important here. This could be other Muslims, who would be expected to keep an eye out for children's behaviour. There were also suggestions that the behaviour of Muslims had to impress non-Muslims, and we could perhaps assume that this is set in the context of some negative expectations. For example Sadeka in her voice diary seems to expect people to think Muslims are 'bad':

'*Da'wah* is, what it is, is like spreading Islam. Yeah. But the way we do it, like, through actions is more subtle, so people can see that Muslims aren't bad, in fact Islam teaches, Islam is all about peace, and it's very peaceful. OK. Salaam.'
(Sadeka Akbir, age 12, voice diary)

[1] In the name of Allah (God).
[2] In the name of Allah, the Most Gracious, the Most Merciful.
[3] There is no god but God, Muhammad is the messenger of God.

95

Mr Miller, himself a convert, puts the importance of his children being ambassadors of Islam in the context of negative press:

'We've really got a thing about them being sort of ambassadors of Islam, you know really being good examples of Islam, so, if they're sort of naughty when they're out in Sainsbury's or wherever the first thing that comes to mind is people are looking at our children and thinking, "Oh this is how Muslims behave", you know, we're really sort of conscious that, that they're sort of ambassadors of Islam and there's so much sort negative...sort of press of Islam that, you know, they've sort of got a burden on them to be, you know, good Muslims and not just good to other Muslims but good to everyone in the West you know, in Cardiff and to sort of be a good citizen of Cardiff.' (Interview with Mr Miller)

So a sense of being a conspicuous minority emerges here. Good Muslim behaviour becomes something that is, at least in part, a defence of collective reputation. There was a fairly high degree of consensus on what good Muslim behaviour consisted of. Becher (2008: 36) also found in her qualitative research a 'remarkably consistent' agreement between children on the appropriate moral code for a good Muslim.

All parents were concerned to manage their children's behaviour as Muslims, to varying degrees. There was more worry about the future and especially the influence of secondary school in the teenage years (see Chapter 6), with some parents talking of going abroad to avoid any difficulties at that particular stage. In some of the families, behaviour seemed to be the primary aspect of religious nurture in middle childhood. For example, in the Fathullah family, despite the father being very knowledgeable indeed about Islam and the children attending a Muslim primary school, the children seemed to have a much clearer idea of 'dos and don'ts' and punishments for bad behaviour, than about other aspects of their faith. This may of course have been due to the practical business of managing a large family (of eight children).

It was noted in Chapter 3 that we used a pots and pasta exercise (Holland and O'Neill, 2006) for children to weigh how important different behaviours were in relation to each other. With parents we did not use the pasta but asked them to talk us through the list of behaviours and comments on relative priorities for them in their parenting. To summarize the results of this exercise, we have produced Tables 4.1 and 4.2 below, which present a quantitative comparison of parents' and children's responses. It is important to keep in mind the limitations of this analysis. It is a retrospective quantification of qualitative data. Parents and children were asked about the list of behaviours in different ways. Neither group was asked to choose their top three behaviours, but we have used this as one feasible approach to retrospective quantification.

Table 4.1. Children's prioritization of behaviour

Behaviour	Number of times in the top three
Respectful	35
Honest	27
Kind	21
Working hard	14
Obedience	13
All behaviours equally important	12
Clean	9
Smiling	5
Modesty	5
Total	141

Table 4.2. Parents' prioritization of behaviour

Behaviour	Number of times in the top three
Respectful	37
All behaviours equally important	24
Honest	19
Kind	17
Obedience	17
Modesty	14
Clean	8
Working hard	4
Smiling	1
Total	141

Despite the limitations, arguably it is none the less interesting to compare the tables, which suggest a reasonably high level of agreement on aggregate between parents and children.

It is not the numbers themselves that are important here; hence we have not set the parents' and children's columns next to each other. The numbers of parents and children completing the task were not the same and the totals agreeing at 141 is sheer coincidence. More important to note is the ranking, hence we have put the behaviours in rank order. Parents were more likely than children to declare the behaviours all equally important. This might perhaps be a gap between rhetoric and practice, with parents expressing the *principle* that they are all equally important for their children and the children who actually have to carry out the expected behaviour being rather more pragmatic in prioritizing some things over others. The children were much less likely to prioritize modesty. This was possibly to do with their understanding of the term. Modesty takes on a different meaning post-pubescence when it becomes associated with body display or covering. For most children aged under twelve if it means anything, modesty will perhaps be associated with not 'showing off'. It is interesting that children were more likely to prioritize working hard than were parents. School loomed fairly large in their lives and school work was maybe what they had in mind in prioritizing 'work', whereas perhaps parents had a more holistic or longer term view on their development. But it can be seen that there was more agreement between the generations on aggregate than there was disagreement. It is probably a feature of middle childhood for most children in the UK, regardless of religion or culture, that their moral horizons are quite heavily shaped by those of their parents.

As would be expected, some parents used tried and tested techniques of parenting that may have come either from secular sources or family and social network traditions, in addition to any religious exhortation. So, for example, Mr Ayub spoke of his friend who used a star chart—a behaviourist technique recommended by parenting professionals—to reward a range of desired behaviours ('If you do that many goods in one day, you will be getting one star'). The daughter in this family (aged seven) illustrated some of the challenges for Muslim parents in a secular context. This family, as noted earlier, live in a district with a low proportion of Muslims. The girl, Iza, questioned rules about what is *halal* and what *haram* and said she wished she was called 'Amy'. Even in a more intensively Islamic environment, however, there can be no guarantee that children's behaviour will be appropriately Islamic. In our observations of Islamic Studies classes, we noted that the girls in one class were pretty disrespectful of the teacher and each other.

Conclusion

To conclude this first qualitative findings chapter, which includes something of an overview of the project, we draw together some of the theoretical strands which have been mentioned at various points.

Early in the chapter, the issue of individualization was considered. It was noted that the parents tend to talk in terms of making choices about their own faith and how to bring up their children. There is also some room for negotiation, for example about school of thought (in some families) or about when it is *really* time to start praying regularly. But the 'choices' being made by parents do not, with the exception of the two liberal families in our sample, deviate from a core of conventional belief and some non-negotiable traditions of religious nurture, most notably the importance of teaching children to read the Qur'an in Arabic.

A separate issue of social and cultural context which is worth high-lighting in concluding the chapter is the way in which structural factors can affect how religious nurture manifests itself. Although our qualitative research design does not allow for robust comparisons between subcategories of Muslim families, there are some indications worthy of exploration in future research. There are constraints caused by the intersection of gender relations, social class and ethnicity, for example where men working in a racialized occupation such as restaurant work have very limited scope to be involved fathers. This example has implications for religious nurture being almost exclusively the domain of mothers in these families.

Then there is the question of why Islam in Britain is relatively successful at inter-generational transmission, as shown in our analysis of the Citizenship Survey (Chapter 2). Three themes emerge from this chapter. Firstly, we mentioned the role of cognitive transmission. Whilst again the study has not been designed to test out these theories, there seems to be obvious salience to Islam, worthy of a dedicated study, of Whitehouse's (2002, 2004) doctrinal mode of religiosity. The way in which frequent repetition of Quranic phrases, in formal readings, in daily prayer and in routine supplication, embeds the importance of the faith in children's consciousness, would seem to fit with the process of cognitive transmission theorized by Whitehouse. Secondly, we can also use a more sociological theory, that of the development of *habitus* (from Bourdieu), to explain the embodied habituation of repeated practices, including prayer, fasting (for older children and adults) and modest deportment. The family is the key unit of socialization for the child's religious *habitus*, although Muslim family and friends would have an important part to play as well. We discuss the wider communities beyond the home in Chapter 6, but at this point we mention in summary the related third theoretical insight into the stronger transmission of Islam—the minority effect. Being in a religious minority which is largely made up of minority ethnic groups and is under a certain cultural pressure in the early 21st century can result in strengthening the importance of faith. In Chapter 4 we have noted that some Muslim children conflate ethnicity and religion, assuming a Muslim identity on the basis of ethnicity. We have also seen that some parents and children explicitly see it as their job to persuade a sceptical non-Muslim public by demonstrating in their behaviour the positive aspects of Islam. We will return to these theoretical perspectives over the course of the coming chapters, to try and make sense of the relative strength of Islam in surviving to the next generation in a generally secular cultural environment.

5

Children in Formal Religious Education

Introduction

Almost all the families in our study recognized the importance of their children learning how to read the Qur'an in Arabic, and acquiring some level of understanding about Islamic beliefs and practices. There is no sense that learning Islamic etiquettes, or learning how to read the Qur'an can be put off to another time, or left to the preferences of children. As noted in Chapter 4, the vast majority of parents in our sample are very clear about their Islamic duties, and the necessity of their child undergoing some form of Islamic education. Fulfilling this responsibility usually involves some kind of supplementary schooling.

The stress that is placed upon learning correct recitation of the Qur'an as part of this educational process derives from the use of Quranic verses as part of ritual prayer, five times a day. Sections of the Qur'an or even entire chapters will be recited as part of *salat* and other ritual prayers, and the ability to do this correctly, using the right vocal sounds and pronunciation (*tajwid*), establishes the validity of the prayer. But the acquisition of a classical language is often also a dimension of strong ethno-cultural identities (Rosowsky, 2012). The conservation of distinct-ive linguistic practices (and thus identity) can seem important when children are more fluent in the majority language (English in our case) than they are in a minority ethnic community language (Rosowsky, 2012). The Arabic of the Qur'an is therefore significant, symbolically, spirituality, and practically.

While the family home is the first and most important site for religious learning during the early and middle years of childhood, many families choose to send their children to 'supplementary' schools of one kind or another, especially in order to learn how to read the Qur'an. This is rather similar to Christian families choosing to send their child to a 'Sunday School' to learn more about the Christian tradition (but rarely a classical religious language), although it is common for Muslim children to attend supplementary education classes more than once a week (see Chapter 4). For the families in our study, the use of such classes was intended to consolidate or enhance family and home-based learning about Islam via input from Muslim teachers. But in a small number of cases, it was clear that families were relying on Islamic institutions to undertake a far more fundamental educational task, perhaps where parents had limited knowledge, or time to invest in their child's religious upbringing. Our findings to some extent reflect those of others: 'Parental involvement in many Islamic schools leaves much to be desired; in fact it has been found that Muslim parents may be even *less* involved' (Merry, 2007: 61). In some cases this may be due to a range of structural or social factors, such as long working hours for one or both parents, or significant additional family/caring commitments.

This chapter focuses upon the views of parents and children with regard to religious nurture via formal religious instruction. We investigate firstly the particular role of religious teachers as people who, ideally, embody Islamic tradition and thus provide role models for young Muslim children to emulate. Secondly we consider the role of other children attending religious classes; what is their contribution to religious socialization and the sense of 'being a Muslim' that children can acquire through contact with peers? Thirdly, we examine the diverse forms of religious education that are delivered to Muslim children in Cardiff, from classes that focus upon the acquisition of Quranic Arabic via fairly traditional forms of teaching and learning, to newer forms of pedagogy that emphasize a deeper exploration of the Islamic tradition in terms of history, moral conduct, and values. Fourthly, we consider the physical and material environment in which classes occur, and the particular value that might be derived from classes that are held in mosques and other kinds of religious space. Towards the end of the chapter, we also consider religious instruction delivered by peripatetic religious specialists in children's own homes. Included in this discussion is the innovative use of new online distance-learning techniques which bring teachers from around the world into family homes in Cardiff, via the Internet.

As we explore these various themes, theoretical ideas such as *habitus*, embodiment and cognitive transmission come to the fore, but throughout the discussion we will repeatedly hear the voices and reflections of children and parents who took part in our research. We shall consider what they found enjoyable and positive about mosque-based and other types of Islamic educational classes, as well as what they found problematic and difficult. What becomes evident is that both parents and children shared some very similar perceptions about the pros and cons of particular teachers or 'styles' of teaching, the influence of other children, or the facilities provided at specific educational settings. As an aside, some of their observations provide an interesting commentary on mosques and Muslim religious teachers in the UK today, as well as pointing towards some suggestions for ways in which formal religious education of children might be developed in the future. Because the world of religious instruction for Muslim children in Britain is largely hidden from view and often poorly understood outside Muslim communities (Cherti and Bradley, 2011), we begin with a brief introduction to the world of Muslim supplementary education.

The Landscape of Formal Religious Education in Muslim Communities in Britain

It is notable that within the overall landscape of British Muslim institution building, facilities for the after-school religious education of Muslim children are relatively numerous and well established. This is a reflection of the importance that post-Second World War migrants from South Asia gave to the religious nurture of their British-born children, especially from the 1960s onwards. This was shaped by perceptions of inadequate religious and moral education provided in mainstream community schools on the one hand, and a concern to retain linguistic, religious, and cultural identity on the other. Supplementary schools emerged 'from the on-the-ground needs of Muslims struggling to retain their identity in an environment indifferent, and in some cases hostile, to Islam' (Merry, 2007: 52). Most of these schools and educational activities are independently organized and unregistered, though organizations that run classes delivered within mosques are likely to be registered charities. Although education is delivered in many different sites, including school halls, private homes, and community centres, the most prevalent place for the delivery of after-school religious teaching is in mosques and family homes (using private teachers). Of course, some communities have also established their own private (or more recently, state-funded) Muslim schools (Meer, 2009). There has been extensive research about these institutions from educational, philosophical, political, and social scientific perspectives (Hammad, 2012; Meer, 2007; Meer, 2009; Merry, 2007; Mogra, 2011; Revell, 2010; Tinker, 2006; Tinker, 2009; Tinker and Smart, 2012), stimulated in part by media and political controversies, driven in recent years by concerns about religious 'extremism'.

Though we were aware of these debates, our research has been far more focused upon the nature and quality of religious education delivered in after-school settings to Muslim children who are attending local community based state schools. Given that only four per cent of Muslim children attend Muslim schools (either state funded or private) (Ahmed, 2012) our research deliberately placed an emphasis on the ninety-six per cent of Muslim children whose formal Islamic learning, where it is occurring, is happening in other kinds of educational setting. Figures for the number of children attending Muslim supplementary schools in Britain today are highly variable. Extrapolating from 2001 Census data, Rosowsky places the figure at around half a million, though he includes those who are attending as well as those who have recently attended such institutions (Rosowsky, 2012). Recent research carried out for the Institute of Public Policy Research has a more conservative figure of 250,000 children in Muslim supplementary education, based in around 2000 *madrasahs* (Cherti and Bradley, 2011).

At this point, a brief word regarding nomenclature is perhaps warranted, because of the diversity of terms that are used to refer to various forms of Islamic supplementary education in British Muslim communities. The most common word is *madrasah*, which derives from the Arabic word *darsun* meaning 'lesson' (Ali, 2009). A *madrasah* (plural, *madaaris*) is a 'centre of learning', but the precise connotations of this word and the levels of education provided within it, are contextually variable. In relation to the UK, it is a term commonly used among British Muslim children and their families, particularly where learning the Qur'an is supplemented by other kinds of Islamic learning (e.g. performance of rituals, an introduction to Islamic law/lifestyles). Meanwhile, a *maktab* (derived from the Arabic word for books, *kuttab*), is the most elementary form of religious education, where the emphasis is squarely upon an ability to read the Qur'an correctly and to use it appropriately within ritual practice.

Many mosques in the UK, of which there are approximately 1600 (Gilliat-Ray, 2010), have an associated *madrasah/maktab* or 'mosque-school', attended by children from as young as five years old, in the evenings, or at weekends. Evening classes usually start on weekday afternoons any time between 4.30 pm and 5 pm, and last for up to two hours. The class is usually divided by gender and ability, particularly if held in a mosque. Newcomers to the class will usually begin their learning with the *Qa'idah*—a short booklet that introduces the basics of classical Arabic and from which eventual mastery of Quranic recitation itself can take place. Great emphasis is placed upon an ability to recite accurately, aloud (Rosowsky, 2012). Children who aspire to memorize the Qur'an, thereby achieving the honorific title *hafiz*, will usually attend classes before school as well, and will extend their learning in the evening and at weekends. One child in our study was engaged in this more intensive process of religious nurture. While boys might well continue to attend supplementary education delivered in mosques after the age of 11 or 12, girls tend to cease regular mosque-based classes at around this age in anticipation of impending puberty, particularly at those mosques that cannot accommodate women. Even so, most Muslim children attending a mosque-school, regardless of gender, will spend a substantial proportion of their childhood between the ages of 5 and 11 learning classical Quranic Arabic. This kind of sustained religious activity, clearly involving considerable mental discipline over such an extended period of time is clearly significant in the process of acquiring a secure Muslim identity.

As was noted in Chapter 1, the demographic of the Muslim population in Britain is disproportionately 'young'. This has consequences for both the scale of, and the levels of demand for after-school religious education in Muslim communities, including Cardiff. Research carried out by the Institute for Public Policy Research (IPPR) found that a quarter of *madrasahs* had over 140 pupils attending each week, were often oversubscribed and/or had waiting lists (Cherti and Bradley, 2011: 4). Our research confirms this general impression of high attendance in some kinds of classes, and significant levels of unmet demand.

In many Muslim communities in Britain, the pedagogical goals and scope of educational provision has widened in recent years to include homework clubs, home schooling, leisure activities (e.g. Muslim Beavers and Scouts), and the development of Islamic Studies classes that focus less upon the acquisition of classical Arabic and learning of the Qur'an, and more on belief, practice, and Islamic history. The range of Islamic educational provision available in Cardiff is probably typical of many other large British cities. As noted in Chapter 4, the classes attended by the children in our sample include at least three main kinds that vary in formality and size. These categories of class could overlap within families, with the same children attending more than one type. Eight of the families in our study chose to send their children to a weekly Islamic Studies class where the emphasis was upon understanding of Islamic sources (Qur'an and *hadith*), and rather less upon techniques of reading and recitation. Fifty-three families were concerned that their child should learn how to recite the Qur'an correctly, and within this group, slightly more than half had chosen to have a teacher come to the family home or for parents to teach Qur'an themselves, rather than relying on an external institution. In one case, this home-based religious instruction was via the Internet. Five of the families, especially those with at least one Arab parent, were concerned for their child to maintain some fluency in spoken Arabic. In these cases, mother-tongue language teaching delivered for several hours on a weekly basis was the primary focus, with some Islamic instruction as secondary.

Educationalists, both Muslim and non-Muslim, have begun to conduct research that considers teaching and learning methods, the curriculum, and the ethos and dynamic of mosque-based classes and other kinds of Islamic educational institutions (Ahmed, 2012; Barton, 1986; Cherti and Bradley 2011; Coles, 2008; Gent, 2005; Gent, 2006a; Gent, 2006b; Gent, 2011a; Gent, 2011b; Halstead, 2005; Mogra, 2004; Mogra, 2005; Mogra, 2010; Mogra, 2011; Rosowsky, 2012; Tinker, 2009). An increasing orientation towards qualitative social science research methods has revealed the importance of *madrasahs* and Islamic studies classes for the cultivation of religious identity, and the scope for children to 'embody' the texts that are studied and the teaching that is provided. Our research builds on this body of literature, while also remaining unique as a consequence of its scale and focus, the use of multiple research methods, and the range of sites from which data were gathered. The degree to which children's own voices can be heard in our study is perhaps also distinctive.

Before examining the range of provision for religious nurture in Cardiff, it is worth noting the degree to which the mosque-based classes we observed were often typical of those that might be found in countries with Muslim majority populations. In many ways, the processes of teaching a child how to read the Qur'an, how to pray, or simply how to behave as a Muslim, are similar the world over and have a rather timeless quality. A *hifz* class is generally recognizable, whether it is in Cardiff, or in Cairo, because of the style and physical arrangements for teaching (e.g. sitting on the floor, placing the Qur'an on a low wooden bench) (Barton, 1986; Gent, 2011b), the gentle sounds of recitation, and the donning of religious dress. A number of studies have been conducted on Qur'an schools in other parts of the world, in terms of what they teach, how they teach, and what all that means for teachers and for children (Boyle, 2004; Heffner and Zaman, 2007b). While these studies have typically focused upon older children, nevertheless, their theoretical significance is relevant for our research that included some very young children. What seems to emerge from this body of literature is that through memorizing the Qur'an or learning specific religious rituals, children are being socialized into a community of religious practice, and they are learning how to embody the knowledge they are acquiring. They are being equipped with the tools to enable them to live as morally responsible and Islamically-informed Muslims in this world, with a view to their eventual success in the world hereafter. Formal educational settings therefore provide children with exposure to the people of knowledge and the community of practice that will, ideally, go on to instil within them a sense of God-consciousness and moral discipline. For example, everyday speech in the mosque (as in the home) will be infused with references to God, via invocations such as '*al-Hamdullilah*' (thanks be to God) or *insha'Allah* (if God wills). Religious nurture in such an environment thus provides a kind of moral 'compass' (Boyle, 2004) to orientate the child in their relations with God, with family, and with the wider Muslim community, not just in the present but in the future.

> '...as the words of the Qur'an are engraved on the mind of the child, they can be retrieved, uncovered, and rediscovered. The meaning of the words unfolds over time, providing insights on how to live.' (Boyle: 92)

These words of Boyle's strike a chord with Whitehouse's (2002, 2004) theory of cognitive transmission via the doctrinal mode of religiosity. Whitehouse has more specific scientific theory for explaining how religious texts become 'engraved on the mind', namely that they are stored in semantic memory. As we noted in Chapter 4, learning of the sounds of classical Arabic without understanding the meaning would seem not to fit with Whitehouse's idea that complex theological ideas are learned this way. However, if we take Boyle's description here as reasonably accurate, then the process might involve a gradual discovery of meaning—retrieval, uncovering and recovering—subsequent to the initial learning of how to sound the Arabic.

If that is some of the theory, what about the realities, as experienced by our sample of Muslim families in Cardiff? What do they most value about the opportunities they have, and what are the challenges and obstacles that they face in trying to educate their children about Islam? We asked both parents and children about their experiences and views of formal Islamic teaching based in mosques and other institutions in Cardiff, and their responses indicated that there were four main themes that were important: the teacher, the other children, the curriculum, and the ethos and facilities of the mosque itself. The degree of consensus among parents and children around these themes was notable, not to mention analytically convenient.

The Teacher as Exemplar of Islam

A range of different people with varying levels of experience and qualification are engaged in the formal religious education of Muslim children in Cardiff. Classes that take place in mosques and distinctively
religious settings are more likely to be delivered by religious specialists
who have undergone some form of theological training (e.g. imams),
often recruited from abroad. A number of British-trained female scholars
(*alimas*) were also involved in mosque-based classes. Educational provision occurring beyond mosques, perhaps in community centres, is more
typically offered by educated Muslim professionals, with or without
conventional teaching qualifications, and who are likely to have been
born in the UK, or living in Britain for a long period. A good deal of after-
school religious nurture, regardless of the setting, also seems to depend
on some degree of unpaid voluntary support. Even this very basic
'mapping' of personnel engaged in religious teaching points to broader
patterns of social capital in Muslim communities.

Within the Islamic tradition, there is an expectation that teachers
should not simply transmit knowledge and information, but should
embody it as well. An ability to do this successfully forms the basis for
their authority. Through moral and personal conduct, 'a teacher should
'exemplify in his/her life the content of that which is taught' (Hewer,
2001: 521). The education and religious nurture that children receive at
home is therefore ideally matched by teachers who reinforce the values
and teachings of Islam beyond the home, thereby enabling children to
understand the holistic and all-encompassing way of life that is intrinsic
to Islam and a secure Muslim identity (Nielsen, 1981).

Perhaps it is inevitable that the children in our study expressed particular delight at the prospect of being with those teachers whom they
considered 'fun', and who made an effort to provide especially child-
focused methods of teaching and learning (such as quizzes). Teachers
who were popular with children also tended to be those who ended their
lessons with snacks/drinks, and who rewarded good learning with
treats. Not surprisingly, some parents also valued teachers for the same
sort of reasons, and expressed their appreciation for those teachers who
were able to make meaningful connections to their children through
fun and relevant activities. One mother was looking for a mosque or
class where it was:

'easier for the kids, to find a place where it is more fun than just sitting there
and reciting for two hours and, you know, not understanding or not getting
the fun side of it so you know that was quite important'. (Mrs Mir)

Alongside these personal characteristics and child-focused methods of teaching valued by parents and children, there were other reasons for appreciating particular teachers. It was evident that children liked being taught by people who could mirror their own multilingual experiences. For example, teachers who spoke the mother tongue of the child, who were fluent in English, and who could translate Islamic terms and ideas from Arabic to English were particularly appreciated. Teaching children how to read the Qur'an is often part of the regular duty of mosque-based imams. But while many mosques in the UK continue to recruit imams from overseas, the consequence is that few have either the linguistic or educational qualifications to carry out this task very effectively. Furthermore, the IPPR research cited earlier also found that 'non-British-born Imams who were trained abroad were recognized as being less able to support children in understanding their dual British–Muslim identity' (Cherti and Bradley, 2011: 6).

When it came to more critical views of teachers in mosques and other Islamic institutions in Cardiff, children and parents had very similar concerns. For example, both parents and children were critical of teachers who used physical forms of discipline, and one parent was especially worried that her child had explicitly been told by the teacher not to divulge this fact outside the mosque. They felt this undermined the necessity for total transparency and open communication about all matters, between a parent and a child. In relation to this issue, one or two parents showed their awareness of child protection legislation, and the fact that mosque-based teachers should be CRB checked. Parents are clearly becoming aware of the legal parameters that increasingly surround contact between children and non-related adults outside family networks. This awareness reflects, in part, the concerted efforts of British Muslim educators within the last ten years to ensure that mosques and *madrasahs* improve their practices and policies (Hafez, 2003).

Given the commitment that parents make to simply getting their children to particular mosques or classes on time, on a regular basis, again, both parents and children were disappointed when they felt that the attendance or presence of the teacher was unreliable. Some reported that the teacher was sometimes absent without any explanation, or was distracted by other matters during the course of the class. Children and their parents regarded it as unacceptable for a teacher to be regularly on a mobile phone whilst a child was taking his or her turn to recite the Qur'an.

Given the number of institutions in the UK for the training of imams (Birt and Lewis, 2010; Gilliat-Ray, 2006; Mukadam and Scott-Baumann, 2010), we would expect cities like Cardiff to have an abundance of religious teachers. Surprisingly, our research seems to show this is not the case. Some parents were clear that there simply were not enough (good) teachers, and they sometimes qualified this observation by noting the particular shortage of female teachers, and teachers who could offer a successful *hifz* class. In relation to memorization of the Qur'an, there is currently more demand for this kind of class than Cardiff can currently supply. As an aside, this is of course an interesting commentary on the apparent vitality of Islamic practice in Wales.

Religious Socialization with Other Children

The sizes of the religious classes that we observed were variable. Some classes had up to seventeen children, others as few as six. In large after-school supplementary schools, there may be up to six or seven classes taking place simultaneously, in order to accommodate groups according to gender, ability, and, to some extent, age. Regardless of precise figures, supplementary school attendance takes place on a significant scale in most Muslim communities, thus making it a distinctly collective undertaking. Where mosque-schools and *madrasahs* are located in the heart of Muslim communities, in close proximity to other Muslim families, to Islamic bookshops, halal or ethnic food stores, a child's experience of attending a supplementary school becomes decidedly social. Their identity as Muslims will be reinforced through the social geography of the community, particularly if they make the journey on foot, perhaps with others. Seen in a broader light, the collective investment that Muslim parents make to the supplementary education of their children is one of a number of 'practices of community' (Clayton, 2011: 1687) within a 'community of practice' (Boyle, 2004:, 25).

> The repertoire of a community of practice includes routines, words, tools, ways of doing things, stories, gestures, symbols, genres, actions, or concepts that the community has produced or adopted in the course of its existence. It includes the discourse by which members create meaningful statements about the world, as well as the styles by which they express their forms of membership and their identities as members. (Wenger, 1998: 83, cited in Boyle, 2004: 27)

Although our research could not quantify this in detail, we gathered evidence that accords with the IPPR research: 'Madrassas also serve a community function—acting as a meeting point for children in the same geographic as well as religious community' (Cherti and Bradley, 2011: 34). So, even before children begin their formal learning, they acquire some degree of social capital by virtue of the relationships and networks they form through going to 'mosque-school', and through feeling a sense of belonging to, and ownership of, the Muslim institutions around them.

From what we know about the relatively high ratio of pupils to teachers in some mosques and classes in Cardiff, the influence of other children—whether positive or negative—is highly significant in the overall view that children and their parents have about the quality of Islamic education on offer. It was clear from our data that parents and their children either value, or find problematic, the same kinds of issues when it comes to the broader social environment of the mosque or Islamic class. For example, some children reported to us that they valued the friendships they had at the mosque, especially when these reinforced existing school based or family related friendships. As one child noted, 'it's really nice there as well, cos... lots of my friends go there as well' (Sadeka Akbir, age 12, voice diary). The world of the mosque and the world of school can meaningfully overlap with each other where friendships from one context are carried over into the other. As we will see in Chapter 6, parents tended to appreciate friendship networks beyond school or family with other Muslims. Some parents also recognized and appreciated the opportunity for their child to learn about Islam alongside other children of very different ethnic or racial backgrounds. For them, this was an important means for their child to start to appreciate the implications of living within a multicultural, cosmopolitan Ummah (although nearly all the mosques in Cardiff are in fact quite ethnically specific).

'(*Our mosque is*) a little piece of going to Hajj every day.' (Interview with Mrs Akbir)

'(*Our mosque*) has a lot of good characteristics, but among them is... the community there is very multicultural, very cosmopolitan. You can be a white Muslim or, you know, Indian Muslim, Somali, Malaysian, you know, it doesn't matter which way, you know, you look. There's so many different Muslims go there from different parts of the world and it's a really beautiful thing to see. It's a really beautiful thing to see.' (Mr Morris)

Not all views about Cardiff's religious institutions and the children attending them were entirely positive, however. Our interviews suggested that some parents were relying almost entirely on Islamic classes for the religious education of their child, and were not necessarily supporting or amplifying this process at home. One of the consequences of this dissonance was the evidence we heard that some children were badly behaved in mosques, and might use bad language or engage in bullying. Referring to other children, one young boy noted that, 'some-time they have a fight in the mosque' (Akbar Khaliq, age 11). One mother (Mrs Sajaad) withdrew her son from a class when he seemed to be encountering from the other boys a glamorizing of 'gangsta' culture, bringing home pictures he had drawn of guns and walking with a limp. This kind of popular culture influence can of course arise in any gathering of children, e.g. in school. Not surprisingly, parents were concerned about bad behaviour in supplementary education classes; children were encountering bad role models instead of the good ones they would expect. But children's perspectives were in many ways more immediate. Quite understandably, they did not appreciate being pushed about, intimidated, or feeling overwhelmed in noisy crowded environments. Some mosques and Islamic classes in Cardiff therefore seem to have a problem with what we might call 'crowd control'. Popular mosques perhaps find it difficult to turn children away in the face of high demand, but when they perhaps accept more children than facilities or teachers can cope with, there are inevitable consequences for the degree to which children and their parents feel comfortable and at home. It is partly for this reason that some parents have chosen to invite religious teachers to their homes instead, as we shall see shortly.

Whatever the problems may be in supplementary schools, children who learn about Islam alongside other children experience a particular kind of religious socialization. *Madrasahs* amplify the meaning and significance of belonging in a locality, and in this sense their education becomes 'a total social phenomenon, in which knowledge, politics and social networks interact in a complex and "generative" way' (Barthes, 1993: 5, cited in Heffner and Zaman, 2007a: 2). Depending on the time of year, children attending these classes will often have the opportunity to perform one of the five daily prayers at the class, thereby introducing them to the gently coercive routines and discipline of congregational worship. Going to classes with other children creates a sociotemporal boundary within the flow of everyday life that becomes conducive to the creation of individual identity and group solidarity...as Muslims. The 'gaze' (Foucault, 1977) of the teacher (and the other children) within the enclosed space of the classroom or mosque renders children particularly visible to the appraisal of others. Being in 'the gaze' can bring about a sense of what is the correct way of doing something. It is here that they are likely to learn what it means to be a 'good' Muslim as praise (or admonishment) is meted out according to the abilities of different children to demonstrate embodied competence as Muslims.

Diversity of Teaching and Learning in Supplementary Schools

Stephen Barton's research in Bradford in the 1980s carries a detailed description of the arrangements for a supplementary 'Qur'an school' based in a mosque (Barton, 1986). His description has a striking resemblance to field notes made at a 'mosque-school' during our research in Cardiff. This suggests that very little has changed in relation to 'traditional' mosque-based classes in Britain that are focused upon teaching Qur'an. In Barton's research, as in ours, children were learning in groups, with each child taking turns to sit on the floor in front of the teacher, repeating what s/he recites. 'Imitation and repetition are the chief methods of learning, and no aids are available other than the teacher and the books' (Barton, 1986: 158). Having learned to recite particular verses, the child returns to their place and continues to practice at his or her own pace. Gent's description of a *hifz* class in Redbridge, London, nearly two decades later is strikingly similar, the only difference being emphasis on memorization of much larger portions of text (Gent, 2011b). Children will begin learning the first *surah* of the Qur'an (*Surah al-Fatiha*) and then work their way through the rest of the Qur'an, starting with the shorter chapters. Every child will learn some chapters 'by heart', in order that they can perform their prayers with increasing validity, in time. 'People outside the Muslim community who regard this method of learning as worthless are seldom in a position to be able to judge its actual value . . . to be internalized the Qur'an must be known by heart' (Barton, 1986: 167).

Considering how hard children must find learning the Qur'an in Arabic there are relatively few comments which show resistance to the process. There is the odd one, however:

ASMA: 'Did you like going to the mosque?'

AWA: 'Erm, yeah, but loads of time you have to do alif ba ta fa jeem ha, wait for our turn to do it.'

FATHIA: 'We have to do it till we know it off by heart.'

AWA: 'Yeah and it was really like, it was really long and I felt like oh I wanted to go home!'
(Interview with Awa Adam, age 6, and Fathia Adam, age 8)

ASMA: 'Ok. Is it a lot of fun going to Mosque? Or is it hard work?'

IZA: 'No it's boring.'

ASMA: 'It's boring.'

IZA: 'It's very, very boring.'
(Interview with Iza Ayub, age 7)

113

In one class we observed, the children were well behaved and seemed to respect the quiet authority of the teacher, but showed their restlessness, and perhaps some degree of subdued resistance, with very frequent trips to the toilet. All this suggests that there are fairly minimal opportunities for children to exercise agency in a context where, like most other children at the same age, their horizons are fairly limited by adult management. However, this may be especially true in Muslim families where regular formal learning about the faith is generally expected. The question of whether children are spending such large amounts of time *productively* is a question that is beginning to increase Muslim educators. Muslim children who attend mosque-based classes for two hours every weekday evening inevitably have less time available for relaxation, social and sporting activities, not to mention homework. 'However, the fact that madrassas offer children a place to go after school which keeps them occupied in a place where they are supervised may have beneficial impacts on their development' (Cherti and Bradley, 2011: 21).

Besides supplementary schools that focus almost exclusively on reading and recitation of the Qur'an, there are a range of other classes on offer in Cardiff, usually held on a weekly rather than daily basis. One of these was a Muslim Beavers group, organized for children aged 6–8 years, prior to becoming Cubs and, later on, Scouts. We undertook observation at a Beavers session that involved introducing children to the rituals of the Hajj. Instead of relying on books, pictures, or even film, the furniture and decoration of different rooms and floors in the Scouting hall were laid out to resemble the key sites associated with the Hajj itself. After some initial preparation about the importance of the pilgrimage for Muslims, and an instruction to come to the session with a white towel (to indicate wearing of the ritual garment, *ihram*), the children 'performed' each of the Hajj rituals, as a group, during a session. There was no doubting the value that parents and children placed on this form of kinaesthetic learning. For children who may struggle with text-based forms of teaching, or those with a tendency to boredom or physical agitation, learning through movement and action can be a powerful teaching technique, contrasting with the largely stationary forms of text-based education that occur in mosque-schools. This was an unusually overt attempt at 'making spiritual realities concrete in children's experiences' (Orsi, 2004: 76).

Between the highly interactive Hajj enactment that was heavily dependent upon the participation of the entire group, and the seated, individually orientated learning at a mosque-school, another educational setting that we observed in Cardiff—an Islamic Studies organization for children—had all the hallmarks of a conventional 'classroom' with children sitting at desks, facing the teacher in a U-shape, working individually, in pairs, and in groups. There was a class textbook, exams, and the emphasis was upon the acquisition of facts and information about Islam. Value was placed upon learning about good behaviour and everyday morality, sometimes using the life of the Prophet in Muhammad as an example. There was also a noticeable emphasis on children 'learning about their identity as Muslims as part of a community' (field notes, 22 May 2009), which we interpreted as centrally to do with religious diversity and community cohesion. It was significant that in this particular setting, the staff had written their own textbook and teaching materials, leading us to conclude that in this particular school, the staff recognized:

> ...the importance of training children to simultaneously identify... as both Muslims and as citizens of the West. Much of the language that Islamic schools adopt to convey their mission is therefore unsurprisingly Western in origin. This includes using the best academic resources, that is, texts, pedagogical tools, and teaching methods. (Merry, 2007: 60)

Each of these three main forms of supplementary education clearly had a rather different pedagogical orientation, and this had obvious consequences for how children learned about their faith. There is little doubt that they are 'internalizing' their learning in one form or another, either through repetition, 'activity', or remembering facts and principles, all of which could be seen as achieving cognitive transmission in the 'doctrinal mode' of religiosity (Whitehouse, 2002, 2004). While there is likely to be some degree of overlap between these different learning styles, each places a slightly different emphasis on what it means to be a Muslim. What is interesting for our purposes is the increasing choice now available to parents (and children, to some extent), about which of these styles of learning is most 'appropriate'. There is clearly a gradual shift away from a complete reliance on 'traditional' mosque-schools, towards the development of newer forms of teaching and learning that are seeking to bridge past and present realities.

Added to this range of choices, some parents are concerned that their child should retain a strong grasp of the parental mother tongue and associated cultural traditions. For example, the one Turkish family in our study, although based in Cardiff, chose to frequent a predominantly Turkish mosque in the neighbouring town of Newport. They felt it was important for their child to retain a distinctive ethnic identity, thereby making some of the mosques and religious classes in Cardiff less appropriate for them.

Amid these various forms of supplementary education on offer in Cardiff, what do parents and children particularly appreciate? In many ways, the answer to this question, at least from a child's perspective, is related to their earlier comments about teachers. In other words, they enjoy the simple pleasure of being read to, such as hearing stories about the Prophet Muhammad, or the early history of Islam. They also enjoy social contact with friends they make in the classes. The most positive and appreciative comments from parents seemed to relate to mosques and classes that did a number of different things. These included the integration of Islamic learning with other activities, teaching children how to pray in congregation, and the learning of not just 'how' to do things but an accompanying explanation of 'why' they were important.

Our data seem to show that regardless of the setting in question, many Muslim parents have absorbed a number of ideas about teaching and learning derived from mainstream educational environments, and in this sense our findings are consonant with earlier research on supplementary education (Amer, 1997). Amer's research on supplementary education in London and Birmingham also recorded the concerns of parents in relation to curriculum and pedagogy. Certainly, most parents in our research were concerned that their child not only learns how to read the Qur'an, but also what it means, and what the implications of Islamic teaching might be for daily life. Our work also accords with Rosowsky, who found that parents 'appear to emphasize the importance of their children's understanding of their respective faiths rather than the meritorious but often meaning-bereft acquisition of the religious classical language alone' (Rosowsky, 2012: 2). Classes that stress this kind of approach, often run by Muslim educators rather than religious professionals/imams, appear to be working towards the development of 'an Islamic philosophy of education that does not eschew liberal demo-cratic values but incorporates them into an Islamic framework' (Merry, 2007: 52). Thus, some of the most popular Islamic classes in Cardiff seem to be those that have found a way of making traditional Islamic educational practices meaningful and relevant in 21st century Cardiff. This does not mean any less emphasis on the importance of learning how to read the Qur'an, but rather an appreciation of how this might be part of a more holistic package of integrated Islamic education. A continued reliance upon overseas educated imams for the delivery of this kind of curriculum is clearly problematic in terms of the evolving aspirations of parents.

Changing parental views appear to be especially significant as a com-mentary on how some Muslims are choosing to shape the identity of their children in a way that is consonant with their faith, and the society to which they belong. The debates taking place at the intersection of these different kinds of educational philosophy and practice clearly point to broader contestations taking place around the construction of diasporic identities. They may mark a development, from what Castells would term 'resistance identity'—shaped by perceptions of external hostility and rejection of dominant secular-liberal values—to 'project identity', that seeks to redefine the social position of Muslims, not through withdrawal to the 'trenches', but through proactive engagement within civil society (Castells, 1997).

Mosque Facilities and Religious Spaces

The fourth prominent theme in our data related to the process of learning to be Muslim refers to the environment in which teaching is delivered, and the meaning that parents and children attach to particular learning institutions. How is learning to be a Muslim influenced by the setting in which it occurs? Some children displayed high levels of self-critical awareness and maturity about the value of mosque-school attendance, while others took a more pragmatic view.

> '(*I'd*) rather go to the mosque than do nothing at home.' (Interview with Haseeb Akhtar, age 12)

> 'I like going there cos it's not just a mosque; it's a place where you basically chill.' (Sadeka Akbir, age 12, voice diary)

To our surprise, the decisions that families made about formal Islamic education for their children were not always shaped by predominantly religious concerns (e.g. choosing a mosque or class because of its 'school of thought'), but often by very practical considerations. For example, some parents chose a particular class or mosque for their child because it was close to home, or it avoided rush hour traffic hotspots in the city, or because it was easy to park in order to drop children off and then collect them later on.

> 'It's harder for us to take all the kids out of home to drop the other two or three to the mosque ... five or six o'clock is rush hour as well. Ilyas did start going to (*the mosque*) but the timing of that was quite difficult ... firstly you have to find parking there, secondly getting there is a nightmare.' (Interview with Mr Hussain)

Parents take a far more strategic and practical approach to the decision about which class or mosque their child will attend than we had expected. They will choose those that that are closer to their home, or timed to be more accommodating to the demands of busy working family lives. In keeping with this rather utilitarian approach to mosques, there is clear evidence that some families are connected to several mosques simultaneously, perhaps with children attending classes at one mosque, whilst the father is reading Friday prayers (*juma*) somewhere else. Sometimes it may even be the case that each parent attends a different mosque. One of the apparent consequences of this strategic way of thinking is that there appears to be a high degree of turnover around the different classes. When families move house, or change their domestic arrangements, children will be put into, or taken out of a class to reflect these changes. This has obvious implications for teaching and learning when the composition of a class is subject to such frequent changes.

However logistically complex it may be for families to attend supplementary schools, it became evident that there can be some unexpected benefits to be derived from the time parents invest in taking their child to a class. There is a sense that going to mosques and classes is a shared social activity, and the very fact of travelling by car or walking to the mosque seems to be valued by some parents and children for the simple reason that it provides a space for them to talk and enjoy each other's company in the midst of busy working and family lives. And even if this is not possible on a day-to-day basis, occasions such as Eid and Ramadan provide a very important opportunity for the cementing of family relationships, and especially the relationship between father and son. Fathers seemed to view occasional religious festivals, as well as routine attendance at mosques and classes, as an important dimension of their son's preparation for, and socialization into, adult membership of the mosque.

Many of the parents in our study regarded the mosque as the basis for their social life and networking, and their children are inevitably bound up with that. Attendance at religious functions or social gatherings such as bazaars provides a sense of belonging and identity. However, an issue that many parents raised, both fathers and mothers, was the question of how and to what extent women were able to access mosques, both on a regular basis and on special occasions such as Eid. Some parents valued a particular mosque or Islamic class for their child simply and solely because it was accessible for women, in terms of them being able to wait inside at collection time, or to speak to the teacher about their child, after the class. This came through as a particularly striking concern. Our data seem to suggest that more mosques in the UK need to move away from being sites for predominantly male religious activity, becoming instead places that welcome all the members of a family, and both genders.

'They wouldn't allow ladies to go in—I think that's the thing I'd really like to change because for us in this catchment area that's the closest (*mosque*) and if we could have women going in to pray *salat* with the men, I mean in a separate room, it would be so much easier—you know, in holidays I could take the kids and the kids could listen to the *Khuthba*[1] because it's given in Urdu, they'd understand it. I used to take my dad at about quarter past twelve and he would go, listen to the *Khuthba* and by the time he would come out it was about half-past one, quarter to two—I was just sat in the car, not able to pray and I had to rush back quickly because, it was winter months I think, so I don't miss my *Zuhr*[2] and I had to pray, by which time it was *Asr*[3], you know. I think that's one thing I'd like to change if I could.' (Mrs Tufail)

The most popular religious institutions in Cardiff seem to be those which provide 'life-long learning', by which we mean the facilities for religious education and nurture throughout the life course. For some of the parents in our sample, the need to pay serious attention to the religious education of their children has been a catalyst for taking their own religious practice and knowledge rather more seriously. As their children start asking questions about Islam, they are conscious of the need to have some answers. Thus, mosques that can facilitate that process, and can support the education of children and their parents, seem to be providing a highly valued service.

If the inclusion or exclusion of women is a key factor determining how parents view a particular mosque or class, another prominent concern relates to the internal workings of the mosque itself. Some parents were critical of mosques which can appear as the exclusive preserve of a single ethnic group—this was in fact true for most of the city's mosques—complete with its own internal tensions and interpersonal rivalries. Cardiff has a long history of migration and settlement by Muslims from very different ethnic, racial and linguistic backgrounds on account of its maritime history. Some parents in our sample were concerned when the spirit of multiculturalism that is inherent within Islam, and which should be especially evident in a city such as Cardiff, was not apparent within mosques.

Many of the Muslim children we met had been effectively socialized into the world of mosques and formal Islamic institutions. For example, they were generally aware of the behaviour that is expected in a mosque, such as making sure they are clean and removing shoes, as the following interview extract illustrates:

---

[1] Friday sermon. [2] Noon prayer. [3] Afternoon prayer.

ANEESA: 'We go in our class.'

ASMA: 'With your shoes on?'

ANEESA: 'No, we take, we take, we go up the stairs, we take our shoes off.'

ASMA: 'Why do you take your shoes off before you get inside?'

ANEESA: 'Because we might step in something dirty. The carpet, we read on the carpet.'

ASMA: 'Okay, so the carpet has to be clean when you are reading the Qur'an, yeah?'

SABAH: 'When we pray.'

(Interview with Aneesa Rana, age 10, and Sabah Rana, age 8)

Children could usually describe what they do at the mosque-schools, the way that teaching is organized and so on, using correct Islamic terminology. One child had absorbed a particular *hadith* relating to the merits of attending mosques: 'you know when you are walking to the mosque every step you take is a good thing and one takes away your bad thing' (Badr Barakah, age 11). So irrespective of progress in relation to formal learning of the Qur'an, children who attend formal Islamic classes are nevertheless also learning other important things about being a Muslim, simply by virtue of regular attendance. They are becoming familiar with the spatial arrangements in mosques, the norms of ritual purity, and the behaviour that is consonant with being a 'good' Muslim in a public religious setting.

Teaching and Learning at Home

A certain degree of privatization of religious instruction and practice was evident among families who, instead of using supplementary classes, had chosen to invite peripatetic teachers to educate their child at home. This sometimes also involved other siblings or relatives/friends, and it was clear that the majority of this kind of teaching delivered in private homes was exclusively geared towards reading and recitation of the Qur'an. The frequency and duration of lessons were variable, but the most general pattern was either a short daily lesson (Monday to Friday), or two to four lessons per week, for about an hour. The reasons families had chosen this form of religious education were varied, but included factors such as flexibility of timing, the concentration of teaching and learning, and improved communications between parents and teachers about the child's progress. Parents recognized the additional expense of private tuition, and the loss of opportunity for their child to perform congregational prayers at the mosque/class. But for some, this was a price worth paying in order that their child could maintain other extracurricular activities, such as sports (see also Østberg, 2006). From the children's perspective, they valued having teachers who were alert to their energy levels (especially after a long day at school) and who could orientate the lesson to their exact level of knowledge. However, some children, and especially those learning without siblings or other children for company found the presence of the teacher somewhat daunting. This problem was largely avoided, however, in the case of one child who was receiving Quranic instruction via the Internet, as a supplement to a weekly face-to-face lesson given by a local Somali teacher. Forces of both conservatism and innovation are evident in the online class involving three half-hour sessions per week, delivered by a company in the United States. Via a computer in the child's bedroom, the teacher was able to deliver a highly interactive but none the less 'traditional' Qur'an class, as these field note extracts illustrate:

'Amina (mother) showed me to Sahra's bedroom which was decorated in pink and lilac furniture. Amina pulled a chair forward for me to sit on a couple of metres away from where Sahra was sitting at the computer desk, wearing her school sports kit. Sahra was also wearing a pair of headphones with a microphone attached but I could hear the teacher clearly from the speakers on her computer. Up on the screen was a grid of short Arabic words and the teacher got Sahra to spell out the letters on each one, correcting her when she was wrong or getting her to repeat after him when she was really stuck. After she spelled out the letters of each word, including the punctuation which changes the sound of the letter, he got her to repeat each word slowly and then more rhythmically and quickly. The teacher had a pen or something that created a red dot on the part of the page he was teaching at any particular time.

. . . After the lesson Sahra told me that she had really enjoyed her lesson and that she prefers it to her face-to-face lesson with her Somali Qur'an teacher, which she still has once a week. She feels that this "virtual" teacher pays more attention to her reading whilst the 'actual' teacher's attention wanders and occasionally he makes use of the family's phone to make personal calls on during lesson times.' (field notes from Adam family, 19 May, 2009)

Whatever the pros and cons of home-based instruction, it is clear that Muslim children may miss some important aspects of religious socialization if parents are relying upon private teachers as their primary means of learning. A private teacher working in a child's home cannot convey the 'pedagogic authority of the school' (Jenkins, 2002: 109) in quite the same way, not least because there is a significant shift in power relations when teachers perform their role, as invited 'guests', outside the spaces that are normally associated with their authority. What appears to be missing is the scope for children to gradually acquire an embodied identity as Muslims, which is reinforced through the discipline and routine of going to a specific place of instruction, negotiating their identity alongside other children, and contextualizing this learning within the wider community of practice.

> Embodiment has to do with the body, but it implies that it is something else, other than or added to the physical body itself, that is embodied, and such a 'thing' often turns out to be an abstract social value, such as honour or bravery. Embodiment thus has to do with values that in some ways are also disembodied or may be thought of separately from the body itself. *Embodiment*, in other words, is a term that belies itself by combining the abstract and the concrete together (Strathern, 1996: 195, cited in Boyle, 2004, p. 87)

By attending supplementary classes beyond the home, children learn the etiquettes of participation in Muslim community life which begins locally, but has resonance nationally and internationally, thereby giving children access to a global community of practice (the Ummah).

Conclusion

Supplementary schools are sites of community participation and active citizenship. They cast children and parents as 'community members' and thus part of a thriving civil society. They extend into and are connected to other Muslim organizations, e.g. mosques, charities, and other kinds of associations (e.g. Scouts), which value community and generate social capital. (Dinham et al., 2009: 198). They are therefore part of a complex nexus of institutions that include mosques, professional and religious associations, businesses, the family, and other educational providers. 'Islamic education is characterized, not by lock-step uniformity, but by a teaming plurality of actors, institutions, and ideas' (Heffner and Zaman, 2007a: 2). Far from promoting isolation or separatism, children who attend formal Islamic institutions learn not only how to be a Muslim, but also what it means to be part of a community and a society. In this way, such institutions are perhaps unique in terms of their scope and significance for the production of distinctive British Muslim identities. The publication of the IPPR report cited at the beginning of this chapter is an interesting commentary on the significance that policy makers now attach to supplementary schooling in Muslim communities, and the role it can play in community cohesion. They concluded that:

> Under the right conditions, they can strengthen religious identity and help children make sense of their life as a Muslim and as a member of the wider

society. They can give children a narrative with which they can explain their religious and lifestyle choices in a non-Muslim environment and this can bring them confidence and self-esteem. (Cherti and Bradley, 2011: 33).

Seen in a far broader perspective, supplementary schools are important sites where one generation of Muslims entrust the continuity of Islam to the next. Our research demonstrates the vitality of this activity in Cardiff, certainly for the time being.

In relation to the question of why Islam is passed on more successfully than other religions, we can see that religious organizations have an important role in shaping children's learning. The pedagogical techniques broadly fit with the cognitive transmission style of the doctrinal mode of religiosity and also help to instil an embodied religious *habitus*, within a community of believers. This is in theory a global community, but in reality the attendance at most of the mosques is dominated by a single ethnic group, reinforcing the identification of religion with ethnicity.

6

School, City, and Society

This chapter deals with children's wider social environment outside the immediate family, i.e. social relations in school, in the city of Cardiff and beyond. There is discussion of parents' and children's views of schooling, with particular reference to religious nurture. Most children attend state primary schools, but some parents have opted for private education or home schooling and these decisions are explored. Wider social and cultural influences on children, such as interactions with non-Muslim peers and interface with popular culture, are discussed and there is a summary of parents' views of living in the city of Cardiff, in so far as it has implications for religious nurture. Finally, there is some discussion of children's contact with ethnic and family networks, both locally and overseas.

In recent years there has been considerable interest from politicians and sociologists in social networks and social capital. Social involvement, reciprocity and trust are seen as key to the well-being of communities and the individuals within them (Putnam, 2000). Understanding the locations of children and families within social networks is important in order to understand their needs (Barnes and Morris, 2007). As Hill (1989) notes, 'from birth, children develop, play and work within extensive social networks'. According to Putnam, there is a distinction between 'bonding' social capital, which concerns the connections between relatively homogenous groups and 'bridging' social capital, a concept which refers to the networks connecting socially heterogeneous people. Bonding social networks are generally thought to be more conducive to well-being than a fragmented social fabric. Furthermore, they tend to have a very important role in reducing isolation within minority populations. However, they can also be constraining and stifling to individual progression and mobility (Putnam, 2000; Holland et al., 2007). There has been considerable attention paid by politicians in the UK and beyond to the supposed problems of Muslims failing to integrate with non-Muslim society, but instead living 'parallel lives' (Cantle, 2001). Some researchers have challenged the assumption that Muslims want to live separately from non-Muslims, citing, for example, fears of racism and the housing market as reasons for geographical segregation in some cities (Phillips, 2006). It is evident, however, that there is considerable social separation and in Putnam's terms this is an absence of bridging social capital. The concepts themselves are contested. For example, Leonard (2004) argues on the basis of research in Belfast that bridging can potentially benefit individuals but not communities. Morrow (1999) sees the concept of social capital as poorly specified as it applies to children, sidelining the importance of social structural restrictions on children's lives and environmental restrictions beyond their control, as well as down-playing children's agency and overemphasizing the influence of parents' networks. Whilst acknowledging there has been much debate about social capital, for the purposes of this chapter we regard the concept as 'a useful heuristic device and a tool with which to examine social processes and practices' (Morrow, 1999: 760). In particular, there will be reflection on bonding and bridging capital.

Morrow (1999) challenges an overemphasis on parents' role in shaping children's social capital. Yet the family remains the primary unit in early and middle childhood for socialization and for the development of social networks. For the children in our study, parents played an important role in influencing and providing access to social networks outside of the immediate (nuclear) family and this is not untypical for this stage of the life course (Borland et al., 1998). The issue of religious nurture and the importance of Muslim identities and Islamic practice are important to parental decisions about schooling and education. Parental decisions related to religious nurture influence children's experiences within formal education and their relationships with their friends, teachers and other children at school. However, as with all social interactions, this is not a one-way process. The barriers between families and the social world are permeable and children play a role in negotiations about which networks are open to them. Children themselves help to build social networks and potentially enable bridging to widen families' contacts and their integration into appropriate networks. Children are not passive recipients of parental social capital but use social capital in many and varied ways to negotiate important transitions and to construct their identities. Children are active producers and consumers of social capital (Holland et al., 2007, James and Prout, 1997). Children can be resourceful and active in developing networks with each other and with adults (Leonard, 2005). The chapter will consider the extent to which Muslim children are actively involved in constructing social networks. We begin by exploring the school context.

Schools

For the Muslim parents in our study it appeared that, for many of them, considerations about their children's education were affected by both their perceptions about the social environment of the school and the social networks with which their children would be engaging. It may be that many of the parents we interviewed did not think in terms of choosing a school for their children but simply sent them to the local catchment area school. However, some parents will have been aware of 'choices' in their area, including a state Welsh-medium school and perhaps a church school. Those who could afford to pay for their children's education also had the options within the city of non-religious private schools, a church-linked private school and two private Muslim schools. There is also a private alternative school for the youngest children. This and the Muslim schools, whilst not run by the state and not free to attend, are none the less substantially cheaper than most private schooling.

It was interesting to note that only a very small number of parents explicitly stated that educational standards were a priority. This might suggest that relatively few of them knew about the choices available or perhaps that the issue of school attendance was not really questioned. Church school and Welsh-medium school may not have been seen as acceptable alternatives to the nearest English-medium state primary and private education may have been impossible. There is no doubt a social class dimension here. Bagnall et al. (2003), writing about the north west of England, describe the different educational horizons according to class, with middle class families maintaining diffuse ties with like-minded people (bridging social capital) and using educational establishments instrumentally to 'get ahead', but working class families being less mobile and more concerned with maintaining tight social networks around kin, residence and leisure (bonding social capital) in order to 'get by'. Many of the working class families in our study were very focused on their local area and perhaps therefore did not consider alternatives to local schools. A small number of parents said they had found state schools in general, or the state schools their children had attended or were attending, to not be sufficiently academically motivating for their children, with large class sizes and high turnover of staff. This was, however, a minority stance, and most parents were very focused on issues of religion and ethnicity. This may be simply a methodological artefact, as we were specifically asking about religious nurture, but it may also suggest that the Muslim parents in our study were more concerned about the moral and religious appropriacy of their children's school than about educational achievement as such.

Parents' views of state schools for Muslim children

In general, state schools were viewed in a positive light by parents in our study. Schools with a mix of ethnicities and religions were generally seen as preferable by parents and schools with a number of other Muslim children/families were even more so.

Attendance at state-funded church schools (Anglican or Roman Catholic) was largely seen as unproblematic and even perceived as advantageous to a number of parents who had made this choice of school for their children. There were, however, some references to questioning by extended family and the wider community of their decision to send their children to these schools, with regard to the impact it might have on the children's Islamic nurture. Some parents saw church schools as providing an opportunity to talk about religion and to teach their children about the differences and similarities between the Christian and Islamic faiths in a positive light and as an opportunity to make conversations about religious beliefs part of everyday conversations with their children, as seen in these words of Mrs Adam:

> 'I mean people were against me putting me them in the church school and I said "Well no, I will teach them the difference". You know at the end of the day our fight is against secularism. Church schools, our principles are the same. But obviously you teach where the difference is with our Islamic values like what we believe in Jesus. So if you can ask them questions about Jesus, they know that we Muslims believe in that he was a Prophet and they know Christians believe in him as the Son of God.' (Interview with Mrs Adam)

Parents gave the impression of schools in Cardiff generally being very accommodating of Muslim prayer, and some even congregational prayer, during the school day. Even where Muslim children were very much in a minority, parents were able to negotiate time and space within the school day for their children to be able to pray and parents were appreciative of this feature of state schools. Nobody stated that children were not allowed to or were discouraged from praying at school.

Ramadan is a key time of the year for schools to demonstrate their accommodation and understanding of the practice of Islam. During Ramadan, children's routines in terms of bed times and meal times at home are significantly different than for the rest of the year. Some schools seem to do some forward thinking, being aware that Ramadan is coming up and making plans for the children that are viewed positively by parents. Most of the parents found that state schools accommodated the requirements of children during Ramadan, although to varying degrees; schools with a high number of Muslim children generally made more of an effort than others. Measures taken by schools included provision of a separate room for children who are fasting to spend the lunch hour and parents being asked to take children who are fasting home during the lunch hour. Mrs Khatun told us about a Muslim teacher who was herself fasting so, 'set an Islamic group, like talking about Islam and fasting and bit of everything'. This approach was said to encourage Mahmood (age 9) in his fasting.

Fasting is one of the pillars of Islam and obligatory on all adult Muslims. Recommendations for when children should start fasting varied in our study: 7, 12 and on reaching puberty, though never younger than 7. However, parents of primary school-aged children considered the age and health of their child before allowing them to complete a whole fast. Some parents asked their children to fast on weekends only, others encouraged their children to 'practise' by abstaining from their break time snacks at school and only eating at meal times. Some parents said they advised their children to break their fast if they felt unwell, tired or hungry, by eating school-provided lunches or making sure their children took a packed lunch with them. Fasting and taking part in *tarawih* prayers (longer prayer taking up to two hours, with most women praying at home and men and boys at the mosque) seemed to be an exciting time for Muslim children, with some keen to participate along with their older family members.

The celebration of religious festivals emerged as the most immediate primary school-related concern for the parents. Some worried that there was confusion for the children in terms of what they were taught about different religions and the precedence given to the Christian festivals of Easter and particularly Christmas. State schools and their curriculums certainly did not seem to be perceived as secular by the parents of Muslim children and Muslim children themselves. Christmas was a particularly difficult time of the year for a large number of parents in our sample, although not apparently as much a problem for children in terms of participation in Christmas plays.

'They're so into their Christmas here, and the concerts and all sorts and singing all those songs and you don't want them to do that but you've got no choice, because everyone else is doing it. The teacher tells them. Sometimes in assembly, songs that they know that they're not allowed to sing, but they get told off if they don't sing. They do have to participate...but it's difficult, like you can't say no to things like that.' (Interview with Mrs Jamil)

One father's decision to move his son from a state primary school to a private Muslim school was influenced significantly by the impact of the celebration of Christian festivals there. He said that Easter and Christmas were given more priority than Eid, which is to be expected when the legal framework specifies that most collective worship should be of a wholly or mainly Christian character. Mr Assad's concern was that his son was 'getting confused and his heart started leaning more towards Easter'. Although the boy 'didn't understand what these celebrations were about', in the school 'he saw more festivity coming from those two traditions than he did from the Eid'.

At Easter, parents have to deal with questions which they find difficult to answer about the differences between Christianity and Islam and explaining that in Islam Jesus is not seen as the Son of God but a Prophet. Parental responses to this issue varied. A couple of parents were relaxed about some aspects of Christian festivals, saying it was fine for them and their children to 'experience the culture' up to a point, for example, by taking part in school Christmas plays. This was in the context of a secure Muslim faith. As Mr Ahmed put it:

'At the end of the day I know they are Muslims, they come home, we teach them about Islam; they know the basics of Islam. So I don't feel threatened or feel fear in any way.' (Interview with Mr Ahmed)

Others chose for their children to opt out of participating in Christmas events. This is not a straightforward issue as children can end up being left out of whole-school activities. Mr Hussain conceded that his children had initially 'felt a bit left out' when not included in the Christmas play, but this had 'worked out over the years'. Mr and Mrs Hussain took the view that this was necessary only when the children were young and impressionable.

'They were young at the time, so we didn't want them to get the wrong influences. Aman was last year, she was part of the play because now she's older, she understands it's just a play; it's not the actual Christmas... The first time, the first year when she said, one Christmas she said, "oh, is Father Christmas coming then?" We said, "no, he's not coming"; she said, "but the teacher said he's coming, you know, we have to go and see him". Obviously the next year it was easier to explain to her even though we had, that year—I think it was probably three years ago, the following year was easier and now, *Mashallah*, she understands ... that it's just tradition rather than actually something happening.' (Interview with Mr Hussain)

There is more discussion of parents' and children's views of non-Muslim celebrations in Chapter 7.

Children's experiences at school

Children gave some examples of difficulties in school which were not specific to their Muslim identity. For example, Fakhir Uddin (age 10) found it difficult when adults raise their voices ('they really scare me and it affects my confidence ... some of my teachers are really mean'). Aamira Miller (age 11) spoke about not really having friends in school ('nobody wants to know me ... I think if I wasn't in school it wouldn't make a difference to them'). This experience might have been related to her religion—she came across as a rather serious girl and this demeanour cannot be separated from her faith. However, it may have been little to do with her religion and more a kind of isolation which could potentially occur for a rather shy child of any religious background.

Very few children related negative experiences at school directly connected to their identity and practice as Muslims. Examples of open hostility were very rare. An isolated example was Ilyas Hussain (age 12) mentioning a fight in school because of religious differences ('kind of like Muslims versus non-Muslims'). It is interesting that, given the high profile of Islamophobia in public discourse, there were not more tales of open hostility. There was, however, a sense in which some children were anticipating difficulty from non-Muslims. For example, Ehlenoor Faysal (age 8) made the comment (no doubt untrue) that she would be expelled for wearing a hijab in her primary school. Her brother Daniyaal (age 10) was outraged.

DANIYAAL: 'Expelled for wearing the scarf? Whoever does that must be insane!'
ASMA: 'Why do you think it would be insane to expel somebody who wore a scarf?'
DANIYAAL: 'I mean it's just a religious sort of thing, it's not like it's going to kill the world is it? It's not going to destroy the school's reputation, it's just a girl wearing a scarf. She's doing what her religion wants her to do.'
ASMA: 'And that's OK?'
DANIYAAL: 'If they just expelled them just for wearing that I'd be going crazy, I'd be like what the fffff, what the beep, my god you are such a beep, stuff like that.'
(Interview with Daniyaal Faysal, age 10)

Now Daniyaal does not present as an especially devout boy. He tells us he is torn between prayer and playing computer games. But in this excerpt he displays what we might regard as a Muslim 'resistance identity' (Castells, 1997). Resistance identity emerges, according to Castells, from stigmatized and devalued cultures which, having been marginalized by dominant discourses, construct 'trenches of resistance and survival on the basis of principles different from, or opposed to, those permeating the institutions of society' (Castells, 1997: 8). This idea is pertinent in a post 9/11 climate where the identity Muslim has become politicized. It may be that overt Islamophobia is not common currency for the children in our study (we return to this issue in relation to adults later in the chapter), but there is a certain expectation of needing to defend Islam, as we saw in Chapter 4, although this has not been a strong feature of the data set. This defence can be related to the pressures of being strongly religious (of whatever faith) in a secular context. For primary school children and their parents, however, the Christian heritage of the UK is at times quite evident, since schools do use aspects of Christian tradition.

The children in our study seemed to have some awareness of other religions, though very few demonstrated any detailed knowledge, but what seemed to stick in their minds more were stories about their own religion when they were told these at school. This is perhaps because these stories are memorable to the children because they are an affirmation of their own beliefs and an (apparently rare) opportunity to talk about their own religion rather than discuss the major Christian religious festivals. For the majority of children in our study the school environment was the only place that they encountered information about other religions. Despite all the religious education and information about Islam they received at home, very little and more often nothing at all was about other religions. This may be a defensive reaction of parents in the face of what they see as the teaching and normalization of Christianity in schools.

There were some examples of religious education that were sensitive to Islam, such as a teacher telling a class that they cannot draw pictures of the Prophet Muhammad. There were also some examples of quite bad practice such as telling a class to draw a picture of God and then apparently sending a Muslim child to the head teacher's office when she refused. This example was given by Madiha Mahmood (age 12). Her sister Fariha (age 10) also said that children are expected to sing hymns unless parents have given a letter to the school. In this school it seemed a special case needed to be made and the girls said this could be embarrassing as you draw attention to yourself and, 'they talk a lot about you'.

In this next excerpt from Fariha, we see how children can in limited ways exercise agency to undermine aspects of school life that do not sit comfortably with their religious beliefs:

'At school I'm gonna work hard, we should work hard in everything...but they do too much about Jesus and on every Fridays we get a certificate but on the starting and on the end to do this prayer, and we always pretend to mouth it. I mouth it but I don't actually. But that sometimes if the teachers spot us, like us go to the front and shout at us to make us sing it.' (Interview with Fariha Mahmood, age 10)

The Rasheed children told a similar story. Theirs were schools with few Muslim children. Fatima and Muhammad were two of only three children who prayed at their school; the third was their cousin. A space was made available for them to perform *salat* at school. However, Fatima chose to hide the fact that she prayed at school from her friends although her friends were aware that she prayed at home. She talked about feeling uncomfortable when one of her friends found her hijab in her school bag once and asked why she had brought it in to school with her. Here, like Fariha Mahmood, the Rasheed children told us they mouthed the words of hymns without sounding them.

MUHAMMAD: 'I hate assemblies in school because they're so boring and...we do activities. The hymns, some of them we have to skip out some of the words, like.'

FATIMA: 'When it says Christ was born, our cousin made up a word and sings 'Chris was born [*laughs*].'

ASMA: 'Is that what you do?'

FATIMA: 'Yeah.'

ASMA: 'Okay, so you feel like you're not saying it, then?'

FATIMA: 'Yeah.'

FATIMA: 'Or sometimes we just don't even sing.'

MUHAMMAD: 'Mouth the words.'

ASMA: 'You mouth them? Because, do you have to say them?'

MUHAMMAD: 'Well, they sometimes, the teachers come and walk around. So I sing it, but I'm not singing.'

(Interview with Fatima and Muhammad Rasheed, age 12 and 10)

This limited agency to resist religiously unacceptable aspects of schooling is similar to what Hemming (2011) found in his ethnographic study of a multi-faith primary school. Although in this school there was an official line of religious inclusivity, what Hemming terms a 'procedural liberalism', some children found the school regime did not fit with their faith. For example, some more devout children who wanted to pray daily—a Pentecostal Christian and a Muslim—ended up praying in the school toilets. This would in fact technically render the Muslim prayer invalid, as the space is not clean, but this girl ended up praying in such a place because a liberal school regime in relation to faith did not allow for the more devout forms of religious practice. Other Muslim children in Hemming's study would change the words of Christian prayers in school assemblies or address Allah in their heads.

Alternatives to state schooling

Parents within our study who chose to send their children to one of the two Muslim primary schools in Cardiff stated they did so because the schools covered the National Curriculum whilst at the same time providing opportunities for children to participate in daily religious education which included recitation of the Qur'an, memorizations of *surahs*, Islamic Studies, prayer and *sirah* lessons. Parents also appreciated the smaller class sizes and they stated that this provided better quality education for their children, although it should be noted that educational standards were not to the fore in these decisions and in fact one of the schools had a somewhat troubled history, including discipline problems, that had put some parents off. Parents also valued the time and space in the school calendar given to the celebration and noting of important events in the Muslim calendar and the opportunity to engage in communal prayer during the school day. Parents spoke about the value of their children learning in a 'Muslim environment' and how this led to children having more secure and rooted Muslim identities and avoided them having to deal with giving explanations for their differences as Muslims. Parents emphasized the importance of young children being educated in a space where Islamic norms and behaviour were the norm and were the natural ways of 'being' and 'doing' to provide them with a foundation for their lives as Muslims in Britain.

As a result of the intensive religious learning and the Islamic environment, parents of children at the Muslim school felt that they were able to take a more a more relaxed approach with regard to religious learning in out of school activities than parents of children in state school. For some families this meant that children had more time to pursue out of school activities. Mrs Ashraf said about stories of the Prophet, 'I haven't done it myself but she, I know she's getting everything from school.' Whilst this mother was happy about her daughter's Islamic education, there was also a sense of guilt: 'I know it's my duty as a mother as well that I should do but I suppose I just get lazy because I think it's getting done.'

Reasons for not sending children to Muslim primary schools included the cost of attending a fee-paying school, although the fees are relatively low in comparison to other private schools in Cardiff. Parents also expressed concerns that placing their children within a Muslim school would remove their children from mainstream society and make it harder for them to function and interact within a secular society once they leave an all-Muslim environment; they would have a lack of bridging social capital. As Mr Mughal put it, this works both ways, with non-Muslims also not being exposed to Islam if Muslims go to separate schools:

> 'There's a concern about Islamic schools but the problem is that if the Muslims, grow up separately from the non-Muslims they will not know how to, the non-Muslims will not know about them. So I am concerned if the children get sent to only their Muslim schools and they'll have no idea, and they won't have any idea and they won't grow up together.' (Interview with Mr Mughal)

Two of the families in our sample hoped to send their sons to a Muslim boarding school in England, either London or Birmingham, to ensure an Islamic secondary education for their children. This appeared to have been a complex decision which included considerations about finances and the personal cost of living apart from their sons but this option was considered due to the lack of a secondary Muslim school in Cardiff. Attendance at a boarding school was not in financial terms an option for most families whose children attended a Muslim primary school. Many of these children would go on to secular state secondary schools and a number of parents were worried about the transition. We return to this issue in the next section.

Home schooling was used by three of the families in our sample for at least part of their children's primary education (see also Martinez, 2009 on the USA). Home schooling makes it easier to give children a concentrated period of learning and particularly the ritualistic aspects of Islam such as prayer and fasting and recitation of the Qur'an without the distraction of the school day. These parents embraced this approach to the education of their children either with reference to an Islamic notion that children should 'play' up to the age of seven and only then should engage in formal learning or with reference to an academically-informed pedagogical argument along the same lines. Two out of three of the mothers who home schooled lived in mixed ethnicity families (one was a convert to Islam and the other was married to a convert) and all three of them sent their children to an alternative school to supplement home schooling. These mothers all belonged to the same social network and attended regular social gatherings together. Two of these mothers sent their children to state primary schools when they were too old (age 7+) to attend the alternative school and one of the mothers (Mrs Morris) continued to home school her children beyond this age. Mrs Morris used a blend of Islamic knowledge and Western educational research evidence to explain the decision to use the alternative school instead of state primary school.

> 'Rasul Allah[1] (Salallaho AluhiWasalam[2]) in the hadith that you should play with your children till the age of seven and then you should teach them as reported by Ali (RadiAllah Anho[3])... and this is something Shaykh Hamza was saying a lot of in his speech. So this idea of playing till then and then formal education. So we kept to that because no formal education till age of seven. And all the research proves that this is very good for children in Sweden, Norway and in all of these places.' (Interview with Mrs Morris)

Non-Islamic Social and Cultural Influences

School provides an opportunity for children to develop friendships and social connections with their peer groups, independently of their parents and at a young age. For many of the Muslim children in our study school was the main location where they had opportunities to interact with non-Muslim children.

Parents voiced some concerns about undesirable behaviour resulting from their children socializing with other children in school, and especially non-Muslim children. There was more apparent concern for children beyond the primary school years and a greater concern over the potential for daughters, rather than sons, to engage in Islamically unacceptable behaviours within undesirable social networks. A number of parents (and fathers in particular) expressed concerns about their daughters' relationships with boys from school without mentioning similar concerns for their sons. Issues about 'undesirable' behaviours and networks cut across ideas about honour and decency in Muslim communities.

Social networks and any bad influences that they may exert over Muslim children seem to be of greatest concern during the teenage/high school years and were not of great concern to parents of primary school aged children. The transition to secondary school is recognized as a stressful and challenging period in children's lives (Holland et al.,

---

[1] The Messenger of Allah (The Prophet Muhammad).
[2] Peace be upon him.   [3] May God be pleased with him.

2007). It is interesting that teenagers are not viewed by parents as being able to manage and negotiate their multiple belongings within Islamic norms and values as well as their younger siblings, or younger children in general, are. It may be there is an assumption of a fundamental innocence of childhood, fading with adolescence, as adult desires develop, since this age distinction seems to be mostly to do with the threat of teenage sexuality. Mrs Fathullah referred to the risk that Muslim teenagers would 'begin to practise the things that they see, the fashion of the non-Muslim people'. Mr and Mrs Ishmael were thinking of moving to an Arab country as they thought the UK was 'very dangerous between (*age*) 9 to 16/17'. Both these sets of parents were more relaxed about the period immediately after the teenage years. For example Mr Ishmael thought it fine for his children to study at university in the UK. Some of the children seemed to already have taken on board messages about the dangers of teenage sexuality. Kauther Khalid (age 10), when asked what he thought of living in Cardiff, spoke of 'Christians live there...young people kissing each other' and her brother Kaleem (age 8) said that if you marry a Christian, 'Allah will punish you and you'll go to hellfire and you burn.' Religious difficulties did not only relate to non-Muslims, however, but sometimes also to Muslims who took a different line about practising Islam. Mrs Adam told us about a party where her daughters were screaming, 'Mum she's eating ham!' when a Muslim friend tucked into a hot dog and said her mother did not mind.

Concerns about contamination of primary school aged Muslim children seem to be focused on issues of dress and food. For example, Mrs Ahmet said her daughter sometimes goes to non-Muslim friends' houses when invited but she has to be told, 'don't eat meat, don't eat gelatine'. A small number of parents stated that they preferred their children not to socialize with non-Muslim children other than when necessary, such as in school hours. However, for others, having non-Muslim friends gave the children early opportunities to articulate their religious practices, as they often had to give explanations for why they did, or did not do, certain things, such as prayer and not eating ham. The process of having to give explanations for their behaviour to non-Muslims was not necessarily a difficult thing for them and at times it seemed almost to be a relief for them to have an opportunity to explain and demonstrate these differences. This was more likely to occur when friends from school visited Muslim family homes rather than taking place at school itself. This excerpt from Mrs Rana gives such an example:

'Her last birthday... we ended up inviting about six or seven of her friends here and then when the *adhaan* came then they got ready for *namaz* so the non-Muslim friends were sitting and watching and they were really interested so then I thought hang on they're upstairs, because they were having a make-up party they were doing nail polish and this and that so next thing we knew they were all reading *namaz, mashallah* ... they were asking how do you pray and what do you have to do and they were explaining the *surahs* and the reasons and stuff that it was more, I think if there's something you find that is natural, it's easy to tell somebody else about it, whereas if there's something that you think is supposed to be a secret or hidden you're not exactly going to go out and spread the news everywhere, so the fact that they enjoy is proven by the fact that they're able to speak about it when anybody else which is really a big step for them, which is good.' (Interview with Mrs Rana)

For the children it seemed that making friendships with non-Muslims was more of a religious challenge when there were not other Muslim children around and they were in a clear minority in school. This was not always a problem but it did mean that some children tried to conceal or tried not to highlight the things that made them different from their non-Muslim friends. For example, Iza Ayub (age 7) (see end of Chapter 3) felt self-conscious about her *halal* diet and told us, 'I don't actually like being a Muslim because I like feel all alone.' However, more generally, children presented a more mixed view of being a religious minority in school where at times it was easy and rewarding to provide explanations and explain differences and at others more difficult, and sometimes these explanations provided opportunities for humour and fun. Norms and religious practices around food, eating and mealtimes were again highlighted as important to children of primary school age as markers of difference. These are concrete material differences from non-Muslim children and are more understandable perhaps at this age than more abstract aspects of faith and possibly also more clearly articulated to children by parents than more abstract beliefs. Becher (2008) found Muslim children of this age (and their parents) to be clear about the importance of food for marking religious boundaries; also some children were less sure about specific restrictions. Nesbitt (2004: 24–25) also notes Hindu children in middle childhood being quite focused on food as an indicator of religious difference.

As well as mixing with non-Muslim peers in school, the children in our study obviously encountered mainstream secular British culture. It is worth considering the issue of how comfortably Islam fits with popular culture for the children in our study, as it is part of the picture when we are thinking about how successfully Islam is passed on to the next generation. There is certainly plenty to protect children from—aspects of popular culture that distract from religious nurture. Daniyaal is very honest about what distracts him:

ASMA: 'Do you think it would make you feel better if you did pray?'
DANIYAAL: 'Well I know it will bring me what we call *hasanah*[4], *Jannah*[5] and stuff like that but I don't see how it makes me any happier, personally.'
ASMA: 'What does make you happy then?'
DANIYAAL: 'It's right over there.'
ASMA: 'What is it?'
DANIYAAL: 'It's the big thing with the screen.'
ASMA: 'The television?'
DANIYAAL: 'And.'
ASMA: 'The computer.'
(Interview with Daniyaal Faysal, age10)

Some children, however, seem to navigate religion and secular entertainment quite comfortably. Tahirah Mahfouz kept a voice diary for us and the following excerpt indicates that she has what Østberg (2006), from her research with Pakistani young people in Norway, has termed an 'integrated plural identity'. She is quite comfortable with watching the X Factor and getting up to pray at six in the morning:

'*Ah lan wa sahlan*, that is hello in Arabic, today we went to see Wall-E in the cinemas and it was my baby sister's first time to go and watch something in the cinemas. We went as a family as it was a very special day for my little sister but then she got a little bit bored in the middle of it so she went to the shops, then as I just said *ah lan wa sahlan*, we went to Arabic class and as you see that is in Arabic, my sister will be talking more about Arabic class but I'll be talking about is we've been praying, we woke up six o clock as usual, to pray *Fajr*. We watched X Factor (*hums title tune*) that's the tune of X Factor's start and here we are, my sister most desperately has been waiting for ages so here we are . . . Layla Mahfouz!' (Voice diary by Tahirah Mahfouz, age 11)

The Mahfouz children are in a fairly small minority of Muslims in a Welsh-medium school, but this display of 'multiple cultural competence' (Jackson and Nesbitt, 1993), i.e. the ability to function well socially in both Muslim and non-Muslim environments without experiencing profound moral tensions or 'culture clash', seemed to be very comfortable for them, apparently as a result of an upbringing geared towards it. They were involved in a wide range of activities. These included formal religious education and Muslim Scouts, but they also

---

[4] Blessings.   [5] Paradise.

completed a voice diary entry after attending an ice hockey match. The local team are the Cardiff Devils and both girls, Layla (age 13) and Tahirah (age 11) told us they were uncomfortable shouting in support of devils, so always prefaced the shouting of their team's name by saying the phrase '*auzubillahi minashaitan nirajeem*' (I seek refuge from the accursed Shaitan [Satan]). Despite this multiple cultural competence, there are limits to their navigation of Cardiff spaces. Layla said she had to turn down invitations to school friends' parties that took place in pubs.

Parents' decisions about navigating non-Muslim social and cultural life are inevitably informed by their own experiences of the same, where they have been brought up in the UK. They emphasize different aspects in different situations and according to their own particular histories. So Mrs Sajaad was keen for Nabeel (age 9) to have a 'normal' childhood, meaning that in addition to his *hifz* class, he was taken to a football club. Mrs Hussain spoke of growing up with 'conflicting personalities' and being effectively a '*gora*' (white person) in school, whilst being Pakistani at home. Her solution to this was to attempt to instil strong Islamic values in her children, for example initially sending Ilyas to one of the Muslim primary schools, until the school had to close for a while and he then moved to the local state primary school. Multiple cultural competence is perhaps not so much something that occurs naturally in children of first or second generation ethnic minority communities in the West, but rather a process which is facilitated by parents and based on reflections of their own childhood and the difficulties they encountered.

Experiences of the City

Parents' views about Cardiff as a place to bring up Muslim children were overwhelmingly positive. They tended to speak of the city as a good place to practise Islam in terms of the resources and facilities available or even as Cardiff as a better place to practice Islam than other UK cities. We should not take this to straightforwardly mean that Cardiff does in fact compare well with other cities in terms of acceptance of religious diversity, as interviewees will have personal reasons for justifying their current location. It is a familiar tactic for people who want to talk up their current living situation to make unfavourable comments about other places they know or have lived in previously.

A number of interviewees spoke about the increasing number and variety of mosques and other Islamic organizations in Cardiff over time. An interesting aspect of the positive views was the way in which Cardiff was regarded as both a big and small city, and also the Muslim community was both regarded as big enough and small enough simultaneously at times. People often referred to the size of the Muslim community as big or increasing and this was seen as positive thing, but it was also good that the community in Cardiff is not 'as big' as those in cities such as London, Birmingham, Manchester or Luton. It was acknowledged that these cities have better quality and more numerous facilities for children to learn about Islam and the lack of a Muslim secondary school in Cardiff was noted by several parents, as well as the smaller number of general services and amenities catering for Muslim people in Cardiff. However, these other cities were also regarded as busy and impersonal and in general the Muslim community life of Cardiff was preferred. Social problems within Muslim communities, as well as hostility from non-Muslims, were generally thought to reside elsewhere.

The relatively smaller Muslim community in Cardiff was valued by some of the parents as facilitating a form of social control over their children. There was thought to be an increased likelihood, because of the city's relatively small size, that behaviour outside of accepted norms would be observed and reported back to parents, making it more likely that children would behave in an acceptable manner. Mrs Akras's words here are an example of this parental view, referring to the increasingly common use of private transport for delivering children to various locations.

ASMA: 'What do you think about Cardiff as a place to practise Islam?'

MRS AKRAS: 'Amazing.'

ASMA: 'Why would you say so?'

MRS AKRAS: 'It's small, yeah, uh, a lot of Muslims, yeah. As well, your children in the community and in the school with a lot of children, they keep an eye on each other—very important . . . If your child starts to go around, the news will come to you . . . It's easy for you, it's a very, very good place to raise the children in Cardiff to be a good Muslim because, they can't lost like in London for example, London or Manchester. Your child takes the Underground from the morning, you don't know where is he going. But in Cardiff . . . personally I advise every mother if she wants, you know, her children to be good, yeah, don't let them go in public transportation. Take your child to school and bring him back from school.' (Interview with Mrs Akras)

Different parts of the city allowed for different levels of practice. The Akbir family had moved from a mostly white suburb to a more central district with a much higher proportion of Muslims and far more access to mosques and local Muslim organizations. Mr and Mrs Akbir spoke of this move as having helped them to improve their practice of Islam.

There were occasions where research participants spoke about Cardiff positively, but when asked why they thought it was a good place to live they spoke about being *allowed* to practise their religion, for example talking about the absence of problems, lack of any verbal abuse and so on. So for these interviewees the bar was set fairly low. A couple of parents brought up in Cardiff referred to childhood experiences of racism but explained that these experiences were in the past. This could be a feature of racism being a commoner experience in childhood than in adulthood or could indeed be an indication of progressive social change over time. There were several indications that children were very aware of any racism being unacceptable. For example, Faiza Tahir (age 7) defined respect as 'not being racist'; something he had learned 'in school'. As mentioned earlier in the chapter there were almost no mentions from children of having encountered overt Islamophobia.

For adults, incidents of Islamophobia or racism were more likely to be cited from other places. For example, Mrs Miller said that her brother who, like her, is married to a white Muslim convert, had experienced hostility in Newcastle. In Cardiff, however, 'there's lots of older converts' and white women who have married Yemeni men, so, 'it's more accepted in Cardiff and you're not frowned upon'. However, Mr Mughal, quite noticeably Muslim in his *jelbaab*, loose trousers and full beard, told us he does not walk alone in Cardiff. Mrs Hussain spoke of 'racist remarks' after 9/11 and having consciously toned down her dress as a result to make herself less conspicuously Muslim. Mrs Rasheed, a white English convert, had experienced hostility which although she has been called 'Paki' is presumably related to her religious identity or perhaps an assumed race/ethnicity because of her religion.

> 'I get the odd, it's funny I get racist things because it's weird, I don't get it very often but like the name calling thing. Cos I've been called "Paki" and "Ninja" and I've been shouted at, "why have you got a sheet on your head?", and all this kind of stupidness but...I noticed one of the talks was about Islamophobia and there's somebody at the university researching into that and I don't know if it comes under that because it's like I've crossed over now. I'm not a White British person any more am I? I am, but I'm not to other

people. And I think that Cardiff isn't so bad for that but I, I wouldn't want to move to be honest I don't know where else I would live I can't go "back home" or anything can I?' (Interview with Mrs Rasheed)

It should be emphasized that such data were rare in our data set and parents were more likely to speak of hostility somewhere else or in the past rather than the present. Talk about Cardiff was overwhelmingly positive. The potential for difficulties was there, however, as illustrated by the above excerpt from Mrs Rasheed.

Informal Muslim Social Networks

Local networks

The children in our study spent time with grandparents, aunts, uncles, friends, neighbours, and babysitters. For almost all families, the vast majority of these informal social connections, even outside the bio-logical family, were with other Muslims and in most cases people from the same ethnic background, with a strong emphasis on bonding rather than bridging. Bierens et al. (2007) argue that social bonds of common ethnicity and religion create a sense of belonging and commu-nity and can lead to the development of stronger cultural identities, which provide the confidence required for bridging to the wider social environment. So strong bonding is required before bridging can take place. Extended kinship networks seemed to be alive and well (see Chapter 7), although these tended to be limited to members of parents' original nuclear families, with a bias towards grandparents, maternal kin and female kin. In the case of the smaller ethnic groups, extended family members were rarely in Cardiff or even the UK, but were more likely to be abroad. Language is a very important enabler of participation in an ethnic community and ensuring that their children learn the mother tongue language was one of the ways in which many of the parents in our sample facilitated their children's acceptance into a minority ethnic community. The exception to the general pattern of same-ethnicity social life was the mixed ethnicity families, who tended to have a more ethnically varied set of social connections, as might be expected, although these were still largely with other Muslims.

The significant amount of time spent with extended family and friends of their parents' choice may be a form of control and a limit to time spent with non-Muslims and exposure to un-Islamic influences. These two excerpts from fathers mentioned the importance of control in relation to social networks. Mr Ibrahim was quite overt in referring to the children's upbringing as a 'project':

> 'I think little bit is different because when we brought up we have our mother, grandfathers, the big family, neighbours. Everybody can teach them part of, but here me and my wife, and you know it's difficult also to control the house. Some time we setting up we watching they have the children channel, yeah I think it needs more control here. More control.' (Interview with Mr Ishmael)

SAMEH: 'So they go to these Quranic classes and they go to the Scouts. Do they have like relatives in the UK or Cardiff?'

MR IBRAHIM: 'Err, no, just friends. Malaysian friends.'

SAMEH: 'They go and visit them?'

MR IBRAHIM: 'Yeah but frankly we feel that, we teach our children actually your relatives, your brothers is who have the same *aqueedah*[6] with you who is willing to I mean, is willing to really implement Islam in life.'

SAMEH: 'So you choose for them?'

MR IBRAHIM: 'Yes, yes. We choose actually. We are little bit selective in terms of their friends. But I think this very important because we want to develop them. If we, I mean, we get them loose then we spoil their development the project that we are doing on him.' (Interview with Mr Ibrahim)

The establishment of close social networks of wider family and Muslim friends therefore serves to maintain a 'moral community' and 'moral space' suffused with Islamic values (Werbner, 1990). It extends the number of spaces compatible with faith where young Muslims can feel 'at home' (Phillips, 2009).

For children, parents are the main gatekeepers and facilitators into an ethnic minority community and control the level of their children's participation in it. For some parents, ethnically specific communities were seen as safe places and social spaces in which children could learn about their religion in a way that conformed to the way in which they themselves were taught and would safeguard against misunderstandings and different interpretations of Islam. Muslims communities in Cardiff, and around the UK, are mainly based on ethnicity. Social class also structures these communities, with different ethnic groups having distinctive class profiles. Chapter 1 noted the high levels of deprivation in the Muslim population (Hussain, 2008), and this is especially evident in Bangladeshis and Pakistanis. Employment tends to be heavily racialized, for example in taxi driving and restaurant work (Kalra, 2000; Tackey et al., 2006), which reinforces ethnically-specific social networks and

---

[6] Belief system or creed.

makes mixing with non-Muslims and those from different ethnic groups less likely.

The organization of formal religious institutions and more informal social structures of communities and social networks on ethnic lines are delineated mainly on the basis of language and culture, though this is intertwined with religious practice and school of thought. There can be further cleavages according to region of origin and regional languages (such as Mirpuris and Punjabis from Pakistan and those from Dhaka or Sylhet in Bangladesh). The more complex organization according to regional differences in country of ethnic origin is probably confined to those groups which have a longer history of settlement in the UK. In Cardiff these are Pakistanis, Bangladeshis, Yemenis and Somalis. Smaller ethnic groups appear to be likely to forego some of the aspects of regional differences such as dialects in favour of maintaining relationships and links with people who share some important aspects of ties to the homeland and particular ethnic, cultural or religious practices. Muslim families who belong to smaller ethnic groups may associate themselves with a notion of a wider Muslim community in order to attain a sense of community.

Belonging to an ethnic community can have positive effects of shared understandings and sense of belonging and kinship networks from countries of origin. However, there are also perceived negative effects. For example, Mrs Adam told us that she hoped in future to move out of her area of Cardiff, one with a relatively high density of Muslim population, to lessen the effects that the peer pressures of belonging to the Somali community might have on her daughters—things like early marriage and low educational attainment amongst Somali women. The distance from the community would mean that she could more easily control the interactions her children had with the wider Somali community. This comment emphasized the potentially restrictive dimension of bonding social capital, in terms of constraints on educational trajectory and social mobility (Holland et al., 2007).

Female family members seemed to have a central role in establishing and maintaining children's social networks outside of school. Nearly all network care arrangements were made by mothers. An aspect of children's involvement in parents' social networks that is especially relevant to religious nurture is the identification of suitable Qur'an/ Islamic Studies teachers. This happened typically through recommendations by friends or other social contacts of mothers rather than fathers. This mirrors the experience of British families in general, where despite changing discourse of fatherhood, women are still largely

145

responsible for care and decision making in relation to young children (Shirani et al., 2012).

Diasporas

International connections with historical countries of origin remained important for most Muslim families. These were the 'homelands' of parents, grandparents or great-grandparents. As Eickelman and Piscatori (2004: 137) put it, 'Somalis in Cardiff or Turin may be consulted regularly on decisions affecting their families or households in Mogadishu'. Identification with a historical homeland is discussed in Chapter 8. Here we present a description of how diaspora features in children's social networks and especially in religious nurture.

The conventional meaning of diaspora relates to the forced dispersal of people and longings and mourning for the lost homeland (Bak and von Bromssen, 2010). More recently the term has been broadened out to encompass the experiences of other groups of people who have experienced large scale migrations, such as economic migrants from Pakistan and Bangladesh. There is a very wide range of views on historical homelands, from Mr Tawfeeq (Yemeni) who saw Cardiff as a temporary location even though he had lived there for nearly forty years to Mrs Rana who told us 'I can't find anything that people would say that they're proud to be Pakistanis for.'

Our findings show that there were some positive effects of being part of a diaspora for families in our study. The existence of a homeland outside of Cardiff (which is home) offered choice and opportunity to participate in social networks beyond the city and country in which they lived. Participation in a transnational network also appeared to allow British-born parents a point of comparison, a measure for their achievements in terms of how well they were able to bring up Muslim children within a secular society.

Reasons given by parents for visits to homeland include visiting family, acquiring or improving language, becoming more familiar with cultural norms and values, attending family events such as weddings and funerals and improving Islamic learning. For children to meet and know their wider family was one of the primary reasons for parents to undertake trips to homelands and indeed some trips were taken up entirely by visiting extended family members, particularly grandparents. These visits were often longer than normal holidays and could last up to a number of months. Parents took their children to a 'homeland' for particular reasons but children formed their own opinions and have their own reflections on their visits. Ollwig and Gulløv (2003)

146

argue that children's places are changed, negotiated and constructed for children by others and modified and imbued with meaning by the children themselves. It should be noted that in our study some children did not display these reflections but almost repeated their parents' desires for outcomes of the visits such as the learning of a language without putting forward their own opinions of the experience. This may illustrate the methodological limitations of one-off interviews, rather than necessarily being proof of a lack of agency on the children's part. Bak and van Bromssen (2010) emphasize the importance of language and its acquisition for links to homeland and transnational networks; however children in our study were more likely to talk about food and dress in relation to trips abroad. As with their experience of being Muslim in primary school, these concrete material aspects seem to be, for them, significant markers of difference. Being part of a diaspora did not necessarily mean that the children liked every aspect of this belonging. However, visits to such homelands left lasting memories and provided an opportunity for children to be outdoors and experience an alternative way of life to that in urban Britain, one involving spiders, chickens, open rooftops, motorbikes and freedom to roam.

It is evident from our study that in addition to the country of origin other significant Islamic places (Mecca, Medina, and Gaza) also evoked some of the aspects of a diasporic consciousness, particularly with regard to collective myth and collective commitment, articulated through the charitable donations, pilgrimage and the display of images of Hajj and mosques in Mecca and Medina (see Chapter 7). There was some evidence of a transnationalism which crosses several national borders, rather than simply a bilateral set of relations between the country of origin and the host country. Although the idea of a global Ummah did not emerge strongly and explicitly from our interviewees, the desire to visit Mecca did suggest a certain sense of a global Muslim identity which was not strictly tied to a country of origin or of current location. The interest in Mecca is of course linked to the Five Pillars of Islam but it could also be seen as similar to the notion of diasporic longing put forward by Bak and van Bromssen (2010), i.e. a sense of being away from a place only known through memory or the collective memory of the family.

Return to a historical homeland, or a stay of several years rather than a trip lasting only weeks, could be a concrete reality for some families due to their close family links. However this was likely to be dependent upon structural constraints and it was more likely to be to an imagined return. In some cases, one parent idealized a homeland and their spouse presented difficulties or contradictions. Other parents did not express a desire to return to their homeland but rather to move to another Islamic country. Serial migration seemed to be an option for some. Despite the practical difficulties of moving a whole family across national borders whilst children are young, there is an acceptance of the possibility, in the context of so much global movement. Some parents had themselves had transnational childhoods.

Conclusion

The overview of children's social networks in this chapter has touched on connections in school, across the city and overseas. In relation to schools, parents spoke primarily of concern over the handling of religious issues and this was more to the fore than concern about other aspects of education such as levels of achievement, although the interview was admittedly focused on religious nurture. There were some problematic aspects of primary school for Muslim parents and children, particularly to do with Christian festivals and collective worship which included elements of Christianity (as the law demands of schools). A few parents who could afford to had chosen private Muslim school for their children or home schooling, and the reasons for these decisions were reviewed. School is the main opportunity for Muslim children to mix with non-Muslims. In general parents were fairly relaxed about this, but many worried about the teenage years and especially about sexuality. Although secular popular culture could be a pull away from religious practice for children, there were also examples of children skilfully blending practice as a Muslim with an interest in aspects of popular culture. Experiences of living in the city of Cardiff were overwhelmingly positive, although a few isolated examples of Islamophobia showed the potential for a Muslim identity to provoke hostility. Children's social networks, in Cardiff and beyond (including overseas family connections) were very largely with other Muslims from the same ethnic background.

To reflect back on the concept of social capital, we argued at the outset that whilst recognizing difficulties with the concept, it is useful as a heuristic device. It has to be concluded from the material in this chapter that there is a lot of bonding social capital but little evidence of bridging. Families tended to put much more time into maintaining links with other Muslims, most often from the same ethnic background, than they did into making social connections with non-Muslims. This should support the minority/ethnic defence theory of religious transmission. It is possible to explain the greater likelihood (compared with other religions) that Islam will be passed on to children with reference to relatively tight-knit minority ethnic social networks which reinforce cultural norms. It should be noted, however, that this process also works the other way round; that is, religion shapes the social networks in so far as parents maintain an appropriate 'moral community' (Werbner, 1990) for their children because of their religious faith. This moral community will inevitably consist of other Muslims, whose moral frameworks can be trusted, and language, cultural connection, racialized settlement of cities and racialized employment all make it very likely that in most families these other Muslims will be from the same ethnic background. There was little evidence of the impact of overt hostility from the non-Muslim population on Muslim identity, but we did note what could be labelled as a 'resistance identity' (Castells, 1997) when a cultural threat to Islam was mentioned. This would fit with the minority defence theory.

Children do in fact encounter non-Muslims if they attend state school—as most do—and a minority of them see these non-Muslim friends outside school. Bridging social capital is therefore not absent and children are in the forefront of it. Children also certainly cannot be wholly protected from non-Islamic influences, as they are exposed to popular culture which can sometimes be antithetical to Islam. In interfacing with non-Islamic social influences, children exercise agency. We saw examples of where, in a very limited way, some Muslim children mouthed the words of Christian prayers and hymns rather than say them out loud, thus undermining the worship while avoiding getting into trouble with teachers. However, taking the chapter as a whole, the children's social networks are fairly heavily circumscribed by parents. It is far from unusual in middle childhood, regardless of religion, for children's routines to revolve around their family and for parents to define their movements. However, the management of children's social contacts does seem to be particularly tight in the families in our study, with some quite openly acknowledging the need to control their children's social lives.

7

Muslim Family Life

> 'Because if I was without my family, the first thing, I wouldn't be made. And if my family, I was apart from, I would be somewhere else without my family, I think I would be nothing without my family. And I think if I was a document and my headline would be my family.'
>
> (Interview with Neda Hooshmand, age 10)

Neda has a rather lovely poetic verbal style, despite only learning English quite recently, which was evident many times during our interview with her. Her document metaphor reminds us of the importance of the family. It was noted in Chapter 1 that in Islam the family is of central importance, as reflected in law and scholarship, with parents and children having clear obligations to each other (Waddy, 1990; Bunt, 1998). Islam does not have the monopoly on the centrality of the family, of course. It should be remembered that in middle childhood in Western countries the dominant model is for children to be very home-based and quite dependent on parents. More generally, the family continues to be the primary unit of social organization throughout the world. Morgan (2011a) has worked hard to move sociologists away from preoccupation with traditional family structures, yet he acknowledges that:

> It is clear that 'family' is not simply just a powerful strand in ideological rhetoric but the relationships and activities that are indicated by the use of the term are important to a wide range of people going about their everyday lives throughout the world. (Morgan, 2011a: 4.3)

This chapter returns to the family, engaging with the sociology of that institution. There is discussion of family structure and family practices and a particular focus on interesting aspects of the 'display' of family religion. There is a dialogue between our topic of religious nurture and the sociology of the family. A dialogue requires two directions of travel. So we consider both what Muslim family regimes of religious learning can tell us about the sociology of the family in contemporary Britain and also how perspectives from sociological research on the family can help us to understand religious nurture in Muslim families.

Family Structure

The concept of 'family structure' seems a rather old-fashioned one in the UK where the field of family sociology has been dominated in recent years by qualitative research on family cultures and practices; a body of work which arose partly in opposition to what was seen as an out-dated focus on family structure. In a global context, however, the term still has resonance and much of the quantitative research worldwide on family sociology does concern family structure. Furthermore, there are traditional models of family structure in Islam. However, discussion of family structure does inevitably stray on to the territory of 'family practices' (Morgan, 1996, 2011a, 2011b). In this section we discuss three issues of family structure: gender, extended families and non-traditional families.

Gender

There are strongly gendered social patterns in many religions. For example, women tend to be more numerous amongst worshippers, often assuming the 'hidden' roles in religious organizations, whereas the status of a religious professional often tends to be restricted to men (Gilliat-Ray, 2000). Religiously conservative movements tend to take a traditional view of gender roles; this is true in Christianity and Islam at least (Tohidi and Bayes, 2001). In Islam it is certainly true that there tends to be gender separation in many aspects of life, e.g. prayer at mosque and many social situations. Exceptions to this in our study included the Shia families, whose communal prayer in a community centre was mixed gender. (The one Ismaili father told us women in his mosque sometimes led the congregation in *dua*.) There was also a fairly clear consensus, against mainstream Western liberal feminism, that mothers and fathers have markedly different roles within families, with mothers expected to do most of the child care; an 'equal, but different' approach (Murata, 1992; Esposito and Mogahed 2007). Most of the mothers wore hijab and encouraged their daughters to do so. Many of the research participants, however, and especially the mothers, made a distinction between conservative cultural practices from Muslim countries of origin and Islam itself. It was noted in Chapter 4 that a religion–culture distinction often led to more conservative interpretation of the 'original' Islam, untainted by centuries of innovation. However, with regard to gender, there tended to be a siding with some elements of a Western liberal feminist equal opportunity agenda. So, for example, there was much criticism of the lack of space for women and girls in many of the city's mosques and assertion of girls' right to education and women's right to employment (see also Mohammad, 2005). The drawing of a distinction between religion and culture also meant, however, that some practices which might potentially have been questioned from a gender equality perspective remained unquestioned because they are specifically mentioned in Qur'an or *hadith*, the most obvious one being the prohibition on girls and women reading *salat* during menstruation.

It was noted in Chapter 4 that the main responsibility for religious nurture tended to lie with mothers. The centrality of mothering to the bringing up of Muslim children is something of a challenge here to the preoccupation in popular discourse with Muslim men (although the media also have a fascination for veiled women). This is not to say that there was no role for fathers. There were examples in our sample of involved fathers; especially those who routinely took children with them to mosque. Becher (2008) describes fathers as fulfilling the role of 'coach' in religious nurture, monitoring religious observance and reinforcing the more day-to-day religious teaching of mothers. Gender differences in parenting seemed to be more observable in the lower social class families. This was at least in part because of work patterns, as noted in Chapter 4, with (male) restaurant workers out of the house at all the key times during the week when children were around. So far as we can tell from interview accounts, there were indications that the more highly educated fathers were more involved in teaching about Islam. Education did not neatly map onto social class, however. There were some highly educated taxi drivers, for example, and a trained accountant working temporarily in a chip shop. Some of the education about Islam was self-taught—the phenomenon described by Roy (2004)—and not based on formal qualifications.

There was a general view from research participants that in middle childhood there is little difference in the religious nurture of boys and girls, as was noted in Chapter 4. Formal learning was organized on the basis of gender separation, but the general view from parents was that at this stage of childhood the content of learning would not be different. Only a minority of girls we interviewed wore hijab habitually, although some were expected do so in specific settings such as Islamic Studies classes. In the various classes and groups we observed, the girls seemed to be very confident and indeed physical in their play and conversation. For example, in the Scouts group they chose to play with a clothes rail on wheels, swinging from it and challenging each other to do a body press on it. They also talked about sports lessons at school, comparing the merits of long jump and shot put. As Chapter 6 has explained, parents' anxieties come to the fore in relation to teenage girls, with typical Muslim models of femininity being very different from some of those on offer in secondary school. For some girls there are changes in formal religious nurture. Some of the Bangladeshi and Pakistani parents spoke of teenage girls not going to mosque because of concern about modesty and lack of space for women. For some adult women too there seemed to be ethnic traditions which restricted their religious involvement outside the family home. For example, the Mubashir family (Bangladeshis) told us it was prohibited for women to 'read' the *zuhr* and *asr* prayers out loud.

Extended families

In many Muslim countries, close relations with extended family are expected and indeed three generations may often live under one roof. In the general UK population, such close contact with extended families is less common. Amongst our sample, third generation families from the larger ethnic groups (Bangladeshis and Pakistanis) were more likely to have grandparents living in Cardiff and involved in children's lives. This is to do with large numbers from these ethnic groups living in Cardiff and their history of settlement (see Gilliat-Ray and Mellor, 2010). Other ethnic groups seemed to have different histories. For example, we were told that despite the long history of Yemeni settlement in Cardiff, only in recent years have spouses started to come over from Yemen, whereas it had previously been more common for Yemeni men to marry local white girls. There was a great variety of extended family involvement, ranging from large families where children had regular contact with aunts, uncles, cousins and grandparents, through to small one- or two-parent family units with no relatives living nearby.

Grandparents, when living nearby (or in the same house) tended to be quite involved in religious nurture. Some children saw their grandparents daily, either because they shared a house or because they went to the grandparents' house every day after school, if parents were working. Several of the parents spoke of grandparents' useful role in teaching children about Islam, sometimes because they were seen as more knowledgeable or more pious or else simply because they had more time. So, for example, Mrs Sajaad said:

'My Dad teaches them about all the different prophets. I don't even know about them myself properly but they know quite a bit about the prophets and then my Dad will read the translation of the Qur'an to them.' (Interview with Mrs Sajaad)

Some children spoke of praying five times a day when their grandparents came to visit, even though usually their parents would not find time to do so. We heard of grandparents teaching children specific practices (e.g. *wudu*), teaching the Qur'an or telling stories about the Prophet's life. Some passed on local family traditions of learning by arranging lessons with particular Qur'an/Arabic teachers. Grandparents were also spoken of in connection with behaviour management. Mr Ishmael expressed regret that his children not growing up with grandparents around would mean less control of their behaviour. Mrs Ashraf described her mother as being very knowledgeable about Islam and when asked in what way, she spoke of the same sense of Islam as a set of behaviour rules that many of the children described (see Chapter 4).

'It's basically just about general things like the mistakes they've made or something that she'll talk to them. She'll say you shouldn't do this because you know this will happen or Allah will be upset or in the Afterlife this will happen, and then just starting from that she talks to them about Islam in that way.' (Interview with Mrs Ashraf)

Mrs Ashraf is divorced and relies heavily on her parents and her siblings for help with the children so that she can work. Mrs Shahzad similarly said she relied on her mother. Although she was married, her husband ran a business in Pakistan and spent most of his time there so she was effectively a lone parent for long periods. She told us that her mother taught the children a great deal about Islam and they took this in 'like a sponge', which was helped by the fact that they 'respect her more in a way'.

It seems, then, that when grandparents were physically available, they were typically part of the micro-social network which shaped the child's religious *habitus*. As noted in earlier chapters, this can take place from a very young age. Sami Shahzad (age 6) told us, 'even when I was a baby I used to learn', referring to his grandmother's modelling of prayer. He said, 'when my Nan do prays, when I was one I used to learn it'. This process also involves cognitive transmission, via frequent repetition of Arabic phrases. So, for example, Mrs Shahzad said her mother taught the children the *Qalma* and *Bismillah*. In his oral diary, Hashim Hamid (age 10) repeated each day, 'I prayed *namaz* with my granddad' and also noted, 'I have to read *Surah Yaseen* every day for my grandma.'

It was not always the case that grandparents were seen as more steeped in Islamic learning or practices than parents. Head covering has become much more widespread in recent decades, in the context of the global resurgence of Islam. Older generations of women can therefore seem 'less Islamic' through not wearing hijab, if they have been socialized into a different religious context. Mrs Ayub told us that her mother, although knowledgeable and a teacher of the Qur'an, is: 'just horrified—why do I need to cover my head?'

Non-traditional families

The traditional model in our sample was of a nuclear family augmented by extended family, with extended family members living locally in some cases but almost all having extended family members living abroad. Within the sample there were also several family structures that departed from this model because of change in the immediate family unit. There were three reconstituted families, one lone parent family following bereavement and three lone parent families following divorce, in one of which the mother had a male partner albeit he did not live with the family. There was one family where the parents lived separately in the same city because (in the mother's words) 'they just argue constantly when they live together'. There was another family where the situation was ambiguous, with the father who had previously lived with the family in Cardiff now apparently away in Pakistan for long periods on business, but the son gave the impression his father was not coming back.

In this section we consider some important aspects of non-traditional family structure, in so far as they relate to religious nurture, namely divorce, separation and reconstituted families. The wider context of intimate relationships in the UK has seen substantial social change in the last few decades. The divorce rate in the UK population increased rapidly in the 1970s although it has been has been fairly stable since 1985 (Wilson and Smallwood, 2008). The other notable change has been the rise in cohabitation, which now precedes 80% of all marriages in the UK population (Beaujouan and Ní Bhrolcháin, 2011).

Sociologists have debated the changing cultural climate of relationships. Giddens (1992) has emphasized the radical nature of the social change—a 'transformation of intimacy' in his terms. He describes a trend wherein people are less likely to accept lifetime marriage as their fate but instead seek a 'pure relationship' based on emotional intimacy and mutual understanding. Giddens strikes an optimistic note about what he sees as the democratizing of intimate relationships, though others such as Jamieson (1998) are less optimistic and emphasize the continuity of power dynamics (e.g. of gender) in relationships.

Most Muslim parents regard it as part of their parental responsibilities to find their grown-up children a marriage partner. There has been a long cultural tradition of seeking a spouse within the extended family. Marriage to a cousin, or another relative is deemed to be less risky, since all parties involved remain bound within ties of loyalty, obligation and honour (Charsley, 2006, 2007). Within British Muslim populations, it has been commonplace to arrange marriages between children born and raised in Britain and kin 'back home'. These arrangements are often a way of consolidating extended family relationships, and fulfilling social or economic ties. However, one of the outcomes of this practice is that the marriage partners may have little in common with one another in terms of identity, lifestyle preferences, or aspirations for the future. They may not even speak the same language fluently. Although many happy marriages can and do occur as a result of these 'arranged marriages', there can be tensions and discord, and despite the efforts that families make to support newlyweds, rates of divorce are far higher than we might expect and lone parenthood has risen substantially in recent years (Qureshi et al., 2012). The practice of 'importing' a spouse from 'back home' remains prevalent, even today.

Despite the changing social mores in the general UK population, there was a sense from the families in our study of divorce still being rather stigmatized amongst Muslim families. For example, in one family, where the father was the biological parent of one child and step parent of the other, we were told there was no public acknowledgement of these differing relationships. There was no suggestion of deliberate deception, but rather because the family had moved to Cardiff since the mother's divorce, other Cardiff Muslims were allowed to assume the family was a traditional one with both parents being biologically related to both children.

As in the general population, however (see Smart, Neale, and Wade, 2001), there is a range of different experiences of divorce and post-separation parenting amongst the families in our sample. Mrs Rana told us her ex-husband was abusive and controlling, isolating her from her family. She spoke of the children not enjoying seeing their father but only doing so to fulfil a legal agreement about contact. In contrast, Mr Asaad was very positive about his child's new step-father, a devout Salafi who sends all his children to a Muslim school. He highlighted the man's positive influence on his son's learning about Islam:

'The husband is nice. He's a decent guy. He's strict with his *Din*[1] ... In my opinion she chose a decent man. He's *hafiz* of Qur'an. He teaches Qur'an as well. So he's getting that ... um so he's getting that benefit at home as well. So not just at home, in Qur'an school, and then you know, his knowledge of history's not as good as mine so I top him up. So Hamza is benefiting all round.' (Interview with Mr Asaad)

This is an important dimension of separation in relation to this book's topic, namely the way in which religious nurture plays out in separated and reconstituted families. It should be noted of course that any issue can potentially become a cause for disagreement after divorce and aspects of the moral framework of a child's upbringing can be debated in any family, regardless of religion. However, there was at least one example in our study of where religious nurture seemed to be the main issue of disagreement between biological parents. The Mir family had recently moved from London, following a divorce. The father of the two older boys was still living in London and their mother had remarried to a man from Cardiff who brought his son to live with his new family. In the interview there were fairly open tensions between the boys with different parentage. The two older boys were quite preoccupied with the difference in religious regime in their new family. For example, they said that 'they', that is, their mother and stepfather, would not let them do the *isha* prayers, as they had done with their father. What was probably an issue primarily of suitable bedtime had been constructed as a religious argument. It was evident from all the interviews with this family that the older boys' father was more visibly practising than their stepfather and that this had become both an issue of disagreement between the adults and also a further justification for the older boys' unhappiness at having moved to Cardiff and been separated from their father.

There was another case, the Uddin family, where the ten year old boy, Fakhir, expressed sadness about his parents' divorce, saying 'because my family is broken I'm heartbroken too'. He did not miss his father, unlike the Mir boys, but clearly the split had been difficult and he thought he was implicated, saying 'it's because of me that my parents got divorced'. He mentioned disagreements about his 'education', though he did not know the substance of these disagreements and his mother did not mention any disagreements about religious nurture, despite the interview being focused on this topic. It was striking how willing Fakhir was to openly express his sadness about the divorce to a relatively unknown interviewer (Sameh). This willingness of children in this age group to be open to relative strangers about family disruption was also noted in the research by Scourfield et al. (2006).

---

[1] Religion.

Family Practices

The concept of 'family practices' puts the emphasis on what gets done within families rather than what families 'are' (Morgan, 1996, 2011a, 2011b). This allows social analysis to move away from a restricted notion of a family unit and pays attention to the everyday negotiation of family life. This is a theoretical perspective very much in keeping with a focus on everyday lived religion. The rest of the chapter presents and discusses findings in relation to some aspects of Muslim family practices. It is not an exhaustive study of this issue. Becher's (2008) qualitative study of South Asian Muslim families is a much more thorough treatment of the topic, in relation to the largest ethnic groups amongst British Muslims. The sections that follow are specifically focused on Muslim family practices in connection with Islamic nurture. Most of these involve what Finch (2007) would describe as 'display'. This, in a family context, is the process wherein people convey 'that certain of their actions do constitute "doing family things" and thereby confirm that these relationships are "family" relationships' (p. 67). As well as displaying family, the practices discussed in the following sections certainly also display parents' credentials as good Muslims.

Asserting the centrality of family

In the words from Neda quoted at the start of this chapter she made it clear she saw her family as central to her life. She has not long come to the UK from Iran and was therefore perhaps more dependent on her family than if she had been in Cardiff longer term. However, the fact that a ten-year-old girl expressed this view would tend to suggest that the central importance of family has discursive power for Muslims. We presented interviewees with a card-sorting exercise for collective identities, which included a 'family' card choice. We acknowledge that 'family' was a different kind of choice from a national or ethnic identity label. Mr Hooshmand, in his interview, told us he thought it was not really an identity. But the exercise did in fact include a range of sources of collective identity, such as gender and locality (Cardiff). The results of the card-sorting exercise will be explained more fully in Chapter 8 and here we consider only the 'family' card. Of the 53 children who clearly chose a 'top three' from the identity cards, 33 selected 'family'. Of the 71 parents who made a clear choice, 24 put 'family' in their top three. Parents, as might be expected, had more positive engagement with national and ethnic identities (see Chapter 8), so for them the family card was up against more competition. For the children, at this stage of the life course in particular, as their lives are very home based and they have little freedom to move independently around the city, family relationships loom large (see Scourfield et al., 2006).

A discourse of family centrality for all religions is revealed in the analysis by O'Beirne (2004: 20) of the 2001 Home Office Citizenship Survey. When asked, 'Which of the following things would say something important about you, if you were describing yourself?', the most popular choice for Christian, Muslim, Hindu and Sikh adults was 'family'. Thereafter, there were differences between the religions, however, with 'religion' being the second most popular choice for Muslims, Hindus and Sikhs but only the seventh for Christians. Field's (2011) analysis of 27 national opinion polls taken since 9/11 found seven-tenths of young adult Muslims believed family obligations should precede individual success.

Family and religion were said by some interviewees to be intrinsically connected. So Mr Ahmet told us 'the family thing comes with Muslim' and Mr Hooshmand said he cared about his family 'because it is my duty as a Muslim'. Zubir Hassan (age 11) approached the connection from the opposite direction, saying he had prioritized the 'family' card over the 'Muslim' card because 'family basically is Muslim because I'm Muslim, my parents are Muslim'.

Another strong reason given for the centrality of family was interdependence. Mr Mustafa told us that 'without family you're lonely no matter how much wealth you have' and Mr Yaqub said he was 'nothing without my family, my family nothing without me'. Hamza Asaad (age 10), when asked why family was important said it was 'because you have to look after them'. Conversely, the need to be looked after was spoken of by Kaleem Khalid (age 8) who imagined that if parents died, 'you'll be all alone and then nobody will help you, only your brother and your sister.' For Mr Khaled, the family was a refuge in old age and a happy place to go at the end of a hard working day.

The other rationale given for the centrality of family was intimate knowledge of each other; as Mr Karmo put it, 'I live with them all my life.' This intimate knowledge can lead to strong bonds—'I see my family as my best friends', in the words of Mrs Ashraf. Family members were said to be 'available to enjoy your good times and also they are there to share your bad times' (Mr Ahmed). We regard this display of family centrality as a fundamental Muslim family practice, but it is of course not unique to Muslims. The O'Beirne (2004) findings noted above found other religions similar and indeed people with no religion would also be likely to assert that family matters more than anything, as that is a powerful message in mainstream British culture.

The fabric of the home

Finch (2007) uses the concept of 'display' to convey how people make their family connections and family cultures known to others. This concept is relevant to much of the current chapter, but it is important to note that as well as displaying family, the parents in our research project were displaying their Muslimness in various social practices in spaces which are private (the home) or semi-private (social networks and religious institutions). This section of the chapter is concerned with the very physical and material display of the fabric of the home. Hurdley (2006), writing about mantelpiece objects, uses the term 'domestic display' for a practice which is in part performance for others but is also a means for the construction of self-identity. Domestic objects are amongst the everyday 'things' which are important for the construction of intimacy and relationality (Smart, 2007). As well as being important in personal life, however, domestic objects signal connection to culture and collective belonging, including religious affiliation. If monotheism shapes your world view, it is likely to shape the way you order your home and this could be seen in the domestic display of our sample of sixty Muslim families. Not only does religious belief have an impact on the fabric of the religious home, as part of the process of materializing belief and making the invisible visible (Orsi, 2004), but this process also works the other way around. Material religion in the fabric of a home is likely to shape the religious development of a child growing up in that home. There is no inevitable process here, but there is likely to be *some* kind of effect on a child's religion of growing up in a home which displays religiosity.

Before even entering a Muslim home, religious affiliation can be evident from the front door, because of the practice of displaying Arabic text on the lintel or the door itself (Metcalf, 1996; Mazumdar and Mazumdar, 2005). The Rafique family, for example had two signs on their front door; one was a *hadith* (Abu Dawud 4/325) 'in the Name of Allah we enter, in the name of Allah we leave, and upon our lord we depend'. The other said, 'you are welcome, sister', both in Arabic with large font and English in small font.

We asked the children how people would know they lived in a Muslim home. In their responses, they mentioned many overtly Islamic objects such as framed Arabic texts, prayer mats, prayer beads, copies of the Qur'an, an *adhan* clock, pictures of mosques in Mecca and Medina.

161

Equally, when a subsample of children undertook photographic diaries about a typical week in learning to be a Muslim, the domestic images tended to feature these same kinds of objects. Children's bedrooms, although perhaps an important private space for them, did not feature in the photographic diaries. They were perhaps not seen as places that are much to do with being a Muslim, which at this stage of childhood is seen as to do with formal learning of the Qur'an or with learning codes of behaviour, as suggested in Chapter 4. There was also a sense in which some non-Islamic elements were allowed—temporarily perhaps—for young children and in their own private spaces. So Aman Hussain (age 8) had Hannah Montana posters in her bedroom, although the downstairs rooms, which non-family visitors were more likely to visit, were rather more staid. This division of childhood interest in bedrooms and more adult-focused respectability in reception rooms would also be found in many non-Muslim homes.

The most common pictures taken by the children were of Islamic 'images', i.e. photos of the Kaaba[2] (Hassan Tahir, age 4, called this 'Allah Miah's house') and Arabic verses in frames (see Figure 7.1), as well as prayer mats. They tended to take photographs in the family home, reflecting the principal physical location of middle childhood. The children seemed very aware of the religious significance of these overtly Islamic items, such as the Arabic texts and photographs of significant mosques, even if they did not fully understand them. Sahra Adam (age 10) told us, 'I'm not sure what it says, but it's in Arabic and it keeps our home safe'. Often they had been told at least some basic information about the texts. For example, Daniyal Kennedy-Shah (age 4), although he had not yet learned any Arabic, could show me framed writing of the words 'Allah' and 'Ali' (his father is Shia). Nabeel Sajaad (age 9) had been told that having Ayat ul Khursi on his bedroom door would stop him being scared at night. This is a verse from the Qur'an thought to give protection against evil. The use of Islamic texts in frames is not necessarily a tradition from Muslim countries of origin, but is more likely to have come from British Muslim practice, although some texts displayed are gifts from Hajj. Figure 7.1 shows examples of wall displays that children included in their photographic diary of a typical week of learning to be a Muslim.

It was also the case that some children took photographs of essentially ethnic markers, e.g. (quoting their descriptions) 'this is rice and curry',

---

[2] The cuboid structure at the centre of the most sacred mosque of Islam, at Mecca. Muslims are expected to face the Kaaba when performing *salat*.

Figure 7.1. Photographs of wall displays taken by child research participants in their homes.

and 'these are Punjabi clothes', or pictures of books in Urdu. Again we see that for some of the children, 'Muslim' implies ethnicity or at least we can say that ethnicity can be wrapped up with religious identity. This is 'religion' plus 'culture', without the distinction that is made by the majority of the parents. Asad Jamil (age 8) took photographs of himself about to perform *wudu*, a copy of the *Qa'idah* for learning basic Arabic, a banana boat in Bangladesh, a Bangladeshi meal, a mosque, and members of his family. Interestingly, when asked about why this last image was an important picture about being Muslim, he told us it was about 'being together as a family', but that this was 'important for everybody' and not just for Muslims. Inevitably it is difficult, if not impossible in practice, to separate religion and ethnicity if their Muslim social networks are dominated by their own ethnic group. So Karimul Azzad's photo diary included images of a Malaysian Eid party— an occasion that was both Islamic and ethnic.

Photographs are in fact a controversial issue for some Muslims. Most of our adult interviewees seemed aware that there was debate about their acceptability, even if they did not usually articulate why that might be the case. Three of the mothers specifically mentioned that they had heard angels would not enter a home with images of living things on the walls. Interestingly, however, two of these women did none the less have family photos on the wall. One said there were just 'a few in the bedroom' and the other that she was thinking of taking them down. There was a general tendency of displaying only small images that were restricted to particular rooms. For example, Mrs Ahmet allowed the children to have class photographs in their bedrooms. The only person who specifically mentioned the rationale for any prohibition on images of people was Sahra Adam (age 10) who said rather tentatively, when talking about reading the Qur'an, 'I think you're not meant to, like, have, um, idols in the room and that, something like that.' This is a very different religious context from the widespread reliance of images of people in materializing religion for Catholic children in Orsi's (2004) work. Another parent, Mr Azzad, had an interesting rationale for deciding to display photographs of family members, despite being aware that they could be thought to be *haram*. He explained that having his own parents and extended family at a great distance in Malaysia meant that his 'values' about the importance of family overrode any potential scruples about displaying photographs:

> 'If you are in my shoes, you are aware that we live in this country, I live in this country, I've got to have the certain values of my family as well, these pictures. Unless otherwise if I stay back home in Malaysia, or where we used to live, but everything is there when we open our eyes, but here, I want to make my children aware that these are my parents, their grandparents, even though we are so far away.' (Interview with Mr Azzad)

Interviewees were asked whether there was any dedicated space for prayer in homes. They were almost unanimous in saying their houses were too small for this, regardless of actual size. Some did tend to use particular rooms most often for prayer, however, even if these rooms also had to have other purposes as well. Mr and Mrs Mahmood differed in their views on this, as on several other issues. Mrs Mahmood, brought up in Pakistan, was keen to have a specific space for prayer that she was sure was properly clean. Mr Mahmood's view was that you should not be too purist; if you were to be purist, he reasoned, you would not pray in the direction of the nearby brewery. In practice, we were told they compromised by having one room which could be used by visitors for whom it is important to have dedicated prayer space.

Almost all had homes had televisions, some of which were very large. There did not seem to be any distinction from non-Muslim homes in this regard, although several interviewees did speak of watching Islam Channel or Peace TV. One parent, Mrs Rasheed, chose to have no television, although they did have some DVDs, including some on Islamic themes, as she felt she had some 'control' over those. Rather than this being primarily an Islamic objection to television content, it seemed to be an aversion to the children going into a 'hypnotic state' in front of the television and the consumerist influence of advertising; an aversion that might well be shared by fellow parents of the alternative school her children attended.

Naming

As Finch (2008) observes, names have a dual function of identifying a unique individual and also making social connections. Names establish an individual's social position through, for example, the marking of ethnicity, or perhaps social class, as well as the marking of kinship that is provided by a family/surname or through the practice of a given name being chosen 'after' a significant person (family member, friend or famous figure). Mateos et al. (2011) have shown that the choice of names tends to maintain ethnic and cultural traditions for generations after migration. In the case of Muslim families there are traditional Muslim names which are often cross-cultural. There is a social expectation that a convert will take a Muslim name, instead of or in addition to their original name. Naming for Muslims can therefore be a religious marker as well as perhaps an ethnic one.

In this section we will often not be attributing quotations to specific individuals. This is to preserve anonymity, as linking the meanings of names to particular families with ethnic backgrounds identified in Chapter 3 could risk identifying research participants. Where there is no such sensitivity, quotations will be attributed. In some places, a real name is replaced simply by 'X' rather than a pseudonym. Sometimes this is because the meaning of the pseudonym does not fit with the meaning of the real name and sometimes, again, it is to distance the data excerpt from any possibility of deductive identification.

The first thing to note is that many of the parents spoke of choosing names with religious meanings. Choosing a child's name with an Islamic meaning was seen to be important by many parents (though not all, as discussed below). This could be a way of marking difference. For example, Mr Sohail, recently arrived from Pakistan, made both a religious and ethnic distinction when he said, 'Indian people give their child Indian name like Priankar, this one, but we give Muslim name'. Many parents spoke of using a book of Islamic names or looking up Islamic name websites.

Many different meanings of names were cited. Naming children after one of the prophets, or a relative or companion of the Prophet Muhammad was especially popular. Other meanings included 'the Virgin Mary', 'seven heavens', 'The Prophet's wife', 'light of Muhammad', 'the journey the Prophet made', 'my judge', 'Allah has heard', 'happiness', 'intelligent', 'gift of God', 'light', 'silk or cloth from paradise', 'the highness', 'a well in paradise', 'verses or miracles or signs of God', 'the signs of the universe', 'somebody helpful', 'colour', 'flowerbed', 'beauty', 'the nurse who cared for the Prophet', 'sweet, gentle', 'new messenger', 'handsome', 'greatest', 'justice', 'the wise one', 'eternal', 'very powerful', 'brightness', 'hope', 'goodness', 'a river in *Jannah*', 'a woman who was a student of the sixth imam', 'one of the roads in Paradise', 'a new Muslim', 'the first prayer', 'the first martyr in Islam'. Usually the reason for naming a child after a specific person in the history of Islam was not articulated, although a couple of parents mentioned an individual having been a 'good role model'. One mother said a particular historical figure had 'very strong *iman* (faith)'.

In some cases, parents seemed content to know that a name was Islamic, without necessarily being clear about its meaning or feeling strongly about which specific meaning they ended up with. Mr Tahir said, 'at the time I did find out the meaning—is it right for a Muslim child?—and they were but I can't remember them now'. Mr Akbir said he and his wife made 'a lottery' of five or six names. Neda Hooshmand (age 10) reported that her mother 'said that I don't care whatever comes', so she 'just opened the Qur'an and the page that came was that *surah* and that's why my name's X'. Mrs Morris also sought religious guidance, but via a more direct sense of divine intervention. Rather than leaving it to the chance of a lottery or selection of a random *surah*, she used *Salat Al-Istikhaara*, a prayer to seek God's guidance in decisions. The name then came to her in a dream, as well as 'appearing everywhere', such as on the radio and in books.

As well as having positive religious meaning, it was also possible for names to be religiously unacceptable. So one set of parents liked the name of a mosque, but then ruled it out when they discovered it meant 'wild tigers'. Another family changed their son's original name, as a shaykh in Bangladesh advised it meant 'a really stubborn person, the really bad person, like Shaitan, so they were like "why would you call your son Shaitan?"' Another family chose a name for their first child which meant 'fragrance', but as the Imam in Cardiff thought it was not religious enough, they chose more pious names for subsequent children.

Not only Islamic meanings were important, however. One father said they wanted a name meaning 'Queen', so they 'checked in the Islamic book if it was there, and it was there'; in this case the Islamic status was secondary to the choice of a name they liked. Mr Akras, who was very knowledgeable about Islam, told us in his interview that there is no obligation for Muslims to have 'Islamic names' and that people tend to use names taken from the Qur'an which are 'nice names, that's all'. There were other examples of where names appealed to parents regardless of any Islamic significance:

'I always loved the name X. I didn't really go into the details on Islam. It's now that I feel it's so important a child should have a name with a good meaning, you know we should really look into that you know. I found X; I didn't really look; I just love the name X or Y.' (Interview with Mrs Hamid)

'It means when you live a nice life, you know, happiness and nice life . . . I don't think it is mentioned in the Qur'an. Maybe it is mentioned, but not as much as X.'

Other parents were not clear about the meaning of names. One said, 'it means faithful I think' and another that when choosing a name she had looked up the meaning but had forgotten what this was and now 'wouldn't have a clue' what it meant. For others, although they may have chosen Islamically acceptable names, it was not the religious connotations that were to the fore, but some connection with the child's behaviour and history. Mrs Yaqub said, 'it's like, you know, the personalities go with their names'. For another mother, a name meaning 'builder' and 'long life, prosperous' was chosen because a child was premature. For yet another, the original choice of a religious meaning had been overtaken in family culture by a popular culture reference:

'We found out that it means mission and apparently, because she's a bit of a handful, so it's like 'Mission Impossible' is her nickname!'

For some parents, a choice of name had ethnic cultural significance. One father said he named his daughter after a famous Arab poet because, 'being in an English environment I wanted to show that I am an Arab and I liked to give my children Arabic names'. One of the Iranian fathers had named his son after an 'old poetry character in Persian literature'. It was especially in the smaller ethnic groups (in the context of Cardiff) that ethnic names were chosen. So both the Turkish and Kurdish family we spoke to had chosen names from their countries of origin. In fact the Turkish family had chosen one Turkish name (after a political leader) and one 'Arabic' and 'Muslim' name. Similarly, one of the Somali families had chosen 'Muslim' names for all but one of the children, with the other child having a Somali name that was not 'related to a religion'.

Names were also sometimes chosen to signal family connection (Finch, 2008). Mrs Mahmood looked up meanings of names in a book and on the Internet, but also chose her mother's name because 'she was a good role model' and because she wanted to get this name 'before someone else takes it!' Mrs Mughal said one of her sons was named after her husband's favourite teddy bear. Some parents told us that family elders had a role in deciding names. This seemed to be especially the case for the Bangladeshi families and we were told by Mrs Uddin this is a Bangladeshi tradition, but it featured in several of the ethnic groups.

Names were chosen by a grandparent most typically, on either side of the family, or by an alternative elder—e.g. Mr Akhtar's father's oldest brother, as the oldest man in the family. Several families spoke of consulting with the extended family about names, including those in countries of origin, rather than relatives simply choosing the name. It seemed more common to display a family connection through this consultation than by naming a child after a relative.

The process of consultation meant it could take quite some time to decide on a name, with negotiation sometimes involved. In the Hussain family there was a tradition of the maternal grandfather choosing the name, but when the time came there was 'a battle' over which name would finally be selected. Mr Akbir said his mother made the first suggestion but, 'it wasn't a good meaning and I said no'. He added, 'we have to honour our mum and dad but on this particularly case we said sorry mum'. Mrs Yaqub was determined to have her own choice of name rather than that of her brother and sister-in-law:

'I thought if I have a daughter she's going to be called Naima so I stuck to my guns. When they wanted to change it I said no, she's going to be called Naima.' (Interview with Mrs Yaqub)

Further to this, a couple of families compromised by allowing relatives to choose a name, but the child in practice being known by its second name or by a 'nickname'.

Some families had different contracts for name selection other than consultation with elders. Mr Saad told us that he and his wife decided he would choose the boys' names and she would choose the girls' names. In the Saad family, the girls were each named after their grandmothers. However, as well as using names of elders, some parents chose names of friends—for Mrs Rasheed this was the friend who had accompanied her when she gave birth.

Several parents were very aware of cultural difference as religious and ethnic minorities, so wanted names which would be culturally accessible outside of their ethnic group; an 'inter-continental name' as Mrs Rana put it. This sometimes came up as an issue for families with two Muslim parents. For example Mr Mahfouz was initially keen to have a name 'that people over here wouldn't have a problem understanding', although as time went by he decided 'there are so many unusual names out there now that you know, it didn't really matter what we chose'. However, it was more especially an issue for mixed ethnicity families, where one branch of the family was not Muslim. There was more of a concern here for a name that is 'easy to pronounce' (Mrs Fatullah) or 'a prophet's name...that's accepted by everybody' (i.e. appears in the

Bible as well as the Qur'an) (Mr Miller) or an Arabic equivalent of a British name (Mr Morris). Mrs Kennedy-Shah, the only non-Muslim parent, wanted a name with 'a Muslim connotation' that would also pass as British name when shortened. There was a sense in which a mixed ethnicity family could most easily be creative with traditions. So Sarah Kennedy-Shah also told us this:

> 'There's a tradition in Ajmal's family of letting a child choosing its own middle name so he hasn't got a middle name, when he's about thirteen when he hits puberty he'll be allowed to choose his own middle name.' (Interview with Mrs Kennedy-Shah)

In a similar vein, the Mabrouk family had a 'what we called a naming day' with her (non-Muslim, white) family. This was consciously drawing on the Christian tradition of baptism, with which Mrs Mabrouk's family was familiar, but without the explicit Christian framework, and it was a family meal rather than any formal ceremony. In a similar vein, but without the same cross-cultural context, the Bangladeshi Chowdary family had a very informal ceremony presided over by the Imam: 'he did a *dua* for her, you know, blessing her and everything and that was it, you know, not a formal ceremony as such.' (From interview with Mrs Chowdary.)

Birth rituals

There are five main Islamic birth rituals which we asked parents about. If they did not mention any we tended to prompt them by mentioning these five. These are all in the category of *sunnah* practices—those which are said to have been modelled by the Prophet Muhammad but are not *fard* (obligatory) for Muslims. They originate in the *hadith*. We outline the five rituals here, with reference to Van Gennep's ([1909] 1960) classic typology of rites of passage as rites of separation (pre-liminal), transition (liminal/threshold) or incorporation (post-liminal), and we summarize the extent to which the different rituals are taken up by families.

The first ritual is to say the *adhan* (call to prayer) in the newborn baby's right ear and *iqamah* (second call to prayer) in the left. This could be seen as a ritual of incorporation, welcoming the child to the human experience, an essential part of which for Muslims should be five daily prayers. In fact early childhood is a liminal or transitional period in terms of prayer, with young children considered too young to pray *salat*. However, this is a rite of incorporation to humanity. Broadly speaking, all parents were familiar with this tradition and almost all practised it.

169

The second ritual we refer to here (not the second in sequence necessarily) is circumcision of boys (*khitan*). This is clearly a ritual of separation, with removal 'from the common mass of humanity' through a symbolic cutting and also permanent incorporation via 'a mark of membership in a single community of the faithful' (Van Gennep, 1960: 72). Parents spoke of circumcision less often than the other rituals, perhaps because it could be seen as a slightly delicate topic, concerning private parts of the body. However, all who spoke of it had carried it out and we did not encounter any parents who had not had their sons circumcised.

The third ritual we refer to here is *tahnik*, the practice of introducing something sweet such as honey or a chewed-up date to a new baby's mouth. It can involve as little as rubbing the sweet thing on the baby's lips. The person who presents the sweet item will be an influence over the child in later life. It could perhaps be categorized as a transitional rite, as it is a food ritual unique to this stage of the life course, involving as it does food which is (in theory) baby-friendly and its effects are long term, with influence stored up for adulthood, rather than immediate. It is ideally performed within seven days of the birth, as are all the rituals discussed in this chapter, other than the *adhan/iqamah* which should be done as soon as the baby is born; they should be the first words a baby hears. It seems that *tahnik* was performed by around half the sample of parents. The fourth ritual referred to in this section is *aqiqah*, that is, the sacrifice of a sheep for meat to feed relatives and the poor, with two sheep for boys and one for girls. This could be classified as incorporation ritual in so far as it involves collective marking of the child's membership of a community. A minority of parents hosted an *aqiqah* themselves in Cardiff, most of these at their mosque, but most marked the ritual by sending money to a Muslim homeland (where you get to feed people who are 'really destitute') and all seemed to be aware of the tradition. Many parents had not heard of the final ritual we discuss here, namely shaving a baby's hair and giving the weight of the hair in silver to the poor. Most parents did not perform this ritual. It is primarily a separation ritual (Van Gennep, 1960: 54), presumably marking separation from the mother's body, involving as it does the symbolic cutting of the 'old' hair to allow new hair to grow.

Despite the general assumption revealed across the dataset that it is good to follow as closely as possible practices from the Prophet's time, it is interesting to note that families did not tend to follow the various *hadiths* about birth rituals literally. A few seemed well aware that whilst it is good to follow the Prophet's example, these practices are not obligatory. The Akras parents, for example, were very knowledgeable about Islam and very observant but expressed their own view that they would only say the *adhan* and *iqamah* and not follow the other rituals. In explaining this they said that their approach was not ideal. There were very few overt statements to distance the interviewees from the *hadiths* on the grounds of them being rooted in a particular historical context. Parents were more likely to be self-critical or to refer to practical constraints (e.g. we could not afford an *aqiqah* at the time) when explaining why they had not followed certain practices. Knowledge of the Islamic sources certainly varied, with some parents clearly unsure of the Islamic character of some practices they had heard about. For example, Mr Abdul-Rahman said of shaving a baby's hair, 'I don't know whether it was from a religious background or whether it was from a cultural background, so I didn't rush to it at all' and Mrs Miller said of *tahnik*, 'my mum does that and I thought it was more culture then religion'. Where a practice was not supported by a parent, there could be a dismissal of it as being rooted in culture, rather than religion. Mr Shirazi's objection to *tahnik* was essentially medical, but he dismissed the practice both with reference to child development and to the origins of the tradition in 'custom' rather than religion:

> 'They would not have solid food before six months, five months. None of my children had, the majority of children they don't do it. So, even if it's the custom or something, it's not religious, uh it's not uh, advised by the uh, general welfare system, so no, nothing like that.' (Interview with Mr Shirazi)

It is interesting that the two for a boy and one for a girl *aqiqah* sacrifice guideline was not rejected, although similar gender traditions were often cast off by parents on the grounds of being 'culture', not 'religion', as noted earlier in the chapter. This perhaps illustrates the reluctance of our research participants to regard religious texts as products of their historical context. Only Mr Islam, clearly the most religiously sceptical of the parents, was able to dismiss the *adhan* tradition by saying that 'new born children can't hear anything, don't understand'.

Birth rituals emphasize the continuing importance of extended family networks, including those in Muslim countries of origin. Those who did practice *tahnik* often used a male elder in the family to convey their character to the child, or a male elder in the (ethnic) kin network was used, including respected scholars ('*maulvi*', '*ustad-ji*'). However, as already implied above in the quotation from Mrs Miller, the parents in our study did not necessarily follow extended family traditions in performing birth rituals—some did and some did not. As noted in other chapters, those without strong social networks based on a particular ethnic group may not have any strong tradition to follow, but may have to be rather more creative. So Mrs Rasheed, for example, a convert to Islam, did the *adhan* for her baby herself; her husband had not wanted to be present at the birth. Practical barriers to performing some of the rituals in a non-Muslim country had been overcome by some— again those with the most well-established religious and ethnic social networks. So a local Pakistani barber was known to be good at shaving babies, *halal* butchers could provide meat for an *aqiqah* in Cardiff and a Pakistani doctor would come to circumcise baby boys in a Cardiff mosque's upper room once there were ten babies waiting to be done. However, we were told that to get the circumcision done in seven days you would need to travel to Birmingham.

Celebrations

First we deal with Islamic celebrations and then with non-Islamic ones. There is an emphasis in this section on children's perspectives. Some families told us they celebrated the Prophet Muhammad's birthday (Milad an-Nabi) but this did not seem to be a major occasion for families and there were no indications of controversy surrounding this event, whose commemoration Salafis would typically reject. Eid al-Fitr and Eid al-Adha were more or less universally celebrated, however. Even the Islam family, who were the least observant Muslim family in our sample, would get together with other Bangladeshi families to socialize, not on the day but at a weekend when work schedules would allow. Some parents told us that celebrating either of these two Eids was a better experience in a Muslim country. Neda, however, ever philosophical, was able to construct the minority experience in a positive way:

> 'When you're in Tehran you can go and meet someone and your family and talk to them and stuff, you go to there and you see your family and there's special things in mosques and it's completely different area for you. It's inside the circle that you should be when you're in your country, but when you're outside that circle you have to like take it and do all the things you can with the things that are outside of the circle. So I think you do it more of your heart when you are here, just because you're forced to do it when you're in your country.' (Interview with Neda Hooshmand, age 10)

Celebrating Eid seemed to be a more communal experience for families from the larger ethnic groups, with an opportunity to meet up with extended family and friends, including those in far flung corners of the UK. In all the families, presents were exchanged and/or new clothes bought, large amounts of ethnic food were consumed and communal prayer would be attended at a mosque or alternative venue (e.g. City Hall). Some attended organized events for Muslim families, such as a party at the mosque or a private booking of a play centre. It was the one time for Fateh Rafique (age 10) when 'we're allowed music'.

Some families seemed to take a view on which of the two Eids would be the primary celebration. So for the Hussain family Eid al-Adha is 'Big Eid', 'because we celebrate a lot more than on the last one' (Ilyas, age 12) and in a similar vein for Mrs Yaqub Eid al-Fitr is *'nikki'* (small) Eid. This relative emphasis might mean presents on only one occasion. Zubir Hassan (age 11) said, 'there's three ones but the first one is where you get money'. Having presents loomed large in children's accounts of celebrating Eid, with many of them referring to these festivals as Muslims' Christmas (see also Becher, 2008). When Nurul Mubashir (age 7) was asked, 'what happens at Eid?' she replied, 'we get presents' and went on to say, 'on the other Eid I weared a pink dress and a pink cardigan and then I weared a pink dress and a white cardigan'. Mrs Rasheed, a convert, was quite relieved that in the context of a consumer-ist culture there was a time when it was acceptable for Muslims to give children presents, both for her and for the children's non-Muslim grandparents. She said her husband 'doesn't believe in presents at all', but although she herself was critical of consumerism, her view was that 'it just seems wrong in this culture to not give them something'. As well as enjoying receiving presents, dressing up and being 'happy because all the Muslims are there' (Iza Ayub, age 7), children were also aware of adults' agendas. Zubir Hassan (age 11) said, 'well, you go to the mosque and they talk a lot'. Not all families had an equally sociable time, however. As we also note in Chapter 8, the Sohail family were quite isolated from other Muslims because, they said, other Pakistanis were suspicious of their asylum claim. They told us there was one Pakistani family they were friendly with, but because this family has 'many, many friends and families' they did not get together at Eid, but rather they stayed in for yet more children's television: 'CBeebies, we see CBeebies[3] all time'.

We consider next non-Islamic celebrations, namely birthdays and Christmas. A large majority of families did celebrate birthdays, albeit in most cases with family members only and with much more emphasis on younger children's birthdays. A small number, mostly from Deo-bandi or Salafi traditions, chose not to celebrate birthdays, apparently on the grounds that the Prophet Muhammad did not himself celebrate birthdays. Some of the children spoke of this rationale. A couple of others simply said birthdays were wrong (*'haram'* or *'gunnah'* [Urdu for

---

[3] TV channel for children age 7 and under.

'sin']). Sadeka Akbir (age 12) gave the reason that 'there is no point because we are going to get like two Eids, like two birthdays'. In some families there was some fairly flexible interpretation of what constituted a celebration. So Sahra Adam (age 10) told us 'we celebrate Eid, Ramadan and we don't celebrate birthdays; we just have a get together with our friends'. The Rasheed children said they could choose what they want for tea and have a cake but not 'have any friends over or anything, so we don't really celebrate it' (Fatima, age 12).

In two families we heard of children marking only their seventh birthday, as the occasion of starting to pray. The Jawad family creatively mixed this Islamic guidance with the secular Western tradition of birthday celebration by making a 'time to pray' cake (Figure 7.2). As Khansa (age 10) put it, 'we don't celebrate birthdays really we just did this one'. In similar vein, Mrs Hamid told us that when her daughter finished the Qur'an, they 'had a little party'. Nesbitt (2004: 16) describes a similar blend of religion and secular celebration on the part of some Sikh families in her research who used children's birthdays 'to reinforce religious and cultural tradition'.

Unlike the Hindu and Sikh families in Nesbitt's (2004) research, who tended to celebrate a secular version of Christmas (i.e. without the Christianity) or even mark the occasion with rituals from their own faith, the vast majority of the Muslim families who took part in our study did not celebrate Christmas. Most children explained this in a fairly matter-of-fact way, e.g. 'it's not part of our religion' (Hajer Morris, age 9). Others expanded on this, for example by saying Christmas is '*haram*' and for '*kufaars* and non-believers' (Hamza Assad, age 10), or that 'we're not allowed celebrate Christmas like Allah might be cross'

Figure 7.2. 'Time to pray' cake—Jawad family.

(Akbar Khaliq, age 11), or that Christmas is the birthday of Jesus who Christians think is 'the same as God' (Hafsa Mustafa, age 10) or with reference to Santa Claus, about whom non-Muslims 'trick their kids' (Asiya Mabrouk, age 8). A couple of parents were relaxed about some aspects of Christmas, saying it was fine for them and their children to 'experience the culture' up to a point, for example, by taking part in school Christmas plays (see Chapter 6).

For those with non-Muslim relatives, Christmas needed rather more careful handling. In most cases, accommodations had been made whereby non-Muslim grandparents would give presents to children at Eid instead of Christmas and this arrangement had generally become quite uncontroversial. The potential power of Christmas remained, however, and Mr Morris told us, 'we try to make a bigger fuss at Eid and we see this as the only way to combat the seductiveness of the Christian festivals in a Christian country'. The Kennedy-Shah family took a rather similar line, although their circumstances were different in so far as Sarah the mother was not Muslim. She said they had decided together to celebrate Christmas but also to 'up-grade Eid ... make a big fuss about Eid', with special dinner, invitations to Daniyal's friends to come over and more presents than at Christmas. Mr Kennedy-Shah further explained that at Eid, Daniyal would get 'more practical presents', whereas at Christmas he would have 'more frivolous presents', which was an attempt to 'hold on to the values'.

Before concluding this theme of celebrations, it is worth noting that not all religiously significant days in the calendar are marked as cause for celebration. The only other Islamic event involving children that was mentioned in our study was the Mourning of Muharram, when Shia Muslims remember the killing of Imam Ali. This is not a celebration, but we mention it here as a significant day for some Muslim families. For the Hooshmand family the whole month of Muharram involves attendance at mosque and in order to remember Imam Ali, in Neda's terms, 'we turn the lights off and everyone they like talk about him in a crying way ... like in a funeral way'. This event is more in keeping with the imagistic mode of religiosity, according to Whitehouse's (2002, 2004) typology.

Conclusion

The main purpose of this chapter has been to provide a rich description of some aspects of Muslim family life which bolster religious nurture. After an initial summary of family structure, there was a focus on family practices and the display of family and good religion. We conclude the chapter with some thoughts, firstly about how a family practices perspective and a focus on display can help us to understand religious nurture in Muslim families, and secondly what Muslim family practices in relation to children and childhood tell us about the sociology of the family and of childhood in contemporary Britain.

Aspects of Muslim *habitus* are revealed by attention to family practices. A central place within homes for Quranic verses and pictures of famous mosques displays a family's religious affiliation and respectability to all who enter and helps to teach children that their faith is all around them and is present in routine places. Parents (see Chapter 4) and grandparents contribute to the teaching of routine embodied religious practices, such as prayer, and the modelling of morality and deportment. The choice of a Muslim name (in most cases) cements a child's identification with a community of believers and perhaps also an ethnic group. Some names are consciously ethnic and others, whilst in fact ethnically non-specific Muslim names, would be assumed by many non-Muslims to be ethnic names. Thus we see the effect of being in a social minority on reinforcing religious identification. We also saw more examples of children conflating religion and ethnic identity, unavoidably so. Most birth rituals do not have a direct effect on the socialization of children but where performed they contribute to reinforcing a whole family's religious identity and their connection with tradition. The one ritual which does stay with children in a direct sense is male circumcision which, in a country where most boys are uncircumcised, is a bodily reminder of religious identity—at the very least the religious identity of the parents who arranged this ritual.

Studying the family life of a social minority can provide a check to potential over-generalizations or ecological fallacies about families in late modernity. Muslims are most often part of a minority population in ethnic terms and they are also a relatively devout religious minority in a generally fairly secular social context.

There is some evidence of individualization but also a great deal of following of tradition. There is a general tendency not to question the principle that Qur'an and *Sunnah* should be literally applied, even if some recommended practices are in fact not followed by many, as in the case of some birth rituals. To dismiss aspects of religious texts as not relevant today because the historical context was so different when they were written does not seem to be acceptable discourse for Muslims. This therefore places very strong limits on individualization and reflexive life choices in relation to religion. Where negotiation led to recommended practices not being followed, it tended to be that parents would categorize a practice as 'cultural' (i.e. not Islamic) or they would be self-critical (I know I should have done it really).

There was some evidence of the continuing importance of extended families and of respected elders, which rather goes against the grain of social change in the UK. In some families there seemed to be clear hierarchies based on age, gender and lineage. However, there was a mixed picture and we also heard examples of parents going against the wishes of elders, in relation to names or birth rituals. There was some accommodation with the majority non-Muslim population, for example through choice of an accessible name. And Muslim family structures are not immune from wider social change. There were families which had experienced separation and re-formation and it was interesting to note that settling on a regime of religious nurture could be an important part of the challenge of merging families.

Finally, we note the religious debates about photographs and birthdays. There has been recent emphasis within the British sociology of the family literature on family practices (which would include celebrations) and items of memory, such as photographs. It is simply interesting to note that these things can be as significant (in religious and therefore sociological terms) in their absence as in their presence, with some families displaying photographs but doing so rather uneasily.

8

Nationality, Ethnicity, and Religion

Identity is by now a well-worn topic in contemporary social science. Social psychologists have had a long-standing interest in the issue, but sociological interest is more recent and coincides with a preoccupation with identity in late modernity (Giddens, 1991; Bauman 2004a). In relation to British Muslims, identity has been a repeated theme of research in the last couple of decades. This interest has coincided with fairly intense scrutiny by mass media and politicians of the cultural and political identifications of Muslims in the UK. One important trend that has been noted by numerous researchers is the tendency to identify first and foremost as 'Muslim' (Modood et al., 1994; Jacobson, 1998; Lewis, 2007; Mondal, 2008, Field, 2011). This is found particularly in younger Muslims who have grown up in Britain and represents a distinct change from earlier generations who tended to identify with countries of origin, prioritizing national identities such as 'Pakistani' (Dahya, 1973, 1974; Saifullah-Khan, 1976). As noted in Chapter 1, this tendency echoes the work of Herberg (1955) on those who are a couple of generations distant from the migration process identifying more strongly with the religion of their grandparents.

There has been particular research attention to Muslim 'youth', meaning people in their teens and early 20s. There has not been in published research the same attention paid to children of primary school age or to the inter-generational negotiation of identity between parents and children. There has also been very little research on Muslim identities in UK countries other than England. Amongst the very few non-England-based studies in recent years are those by Hopkins (e.g. 2007) on Scotland and Gilliat-Ray and Mellor (2010) on Wales. Hence this chapter will present analysis and discussion of data on collective identities from our qualitative research, with particular emphasis on the intersection of religion with ethnic and national identities. Although a focus on identity in middle childhood is more original for research on Muslims in the UK, we also discuss what parents have to say, as parents are likely to make an important contribution to children's identities.

The Challenge of Researching Identity

Researching identity is not a straightforward matter and the issue of the appropriate methods of enquiry is not uncontested. Anthias (2002), who questions the usefulness of the term 'identity' and prefers instead to write about 'location' and 'positionality', makes the following statement about identity research:

> Researchers in the field often know that they cannot find useful or interesting answers by asking direct questions about identity. Asking someone a direct question about their identity often produces a blank stare, a puzzled silence or a glib and formulaic response. (Anthias, 2002: 492)

The blank stare is arguably more likely to be an issue with majority ethnicity participants who may not have reflected on taken-for-granted identities or may indeed not consciously have an identity. For people with a minority ethnicity or minority religion, however, identity is likely to be a live issue. In fact Anthias, despite being critical of the social scientific use of 'identity' as a concept (see also Brubaker and Cooper, 2000; MacInnes, 2004), acknowledges that the term 'identity' is socially meaningful in so far as people use the term in everyday discourse.

We do write about 'identity' in this chapter, for several reasons. Firstly, the question of 'who do we think we are?' (Abercrombie, 2004) does matter. It is not the only sociological question or the most important one, but we regard it as one of the important questions that need to be asked in contemporary social research, both more generally and specifically in relation to Muslim families. Secondly, identity is familiar territory for Muslims in the UK. As noted above, it is a socially meaningful concept. Thirdly, a chapter focusing on identity allows for discussion of how different collective identities intersect. This intersection and its constituent parts have important implications for how religion is maintained (or not) across generations. As has been already noted in earlier chapters, minority status in religious affiliation and ethnicity is important to the process of learning to become a Muslim, so has to be considered in several of its facets. One of these is collective identity.

We acknowledge, however, that identity is complex and researching it is methodologically challenging. We took the decision to produce prompt cards with commonly used identity labels on them, as well as offering blank cards to be filled in by the interviewee. For this project we were interested in how the parents and children discussed the identity options available to them, rather than in quantifying their responses. A different research design would have been needed for any robust quantification. We do, however, give a flavour of the numerically dominant responses in the next section of this chapter, with reference to 'top three' choices. The one collective identity we presented to interviewees but which is not discussed here because it has already been covered in Chapter 7, is 'family'.

We decided to overtly ask about identity as even if it did produce some 'formulaic' responses (see Anthias quotation above), the discursive power of these formulas is interesting and revealing in itself. The use of cards also broke up the interviews and provided a useful visual distraction. The children in particular enjoyed the process. Fakhir (age 10) said it was a bit like a TV talent show when you are wondering who is going to be out first. The only negative note was struck by Neda (age 10), who expressed concern that the choice might 'come out racist or anything'. This emphasizes the sensitivity of ethnic and national identity.

A few of the interviewees struggled to choose identity labels. Mrs Khatun said she felt 'like an alien' because she felt pressure to put Muslim 'at the top' (see later section headed 'Muslim first') but in fact could not prioritize and took the view that 'everything is important'.

'Being Bengali is really important, being a Muslim is important, being British is really important. I mean, speaking English is important, even Cardiff is important. Everything is important. I can't let one go and say this is not important because it is important because I live in Cardiff and I love it, you know what I mean? I can't be a Muslim and not like Cardiff. It's not going to work that way.' (Interview with Mrs Khatun)

This is in keeping with the opinion poll findings summarized by Field (2011), which showed around half of young adult Muslims making no distinction between their faith and nationality.

A couple of the parents were quite sociologically reflective about the identity options. Mrs Sabiha Morris commented that 'you ask someone what British meant 20 years ago; it's so different from now'. Some of the interviews veered onto the issue of collective identities as contingent on social interaction (Goffman, 1990 [1959]) and therefore potentially changeable according to social context. So Sabah Rana (age 8) told us that 'Muslim' would be the most important identity label at home and in the mosque, whereas 'Cardiff' would be most important in school. Ilyas Hussain (age 12) said he would be more Pakistani when with his grandfather.

Overview of Inter-Generational Identities

We begin the discussion of the data on nationality, ethnicity, and religion with a summary of the inter-generational patterns across the sample of families. It is not possible to comment on the whole sample. The 'top three' card choices were only comparable between parents and children for 33 of the families. In the other 27, there was too much variability in interview interaction for any fair comparison to be made. Even in the 33 where some comparison is possible, it should be remembered that we did not initially set out to quantify responses, so this summary is only a post-hoc quantification of primarily qualitative data, with the limitations you would expect from such an exercise.

With these provisos in mind, it is interesting to note that there were only two of the 33 families where at least one of the top three cards chosen did not match across all interviewees. So 31 out of 33 (94 per cent) did agree on at least one of the top three. Both of the two children whose choices did not match any of their parents were amongst the youngest we interviewed (one age 4 and one age 5) and there could be an issue of child development. There is a general consensus, for example, that the importance children attribute to national identity increases between the ages of 5/6 and 11/12 (Barrett, 2005). Before they reach the age of 5/6, children often have less awareness of collective identities other than gender. In that regard it should be noted that two of the three youngest children in the study chose a gender card ('Boy' or 'Girl') in their top three. It is also interesting that of the two children whose top three choices did not match both their parents' choices, one was from the only family with a non-Muslim parent. In the 31 families where at least one of the top three identity cards matched across all interviewees, this card was 'Muslim' in every family except two (i.e. 29 out of 33, or 88%). In these two, it was a minority ethnic identity that all interviewees agreed on.

It is just about possible to apply inferential statistics to this card choice, to take account of the role of chance. If we use a binary of 'all chose Muslim card v. not all chose Muslim card' for adults and children separately, we can generate a 2×2 table which can be analysed using Cohen's Kappa (Cohen, 1960) to assess inter-rater agreement. This is a very conservative test, because research participants were not in fact offered a binary choice, but the Muslim card was selected out of a wide range of identity choices. However, if we do use this very conservative binary, we calculate a Cohen's Kappa of 0.84 which indicates a very high level of agreement (>0.75 is usually considered excellent agreement).

It was noted in Chapter 2 that in the Citizenship Survey 2003 the agreement between young people aged 11–15 and their Muslim parents on religious affiliation was 99.6%. Although the question being asked in our qualitative research is not the same, the data from the Young People's Survey do indicate the salience of a Muslim affiliation and the prevalence of cross-generational agreement on this.

In 20 out of the 33 families where comparisons are possible, there was agreement between all interviewees on at least two of the top three cards. For eleven of these card choices, the common choice (in addition to 'Muslim') was 'Family' (see Chapter 7) and for nine it was a minority ethnicity (e.g. 'Pakistani' or 'Indian').

The theme of child development is an important one. Scourfield et al. (2006) have argued that despite the apparent rejection of the whole discipline of developmental psychology by some prominent sociologists of childhood, it is important when studying identities in childhood to keep in mind patterns of cognitive development such as, for example, at what age children typically understand certain geographical concepts. Certainly it is crude to only consider age-bound stages of development—Roehlkepartain et al. (2006b) note this point in relation to research on children's religious and spiritual development—but our data do show some children confusing collective identities. For example, Asiya Mabrouk (age 8) said 'Welsh' was 'a language and a city too' whereas Cardiff was 'a country'. In a similar vein, Abbas Hussain (age 5) spoke of the 'Cardiff flag' with a dragon on. There are several different boundaries that crop up in discussion of national and ethnic identities—city, county, country, Wales, Britain, UK—and the difficulty for younger children to understand the differences should not be underestimated.

One respect in which the confusion of concepts is especially important to note is children's conflation of ethnicity and religion. Whether or not this conflation is in part to do with cognitive development is not our concern. Rather it is the social meaning of the conflation that is important and can shed light on the transmission of Islam. So despite the tendency for adults to distinguish 'religion' and 'culture', for many of the children, to be from a particular ethnic background is to be a Muslim and vice versa. Here are a few examples, some of which are from children who are old enough that their cognitive development certainly would allow them to distinguish concepts.

ASMA: 'You tell me, what does it mean to be Pakistani? How does one become Pakistani? Am I Pakistani?'
NABEEL SAJAAD (AGE 9): 'Don't know.'

AYMAN SAJAAD (age 6): 'She wasn't born in Pakistan.'

NABEEL: 'Shalwar kameez, languages and like if you read Qur'an and the food.'

ASMA: 'Do you feel like you're Pakistani as well as being Welsh and English and everything else?'

KHALIQ children (together): 'Yeah.'

ASMA: 'Why? What is it about yourselves that you see as Pakistani?'

SAIMA (age 13): 'Because like we know more people and like cos some people are like that Christian, stuff like they're non-Muslims and stuff cos they take drugs and wine and that's not like good and stuff. But when we're like Pakistanis like we can know more people and they would be like kind and stuff.'

ASMA: 'Why do you think Somali, being Somali is so important to you?'

ADAM OMAR (age 11): 'Because it's like my religion.'

ASMA: 'Do you think you are Welsh?'

AYMAN SAJAAD (age 6): 'A little bit Welsh.'

ASMA: 'Why are you a little bit Welsh?'

AYMAN SAJAAD: 'Because I'm really a Muslim but I learn that Welsh though.'

This conflation matters because it suggests reasons for keeping faith alive across the generations. Religion here is part of the culture of an ethnic minority. As has been noted in earlier chapters, in a social minority context, when ethnic culture is likely to come under pressure from majority values and practices, religion can be one way of maintaining distinctiveness. If a child sees religion as intrinsic to their identity as (e.g.) a Pakistani boy, then it is not inevitable that the religion will be meaningful to him but this connection does result in social encouragement to identify as Muslim.

Most parents were keen to make a distinction between 'religion' and 'culture'. However it was possible for parents as well as children to connect ethnicity with religion. Mrs Mahmood was brought up in Pakistan and had a lively debate with her Cardiff-born husband about the importance of Pakistani culture (see Chapter 4). When he rejected a 'Pakistani' identity ('except through birth or descent'), she asked him if he had kept his religion. He then asserted that you do not have to be Pakistani to be Muslim; she agreed but also insisted that for her a connection was in some ways meaningful, saying this:

'No, the country doesn't have a bearing on the religion, you can come from any country but it's what is inside yourself, what culture you choose to follow, what things you become part of, who you are, praying, what type of behaviour you use.' (Interview with Mrs Mahmood)

Not surprisingly, the children in our study were less fluent in discussing identity than their parents. Arguably, the whole question of identity is perhaps less salient to them. At their stage of the life course, middle childhood being quite socially constrained (quite apart from the issue of cognitive development), they are fairly unlikely to have been faced with options about collective identity. They are more likely to describe themselves straightforwardly as what they 'just are'. There are some subsections of the chapter where adult data predominate. We do, however, note in each section the responses of children, even if that is simply to record that they had little to say on a given theme. We consider, in turn, in different sections of the chapter, the following identities: Muslim, British, English, Welsh, Cardiff, and minority ethnicity.

Muslim First

There was strong evidence of a 'Muslim first' discourse when it came to weighing up collective identities. It was noted above that in all but two of the families where parents and children agreed on at least one identity card choice, this choice was 'Muslim'. Many of the parents in particular insisted this was the one most important identity label. Insights can be gained into reasons for this choice by examining the qualitative data—mostly data from parents, as the children, even if they did tell us the Muslim card was the first and foremost for them, tended not to articulate the reasons why.

The first point to note is that religious identity was said to trump ethnicity. Mr Khalid had a fairly typical view, acknowledging the salience of a national or ethnic identity but telling us that to be a Muslim is more important:

'Somali, Somali, okay is my belonging but, first of all, I think for me the most important thing is to be a Muslim under Allah. And I will always thank to God to be born in a Muslim.' (Interview with Mr Khalid)

However, some other parents were more uneasy about ethnic or national labels and told us they were *not* important, when compared with religious identity. Mrs Ayub was not keen to choose the labels 'British' or 'Welsh' or 'Pakistani' as 'these are just places'. Mr Ahmad was born and bred in Cardiff but considered himself nothing but Muslim, 'full stop'. Mr Mahfouz was proud to claim the identity 'Welsh' and had learned the Welsh language to fluency, but he said, 'all languages are equal, all countries are equal, you know, so being a Muslim is more important than being Welsh'. The implication here is that there might be inequality set up on the basis of nationality or language. Islam, in contrast, is seen as inclusive. Fakhir Uddin (age 10) told us that 'in Islam we are all brothers and sisters'. Mrs Rasheed understood a Muslim identity to be anti-national. She is a white convert, with children of mixed ethnicity.

> 'I don't like nationalism basically, I don't like flags at all so you won't be finding any Cardiff, like Welsh flags hanging outside 'cos they cause a lot of problems between people and I think Muslim is the most inclusive because it doesn't matter where you're from and you can change to it and you can be accepted for it, for whatever and I think that's what Malcolm X, when he went to Hajj, that's what he felt and he hadn't felt that ever before so I feel that.' (Interview with Mrs Rasheed)

There are echoes here, in the distancing from ethnic and national identities, of the 'deculturation' described by Roy (2004). There was very little explicit reference made in the dataset to the concept of the worldwide Ummah, although Mrs Akbir did note that 'because nowadays we have to be all Muslims united together otherwise we will be punished . . . we are punished in Iraq, Iran, and Palestine'. There were some other indications of a Muslim identity being prioritized as a defensive strategy in the face of potential criticism. Mr Mughal told us that he had started to wear a *jelbaab* with loose trousers in secondary school, deliberately making himself conspicuous and he has dressed in this way ever since. There was a sense that he was 'not going to change for anyone' and was almost enjoying the tension of standing out from his peers. For the one African-Caribbean parent in our sample—a convert— there was evidence of a Muslim identity being rooted in racial political solidarity. He said this:

> 'I grew up with a lot of Muslims. I knew a lot of Muslims as well in the community you know. So you know, because there was a lot of racial tension in those days and stuff, you know, a lot of minority groups were forced to, you know, to become a community. So I think that's when it became time when I wanted to become a Muslim.' (Interview with Mr Assad)

So far we have noted a discourse of anti-nationalism and a defensive Muslim identity. Mr Mughal justified his top choice of a Muslim identity more purely in religious terms, by arguing it is a religious duty to prioritize this over other options.

> 'I think the primary thing is that when you're going to be identified with the Day of Judgement, this is what you're going to want to be identified as, so in your heart it's the most important. If this identity defines your entire role, then maybe keep that in your mind and *Inshallah*, the Day of Judgement, that is what you're announced as, as well. Whereas if you keep saying I'm this or that, then you keep saying this is more important to me than being a Muslim; then maybe this will define who you are.' (Interview with Mr Mughal)

There seemed to be a perceived pressure to prioritize a Muslim identity over others. Although Mr Mir did in fact place 'Muslim' in his top three identity cards, it was alongside 'Cardiff' and 'family', and 'Muslim' did not for him have priority over these other cards. He was apologetic about his choice, saying 'I suppose I don't put so much focus on the religion' and going on to explain that he does not really practise, not praying regularly and so on.

The correspondence between parents' and children's Muslim identity choices might imply some overt parental encouragement of or even pressure on children to prioritize religion over other available identity sources. We witnessed parental approval in this exchange during the mother's research interview:

MRS FAYSAL: 'Yes. What did you put Daniyaal?'
DANIYAAL (age 10): 'Muslim, family and Arab.'
MRS FAYSAL: 'Good boy, well done!'
DANIYAAL: 'I chose Muslim first because we have to love Allah more than parents.'
MRS FAYSAL: 'That's right, good boy, when you love Allah you love your family automatically.'

Some of the children were able to articulate their reasons for putting 'Muslim' first. Although they were not expansive in discussing their choices, as were some of the parents, we see can in the excerpt below how one child did none the less express himself in quite a powerful way:

ASMA: 'What about Muslim?'
NADIFA RAHMAN (age 8): 'Um, yes, I am more Muslim.'
ASAD (age 11): 'It's really important.'
ASMA: 'Really important?'
ASAD: 'Yeah. I think being Muslim is like my life.'

This idea of being a Muslim as fundamental and all-encompassing was also expressed by some of the adults. For example, Mr Hooshmand said, 'I do everything because of my religion, only that.' Amongst the children, there was no evidence of them distancing religion from ethnic or national identity as did some parents (see above). Given there is evidence of conflation of Muslim identity and ethnicity from some children, we cannot be sure that when they selected a 'Muslim' identity card they were not also implying minority ethnicity.

There was relatively little resistance to the ideology of Muslim first. Mrs Khatun's refusal to narrow down her identity was discussed above on p. 181. Some resistance also came from Mr Miller, a white convert, who insisted on a *British* Muslim identity. He referred to perceived pressure both from non-Muslims (e.g. via the media) and from Muslims to decide whether he is British *or* Muslim. He said it annoyed him to be presented with this dilemma and he argued strongly that he could not choose, saying, 'I'm British by culture, birth and I am Muslim, so I am both. I can't, whatever I do, I can't, it's not my choice to choose to be British or Muslim because I am!'

Mr Rahman had an interesting angle on the prioritization of a Muslim identity over other options. He told us his view had changed over time. Whilst this might also be understood as a response to shifting discourses in wider culture, he saw it as connected to his age and parental responsibilities. He described himself as having gradually drifted away from the non-Muslim friends he had from school days. He referenced the idea of parallel lives (Cantle, 2001), explaining that the differences in lifestyle between him and his friends had become too great. He saw a primary Muslim identity as the 'natural' one for him:

> 'I do think that the answer would have been different that you got from me, about 10 years ago. About 10 years ago maybe I would have said, I do feel that people identify to their natural, their natural background, as they grow older, and especially now, you know like, um, being Muslim is forefront. All the people I know whether they are you will not, you can define themselves as you know, like, there where their roots are, which is Islam. And yeah, I think I've changed, since I've had a family, yeah. Um, my school friends were all non-Muslim, um, I did keep in touch with them for a little while, but as I practised more Islam, they became distant and eventually disappeared. I've run into my school friends many a times, and I've always taken their numbers, and never get in contact with them ever again, because you know, like, what am I going to go with them? Can't go to the pub with them, they're not going to come to the mosque with me.' (Interview with Mr Rahman)

Being British

In this section we focus on what being British meant to our research participants. Field's (2011) overview of 27 opinion polls since 9/11 of young adult Muslims describes a complicated picture, with a large majority being loyal to Britain but a fluctuating minority being uneasy with how a Muslim identity sits alongside British citizenship. Many times more people identified themselves in opinion polls as primarily Muslim than identified as primarily British but, as noted above, close to half of those polled saw no distinction between faith and nationality.

Very few children in our study were interested in a British identity. Out of 53 children who expressed a fairly clear preference for one or more identity labels, only four included 'British' in their top three. This fits with the research on children's national identity by Scourfield et al. (2006) which found little interest in Britishness in a mostly non-Muslim sample of 8–11 year olds across Wales. This is not to say the children in either study were actively opposed to the idea of Britishness, but rather to note that it had little salience for their self-identification. Most of this section relates to parents we interviewed, as 'British' was a much more popular choice for parents than for children, being in the top three cards for 26 out of the 71 parents who expressed a clear preference (37%). Although a British identity had little salience for children, its importance for parents is still arguably relevant to the issue of religious nurture, as families' negotiation of discourses of Britishness can still have an impact on the children as they grow older.

Several of the parents responded to the mention of being 'British' with reference to official nationality or British citizenship. Passports were mentioned several times, with one father noting that you can only have a British passport and not a Welsh one, hence he would prioritize that identity label. It is not clear whether or not for these particular parents 'British' speaks to anything profound about their sense of belonging of their cultural identity, but the term was for them most associated with legal status. This was especially true of those who have moved to the UK from abroad at some point in their lives and therefore acquired British citizenship. In fact Mrs Rahman explicitly said that for her it only meant legal status: 'I'd say Muslim first, Djiboutian, and even though I've got a British passport it just doesn't come into my mind.' Mr and Mrs Sohail, though at times conflating English and British, were especially enthusiastic about Britishness. This was in the context of their seeking asylum and apparently wanting to come across to the interviewer as good future citizens. The idea of a British 'umbrella' identity, again emphasizing citizenship, was explicitly mentioned by two of the parents, but, also, more often this idea was *implicitly* present in several interviews. Mrs Rana, for example, chose the British card because she thought it included both English and Welsh. In part because of its 'umbrella' nature in a country of four nations, Britishness has been described as 'fuzzy' (Cohen, 1995) and it can even be confusing: 'I wouldn't even know what Britishness means, you know', as Mrs Yaqub put it.

There was some positive and negative framing of British culture from the adult interviewees, that was occasionally also reflected in the children's views. The quotation below from Mr Azzad sums up much of the behaviour that was spoken of positively and negatively by several inter-viewees—treating other people politely and respectfully, but having loose morals with regard to drink, drugs and sex.

'We can find some of the good points, good values of the British culture, British people. And comparative to the Malaysian culture, I'm speaking about culture in the people, because of like punctuality, honesty, bit of cleanliness, bit of courtesy, loving, kind, it's part of the British values which very good... they are so much positive, but drinking, drugs, free sex and all that I'm not like.' (Interview with Mr Azzad)

One mother, Mrs Adam, spoke of 'British' values as middle class inten-sive parenting practices—avoiding junk food and strict bed times. Class and status also came up in interviews where parents told us that outside of Britain, being British could bring a certain cultural cachet. For Mrs Ashraf, being British meant 'you just get a bit of, like, authority... you get treated differently when people know you are British'. But on an international level there is also British foreign policy, which was spoken of by several interviewees as preventing them from identifying closely with the label 'British'. Mrs Adam revealed the cultural tensions that Muslims in Britain can face. As noted above, she embraced what she saw as 'British' parenting and also punctuality—always arriving 10 minutes before an agreed time. However, she was unhappy about other aspects such as feeling pressurized to go to the pub, girls having boyfriends at a young age and foreign policy that involves 'fighting other Muslims'. The Rasheed children also illustrate this ambivalence, taking different views on the British identity card:

ASMA: 'What do you think; is it important to be British?'
FATIMA (age 12): Yeah, I want to be British.'
MUHAMMAD (age 10): 'British, sometimes they're not nice.'
ASMA: 'Who aren't they nice to?'
MUHAMMAD: 'Some of the army when they used to like, bomb and stuff.'
    (Interview with Rasheed children)

Some parents, when asked their views on Britishness, spoke of post-9/11 hostility they had experienced, especially when wearing Islamic dress (see also Chapter 6). Mrs Uddin said this affected her view of her British identity: 'I did get a lot of nastiness so I tend to be less so in love with the word British as I used to be.' Mrs Faysal said, 'they still look at me as if I'm not part of them, even when I'm working here'. There was a sense from several of the parents that it is not easy being British (Modood, 2010). Some openly struggled between what they saw as positive and negative aspects of British culture. In middle childhood we would not expect to see too much awareness of the debates that some Muslim adults engage in about British culture and indeed there was little evidence of this. Furthermore, as noted above, for the children we spoke to, the identity label 'British' had little salience.

What Does 'English' Mean When You Live in Wales?

The identity card 'English' was a more popular choice with children than 'British', being in the top three for seven of the 53 children who made a clear identity card choice. It was more popular than it was for adults, amongst whom only two put 'English' in their top three. The main reason for it having a certain appeal to the children seems to be conflation of language and identity. There were numerous examples of children assuming the term 'English' meant the English language. This is especially to be expected of children who are bilingual or multilingual, which most of our sample were. Such children are less likely to take language for granted than mono-lingual English-speakers. The conflation of 'English' with language also tells us something about Wales, where although in Cardiff 84% of people have no Welsh language skills (2011 Census), all children study the Welsh language as a subject in school. In this context, children may assume the Welsh–English distinction refers to language use, rather than nation boundaries. They may encounter the Welsh language more or less every week in school, if not every day, and they probably see bilingual notices around the city on a daily basis. Five of the children we interviewed attend Welsh-medium school where all lessons except for English take place in Welsh. In contrast to this familiarity with the Welsh language (albeit a surface familiarity for children in English-medium schools), however, national boundaries may be hazy to some of them, perhaps because of their level of geographical knowledge or because a distinction between English and Welsh nations has little social or cultural importance in their everyday lives. So, for example, Isra Ahmet (age 8) said she was English because 'I speak English, I live in an English place, mostly I speak English and I go to English stuff.' When asked to clarify what she meant by 'English stuff' she said, 'lessons in school'. Hafsa Mustafa (age 10) told us the 'English' card was important to her because 'that's the main language I speak'. There were numerous other examples.

This same tendency to associate the national label 'English' with language rather than national identity was found in Scourfield et al.'s (2006) study of children across Wales. It is possible that it takes the place of 'British' in symbolizing identification with English-speaking UK

191

culture. Sadeka Akbir (age 12), for example, was clear that she was Welsh because she was born in Wales but none the less wanted to keep the 'English' card, saying, 'yes, it's part of my identity because, I am English, we are British citizens, and I know the English language'. Here 'English' seems to be more or less synonymous with 'British', in the way the term is used internationally to refer to people from the UK.

Although many of the children were very positive about the label 'English' and several put it in their top three, amongst the parents there was more of a tendency to distance themselves from it. Some were aware the term could refer to a language rather than a national or ethnic identity and explicitly drew a contrast between the two. Mr Ahmet, for example, said, 'as a language it's OK—English is like a universal language—but as an identity, ethnic identity, no'; Mrs Barakah said, 'I speak English but I'm not English.' As Scourfield et al. (2006) noted, being Welsh could be defined primarily as not being English (see also McIntosh et al. [2004] on Scottishness). So Mrs Uddin said, 'you can bin that one!' when offered an 'English' card explaining, 'it's that Welsh thing isn't it? Am I Welsh or am I English, where are my allegiances?' A couple of parents said they saw 'English' as to do with 'race', not nationality. Interestingly, two white mothers who were brought up in England spoke of 'negative connotations' of Englishness. Mrs Kennedy-Shah referred to difficult historical relationships with both Ireland (where her mother came from) and Wales. She told us she had recently decided to abandon her ambiguity about being English (a phenomenon described by Condor, 2000); to 'accept' her English identity and no longer be 'ashamed' about it. Mrs Rasheed distanced herself from Englishness because, for her, 'to be honest English is just mixed with so much other stuff which comes with racism', mentioning the BNP and National Front. For Mrs Sajaad, Cardiff born with Pakistani parents, English people were 'more snobby than the Welsh people...they always look down at everything'. The Scourfield et al. (2006) study found this same view being expressed by some children (age 8–11), but children in the current study did not voice these views.

Welshness

Positive statements about Welsh identity were more common from parents than from children. Some children said that if you were born in Wales you could claim to be Welsh, with the implication that you could not if born elsewhere, but as noted above, only 6 children (out of 53 with comparable data) kept the 'Welsh' card in their top three. Of the parents, 13 put the 'Welsh' card in the top three (out of 71 with comparable data). Parents also more often made positive comment about the Welsh language than children. (We return to children's views of the Welsh language below.) For example, Mr Morris, a white Muslim convert, mentioned the discourse—familiar in Wales (Roberts, 1995)—of mourning the loss of the language in his relatively recent family history.

One reason given by parents for valuing a Welsh identity was pride in difference, i.e. being from the UK but not being English. This is certainly something that comes from moving around in the world and is therefore less likely to be encountered in early and middle childhood. So Mrs Khatun said, 'I just feel proud when I meet someone from England it's like "oh we're Welsh, we're not English!".' Mr Mahfouz told us he was proud to have been mistaken for Scottish in London. This seems to be a pride in a minority status within the UK.

For others, Wales was just what they know, from having lived in it for some time. This was expressed in fairly matter-of-fact terms. Mrs Uddin's interview was interesting, as she was quite ambivalent about Britishness, on the basis of hostility experienced in the wake of 9/11 (see section on being British above), but Welshness seemed to escape this taint:

> [*laughs*] 'It's more important than English I think! Welsh because it's a beautiful country, it's my home, my partner's also Welsh, born in Wales, my sister-in-law is Welsh, you know white Welsh or whatever you want to call it. It's the people I know, it's the culture I know. I may not know the drinking side of it or the booze culture or the dress culture or whatever, I may not know that side but it's part of who I am, I know what goes and doesn't go, that kind of thing so I'd have to say that, yeah, Welsh is part of me as well.' (Interview with Mrs Uddin)

Mr Tahir made an interesting distinction between 'having Welshness' and being Welsh through long-term residence. There is a tension here between belonging to a multicultural place and belonging to a specific (and narrower) idea of culture.

> 'Well you gotta class yourself as Welsh anyway living in Wales innit? Like if you live in Scotland you're Scottish so yeah, I haven't got any Welshness in me, I can't speak Welsh at all, but, yeah, when you live in that area you become a sort of, yeah, I do.' (Interview with Mr Tahir)

To continue a theme mentioned in the previous section on being English, some parents made comparisons between Wales and England that favoured Wales and Welshness. The converse of English people being 'too snobby' was that Welsh people were seen as more 'down-to-earth' and less money conscious (Mr Azzad). Mr Hussain saw Wales, in contrast to England, as having some traditional values, being 'close-knit' and respecting elders, rather like Pakistan. He also described Wales as 'a bit more liberal' than England, where is it 'harder to be accepted'. In a similar vein, Mrs Rana was positive about a Welsh identity because she did not experience racism when growing up. There is a contrary example, however, of Mrs Mughal, who said, 'I think English people are more friendly than Welsh people.'

Although he was one of those to declare himself 'Muslim first', Mr Mahfouz told us he got to a point in his life when he consciously wanted a national identity as well as a religious one. He decided to learn Welsh to fluency to prove it was possible to be Muslim and Welsh ('in that order'). Again we see here a restricted notion of Welshness that necessitates speaking Welsh (see also Scourfield and Davies, 2005; Scourfield et al., 2006). Mr Mahfouz noted the presence of a more exclusionary discourse, wherein it is impossible for someone from an ethnic minority to become Welsh even by learning the language: 'I've had people come up to me and saying, you know, cos I've learnt to speak Welsh, um well the classic statement was, a dog born in a stable doesn't make it a horse.' Bond (2006) notes comparable findings from Scotland, with minorities perceiving themselves excluded from Scottishness on the grounds of ethnicity or ancestry. He writes that 'the kind of open, inclusive Scottish national identity promoted by the Scottish Executive does not necessarily match the perspectives of those in the wider population' (Bond, 2006: 623).

More inclusive discourses of Welshness are also available, however. In fact, Mrs Omar described white work colleagues ascribing to her a Welsh identity she did not want. She seemed to be rather baffled by this ascription.

MRS OMAR: 'I'm sure it does cos they, I don't what the fascination is, they know I was born here and whatever they class me as Welsh, do you know what I mean?'

ASMA: 'Who's that? At work?'

MRS OMAR: 'Work [laughs] they do it's amazing isn't it? I think it must suit them for strange reason, I don't know why. But I always do tell them I am Somali but they're saying "you're Welsh".'

The children in the study were, however, mostly negative about the identity label 'Welsh', associating it only with the Welsh language, which they did not enjoy learning in school. The only exceptions were, not surprisingly, the few children in the study who attend Welsh-medium school, who get very positive messages about Welsh identity from teachers. Layla Mahfouz (age 13), daughter of Mr Mahfouz who learned Welsh to fluency, said, 'in like school and stuff they always do stuff like how important it is to be Welsh ... I don't really think about being British I think more about being Welsh.'

Conflation of the identity 'Welsh' and speaking the Welsh language was very common, especially from the children but also from a few parents. Here are just a few examples:

SAMEH: 'OK, what is the difference between British and Welsh?'
MUSA: 'Welsh is a language, while British is a country.'
  (Interview with Musa Tawfeeq, age 12)

ASMA: 'And Welsh isn't important to you?'
YUSUF: 'I don't even know how to speak it.'
  (Interview with Yusuf Mir, age 8)

ASMA: So why do you dislike Welsh and British?
NEDA: 'It's got too many LLs in them!' [laughs]
  (Interview with Neda Hooshmand, age 10)

JONATHAN: 'What about Welsh, why did you get rid of it?'
AMAN: 'Because we don't really talk Welsh at home, only in school.'
  (Interview with Aman Hussain, age 8)

Along with this conflation went negativity about the language from some of the children. These negative views are not necessarily specific to Muslim children, but similar views would perhaps be expressed by some of the white Welsh children who attend English-medium schools, but have to study some Welsh from age 5 to 16. Similar views might in theory be expressed about any language children were made to learn in primary school. So Daniyaal Faysal (age 12) and Ayaan Islam (age 12) both said they 'hate' learning the language. For Daniyaal it 'sucks' and he did not think he should be learning Welsh. Some parents also expressed the view that it was not an important language to learn. For Mr Ahmed it has 'a very limited use'. Mrs Mabrouk, a white Welsh convert, said that although she felt 'a bit of a traitor' to be saying so, she had no desire to learn Welsh and that she would rather learn Arabic.

One negative view about Muslim Welshness was an assumption that the label 'Welsh' refers to an ethnicity rather than a form of citizenship. So Mr Akras explicitly told us he could become British as a British citizen, but his 'ethnic origin' (the category into which he put Welsh) would always be linked to his Palestinian origins. Although a Palestinian identity is especially politicized, so this example is not typical of Muslims in the UK, he was making a point of more general salience to our study. It was noted earlier that 'British' meant citizenship for many of the parents. 'Welsh' seems to mean an ethnic origin for some, meaning that it would compete with an ethnic minority identity rather than existing alongside it. This is perhaps what Ahmed Akbir (age 9) meant when he said (leafing through the identity cards), 'Male, female, brother, sister, Arab, English, Bengali, Welsh. I don't know any Welsh Muslims!' Perhaps the problem here is a narrow notion of 'Welsh' as implying certain cultural values and interests which do not encompass non-Welsh-speaking Muslims. Mr Assad, an African Caribbean man brought up in Wales told us:

> 'No I wouldn't describe myself as Welsh, because they have a distinct culture and understanding to what it means to be Welsh and it doesn't represent me. I was just born here.' (Interview with Mr Assad)

His comment 'I was just born here' may relate to the resistance to national identities we mention above in the section on being 'Muslim first'.

To end this section, it is worth noting that Welsh identity, like any other, is contingent and contested. Mrs Hussain expressed this dimension of social identity when she described her different selves with different groups of people and different social contexts (Goffman, 1990 [1959]). She was noting that Welshness would not be so important to a group of Muslims, but that this national identity might be important to acknowledge (as well as religious identity) in the company of non-Muslims.

> 'I suppose I could say this to you. If I was with Muslims, obviously I would say, "yeah I'm Muslim", but if I was with a group of non-Muslims I'd be more inclined to maybe say, "I'm a Welsh Muslim". I don't identify myself really as Welsh because I don't speak the language, but if I did speak the language I'd be saying – yeah I am I'm Welsh. But living in Wales, I know I am a Welsh Muslim, but not having the language makes me feel like sort of I'm not actually Welsh, you know, but—it depends on what situation I would be in really.' (Interview with Mrs Hussain)

Identification with Locality

The research participants' views of Cardiff as a city were discussed in Chapter 6. Here we give a very brief overview of themes that arose when discussing locality as a source of identity, via the card-sorting exercise.

Eleven parents (out of 71 with comparable data) and five children (out of 53) chose the 'Cardiff' identity card in their top three. For some children there was no meaningful distinction between this identity card and the 'Welsh' one. Litan Akhtar (age 14) told us the two cards were 'the same'. For others, the only way in which Cardiff would be significant to identity would be in terms of support for the football team. This speaks to the rather artificial character of identity research, in so far as for most people it may be that collective identities do not have any particular significance outside of sports events or national celebrations, as they are taken for granted aspects of social life.

Some interviewees overtly compared Cardiff with other places. Farid Ibrahim (age 10) said, 'I like it here because you get lots of free time to do many things and the school don't use child abuse', perhaps implicitly contrasting it with physical punishment for school children in a Muslim country he had at least heard of, if not encountered (he had spent time in Malaysia). In contrast, Fateh Rafique (age 10) chose 'Dakar' as one of his top identity cards, choosing to create this from the blank card that all were offered. He possibly thought of this because Cardiff had been offered. He said of Dakar, 'I'd have loads of friends to play with and it's wide open, I like it', although he said he preferred living in the UK.

Some parents asserted their affiliation with Cardiff in contrast to alternative collective identities. So for Mr Mir, being from Cardiff means you can 'make fun of the Welsh people', by which he means 'the real Taffys' and people from 'anywhere that's not Cardiff'. Cardiff he sees as having 'its own identity itself . . . it is Welsh but you can keep jumping ship'. A similar city chauvinism might be articulated in any geographical location, but it should be noted that there are particular fault-lines in Welsh identity. There are claims and counter-claims about the essence of Welshness; as Dai Smith (1999: 36) has noted, 'Wales is a singular noun but a plural experience'. Cardiff, with a large English-born population and a low concentration (though a large absolute number) of Welsh speakers, does often have its true Welsh credentials questioned; in this context, Mr Mir might, in asserting his Cardiffian identity, be implicitly giving out the message that 'no matter how Welsh you think I am, my pride in Cardiff is more important'.

Minority Ethnic Identities

In this section we discuss minority ethnic identities from families' countries of origin (also see Chapter 6 for a description of the role of diaspora in Muslim children's social networks). In nine families out of 33 with comparable data (i.e. 27%), in addition to agreeing on the choice of 'Muslim', all children and parents also chose the same minority ethnicity card in their top three. Of the whole sample, 39 out of 53 children who declared a clear preference for certain identities (74%)

chose at least one minority ethnicity within their top three. For parents, the figure was slightly lower at 45/71 (63%).

There is a clear sense in which even in a post-traditional and individualized social and cultural context, officialdom can define and restrict collective identities. Citizenship status and possession of passports was mentioned earlier in the chapter. Equally, ethnic monitoring systems contribute to the non-choice of identity labels. So Mr Islam said of his daughter, 'I think the official ethnic origin system makes her Bangladeshi as well; she can't tick White British isn't it?' This could be seen in a negative light. Mr Hooshmand, from Iran, said he struggled to fit into the categories provided by ethnic monitoring. Mrs Tufail spoke of an ethnic monitoring form from her child's nursery, saying, 'yeah, Indian–British, so they are doing it for us already, so you know identity is already picked up', and implying that this ascribed categorization was unhelpful or even linked to discrimination. Aside from officialdom, there is anyway the potential for minority ethnic identity to be ascribed, even when not embraced. Mr Mahfouz said people would see him as Egyptian rather than Welsh. His daughter Tahirah (age 11) spoke of how in school the Egyptian identity was a subject for humour, with children doing a comic Egyptian walk.

There were many examples of positive talk about minority ethnic identity. One interesting example was Sadeka Akbir's (age 12) view that being Bengali 'means that I have a culture, that you actually have a culture...and I know another language, I'm bilingual'. This is a pride in cultural and linguistic difference but it also reflects a deficit view of white Britain as lacking any culture; as culture-less (Hewitt 1996: 40). Some parents spoke of the importance of passing on their native language to their children and the difficulty of this. Mr Abdul-Rahman said he would rather the children learned Somali than English and he fears they will lose their Somali: 'it's our language, it's the mother tongue, and...my mum always says to me, when she phones, you know, make sure they speak their own language, because that fear is there'. Strength of historical roots was a common theme in relation to minority ethnicity, with identities often being clearly passed on from parents to children. Umaira Tufail said this:

> 'Well, my parents made me Indian because they're Indian and so I am Indian as well...my parents were born in India and their parents and my parents' parents were born in India. And my grandparents were born in India. And then my great-grandparents were born in India and so on.' (Interview with Umaira Tufail, age 9)

In some families, whether or not a child identified with a family ethnic origin depended on their place of birth. For other children, parents' place of birth was significant (see also Scourfield et al., 2006). Aman Hussain (age 8), despite being born and bred in Cardiff, rejected the 'Cardiff' card, saying, 'we're not really from Cardiff; we're actually from Pakistan'. For some of the parents who had lived most of their lives outside the UK in a Muslim country of origin, there was an understandable affiliation with place in which they were brought up. Mr Ishmael, despite leaving Sudan as a refugee, said he had to identify as Sudanese, 'because if I live here all my life I'm belong there . . . East or West home is best as they say.'

For Mr Hooshmand, a Shia Muslim from Iran, there was a sacred duty to identify with his country of origin. He told us, 'Islam said your home or your country is a part of your responsibility', and he spoke in the same context of the Islamic duty to give money and help others. His daughter Neda also spoke of a profound sense of duty to Iran:

'Because it's like my home country, it's where I belong. Like when I came here, when I first came and still now I feel as though I'm just a guest; I'm not someone who belongs here. It's not my place and it's not my duty to be here or anything. But I feel that even though I might not be important to many people I think it's my duty to be in my country and I belong there, somehow.' (Interview with Neda Hooshmand, age 10)

In this family there seems to be a very strong narrative of duty to country of origin. Neda and her mother seemed to be genuinely amazed when Mr Hooshmand decided against keeping the 'Iranian' card in his top three.

In keeping with the 'Muslim first' ideology and an accompanying opposition to national identities, some parents distanced themselves from their ethnic origin, even when this was a country of birth. Mr Mustafa, for example said, 'Bengali is just the consequence of where you were born you know; I could have been born anywhere.' Some parents on the other hand distanced themselves from a country of origin that belonged to previous generation, since they themselves were born and/or brought up in the UK. Mrs Mir said, 'I don't see myself as Pakistan is my home country or anything; we've grown up here, I am British.' This distancing went further with a few parents. Mrs Sajaad questioned how 'Muslim' a country Pakistan can claim to be:

'They call themselves Muslims in Pakistan; I don't even know why it's called a Muslim country because it's not, yeah? It's like, there's people dying, they don't help you until you throw a bundle of money, they don't do anything for you. They don't respect women. It's so bad and it's supposed to be a Muslim country. When you look at it you have more self-respect in this country. Why not just live here for the rest of your life?' (Interview with Mrs Sajaad)

Mr Sohail spoke of the negative experiences his family had of Pakistani people in Cardiff. The Sohails were seeking asylum. They spoke of their lives being threatened in Pakistan after a family dispute. In Cardiff they were quite isolated. They met other asylum seekers at English language classes and spoke very warmly of the material and social support provided by the Catholic nuns they met at a church-run drop-in centre. They said that local Pakistanis, however, had been hostile to them: 'they ask questions—"Why you come? How you come? When you go back? What you problem?"' It seems the hostility was because of suspicions about the veracity of their asylum claim. There may here be a desire to keep their distance from a stigmatized group (asylum seekers). In the words of Bauman (2004b: 57) 'the very idea of "asylum", once a matter of civil and civilized pride, has been reclassified as a dreadful concoction of shameful naivety and criminal irresponsibility'. The stigma of this group, when many people seem to assume (in line with the dominant tabloid narrative) that most claims are 'bogus', might even be seen to threaten the acceptance by the white population of established minority ethnic people.

We end this section with an excerpt from Mrs Fatullah, as she spoke of ideally wanting to mix the best of Cardiff and the Middle East. She herself is a white Welsh convert to Islam and when asked if her children preferred their father's country of origin, which they visited, or Cardiff, she replied:

'I think they like both, you know, because when they live here, they sort of get sick of some things, and when they go there they get sick of some things, so it's kind of like a bit of this and a bit of that makes the best, you know, because there's things here that they dislike, and there's things there that they like, so even for me, it's the same thing, there's things there that I like, it's a shame you just couldn't mix them up and juggle it.' (Interview with Mrs Fatullah)

Conclusion

Identity is of course a complicated business. In the varied understandings of collective identities that were discussed in the chapter, we see evidence of individualization, up to a point. The range of options are, however, limited, even for children and parents from minority ethnic backgrounds, who have arguably more room for manoeuvre than the majority white population (in the sense that there may be more than one nationality they can choose to affiliate to). It is possible to sum up the main trends that emerged from the chapter. This does involve some quantification of qualitative data about which we need to be very cautious, but the difference in popularity of the various identity choices was quite marked, so even on the basis of less-than-robust measurement, it is worth noting again in conclusion.

There was a high level of inter-generational agreement. It was not that children and parents agreed on all the collective identities we presented them with, but there was considerable overlap and evidence of transmission of identity, at least at this stage of the life course. An especially dominant theme was the importance of prioritizing Muslim identity. In addition to this, we saw quite a lot of agreement on the importance of family (see previous chapter) and minority ethnicity. As well as parents and children within the same families identifying with a common ethnicity, more generally it was a very popular choice for both parents and children to identify with a Muslim country of origin. The fairly high levels of agreement would suggest that collective identities are an important part of a Muslim *habitus* and potentially reinforce religious transmission.

A British identification was quite popular amongst parents but not at all amongst children. 'Welsh' was also unpopular with children and more so than English, apparently because of a tendency for children to conflate the labels English and Welsh with language. Child development is part of the picture. Some younger children were confused about geography, with inevitable implications for local and national identity. There was some evidence of Islam being conflated with ethnicity and we might speculate that in fact for many more children, being Muslim might be inseparable from ethnic origin and perhaps for most children, the religion–culture distinction that some of the parents are fond of making might be fairly meaningless. Being part of a social minority which is ethnic as well as religious may well have the effect of reinforcing the transmission of religious identity, if not practice, if being Muslim is synonymous with being (for example) Yemeni.

Middle childhood is not a stage at which the political discourses of identity are usually engaged with. The parents' expressed views were inevitably more complex, because they have encountered much more of the world (and also because of cognitive development). There were therefore rather richer data from parents and more tensions revealed in their identity talk.

The chapter reminds us that cultural representations are extremely important but that hard structures—e.g. state bureaucracy and formal citizenship—also have an impact on collective identities. The global political context plays its part, but so does the immediately local level, and perhaps this is especially so for the children, whose lives are spatially restricted in early and middle childhood. Their identity affiliations are more likely to be influenced by classroom interactions (e.g. not liking their Welsh lessons) than by anything happening in the Middle East.

9

Conclusion

The secondary analysis of the Citizenship Survey presented in Chapter 2 left us with two main questions in relation to Islam. One was the question of why the inter-generational transmission of Islam seems to be markedly higher than that of Christianity and also higher than that of other non-Muslim, non-Christian religions when these are collapsed together into one category. (This had to be done to achieve sufficient power for the statistical analyses, but 'lumping together' Hindus, Sikhs, Jews and Buddhists does of course mask the differences between them and it may be that one or more of these religious groups in fact has a rate of transmission which is equal to or higher than that for Muslims.) The second issue for exploration was the interesting differences in rates of transmission between Muslims. Unlike all survey respondents brought up in a religion, for whom the association between religious transmission and socio-economic position showed a mixed picture, for those brought up as Muslims there was a more consistent pattern, with people in more manual occupations, with lower incomes and lower educational qualifications being significantly more likely to still be practising as Muslims.

It has been explained that the qualitative study of Muslim families in Cardiff has not been adequate to robustly explore differences between Muslims according to class, education, ethnicity and so on. A mixed-method study with large subgroups and probability sampling would be required for valid research on differences between groups of Muslims. It was important for the representativeness of our study across the social spectrum to achieve a diverse sample, but a different kind of study would be required to shed light on those interesting findings from the Home Office Citizenship Survey (HOCS) on class, education and the transmission of Islam.

The best that could be managed was some tentative comment in various places throughout the book on differences between groups of Muslims. A picture emerged of the larger ethnic groups having more set traditions of religious nurture, whereas those in the smaller ethnic groups, and especially the mixed ethnicity families with one convert parent, found it easier to make creative choices. There may be a connection with social class here, as national statistics show the larger ethnic groups (Pakistanis and Bangladeshis) experiencing more socio-economic deprivation (ONS, 2006). We noted the racialized occupations of many fathers, with implications for their involvement in religious nurture. We also noted differences in parents' own level of education about Islam, but that this did not necessarily map neatly onto formal qualifications or social class. In fact the business of categorizing families by social class and school of thought was complex and difficult. In some ways the study threw up more questions than it answered about diversity between groups of Muslims. Although we worked hard to achieve a diverse sample, it has to be acknowledged that only parents to whom Islam was meaningful would volunteer to take part in research about religious nurture. It is doubtful therefore that our sample included people who would identify as Muslim only because of overlap with cultural and ethnic identities, but neither believe in nor practise their faith (with perhaps one exception, the rather unfortunately pseudony-mised Islam family).

It may be that the more successful transmission of Islam in less educated, lower social class Muslims found in HOCS is primarily explained by the effects of education, although this connection is speculative rather than rooted in our data. The dominant approach to Islam we observed was of the Qur'an being seen as the word of God for all time rather than a document limited by its historical context—that observation we can support empirically. In the light of this, we can speculate that greater exposure to secular and/or critical educational approaches might—at least for some people—challenge literal approaches to the core text of Islam. In the absence of an established liberal Islamic Studies tradition which takes a critical approach to the Qur'an, scholarly questioning by more educated Muslims might lead, for some, to a weakening of faith rather than an intellectual accommodation as you might find (for example) in liberal Christianity.

We could also note that the tendency in families from the larger ethnic groups (Bangladeshis and Pakistanis) to follow local ethnic traditions of religious education, rather than working out their own creative approaches, might also help to explain the relatively successful religious transmission in lower social class Muslims if we make assumptions about social class on the basis of the socio-economic profile of these ethnic groups in the UK. Making this connection between local traditions of religious nurture and the success of religious transmission makes sense if we assume different approaches to religious nurture in different ethnic groups indicate that individualization varies according to social class. Although individualization can lead to a more conservative religiosity (Roy, 2004), de-coupling religious practice from community tradition does also risk the dissolution of faith. There are several questionable assumptions here, however, and we do not have direct evidence from our study that following ethnic traditions leads to more successful religious transmission.

Although we cannot end the book with robust conclusions about differences between groups of Muslims, we will in what follows come back to the other question raised by the HOCS analysis, namely why is the rate of transmission of Islam so much greater than the rate for Christianity and also slightly higher than the rate for other non-Christian, non-Muslim religions? Woodhead (2011) identifies five different concepts of religion in social scientific writings. Whilst we applaud the conceptual clarity of delineating different theoretical assumptions in academic writings, our position is that more than one of these concepts of religion is needed to make sense of the transmission of Islam in the UK. The four theoretical angles introduced in Chapter 1 all proved to be relevant to our qualitative findings. Figure 9.1 illustrates quite simply

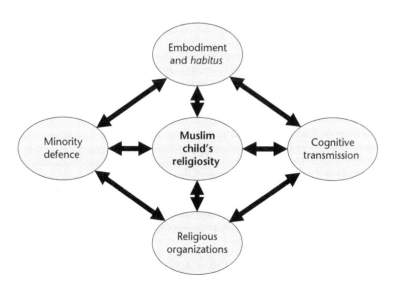

Figure 9.1. Influences on a Muslim child's religiosity.

that they are all required for a thorough understanding the religiosity of a Muslim child and each of the theoretical perspectives is connected to at least two of the other perspectives.

Making Sense of Islamic Nurture

Cognitive transmission

Accepting a role for cognitive transmission means acknowledging that humans are not a blank slate at birth. As Pinker (2003) argues, blank slate theory has become an underpinning assumption, tacit or not, of much social science. It effectively denies any cognitive architecture which humans bring to their social existence. Cognitive science theories of religion acknowledge that there may be some universal processes involved in becoming religious as well as context-specific ones. Because this is primarily a sociological book and the main study has not been designed to test cognitive science theories, the best we can do is reflect on the relevance of just one approach which has been influential in the field, namely Whitehouse's (2002, 2004) modes of religiosity.

Evidence is limited from our study, which was not designed to test out cognitive transmission and the storage of knowledge in different kinds of memory. However, in interpreting the data there are some clear elements of Islamic nurture which fit with the doctrinal mode and therefore we would suggest that this mode of cognitive transmission helps to explain the apparently relatively successful rate of religious transmission in Muslims. Frequent repetition of ritual, from a very young age in some cases, allows bodily practices to be stored in implicit memory. Frequent repetition of religious teachings at home, in formal classes and through informal social interaction with Muslim friends and wider family members allows for the storage of these messages in semantic memory. This may be happening despite the language barrier for most learners of the Qur'an being read in classical Arabic, in which they lack fluency. These processes of transmission arguably apply to any Muslim children who are brought up in their faith. They do rely on parents teaching children at least some messages about Islam and usually on supplementary education. In addition to these cognitive processes, Shia Muslims typically have a religious experience in the imagistic mode if they mark Muharram, the martyrdom of Ali, which is a highly emotional event.

Islam is not uniquely placed in the doctrinal mode of course and this mode alone cannot explain why inter-generational transmission seems to be relatively successful. Many anthropologists have asserted strongly the need to understand the specific context of any religion being studied. In the words of Berliner and Sarró:

> 'Acquiring religion' is not merely a cold-blooded technical process of cognitive downloading. It takes place in a specific interactive social and cultural environment, and one must, therefore, also examine it as a 'dimension of social practice' (Berliner and Sarró, 2007b: 10)

It is not enough to consider cognitive processes alone and neither do advocates of a cognitive science of religion claim that it is enough. Some Christian churches also have worship which is firmly in the doctrinal mode but may not be holding on to their children and young people as successfully. Cognitive science explanations, although coming first in our list of perspectives, are far from being our primary theoretical reference point. Additional theoretical contributions from social science are needed to more fully understand the relative strength of Islamic nurture. However, we start with cognitive science in recognition that a blank slate approach would be inappropriate for making sense of how religion is learned.

Embodiment and habitus

A more sociological concept which deals with some rather similar processes of learning is that of *habitus*. This is the development of deeply-rooted social dispositions such as taste and physical deportment via micro-level socialization within families and communities. It is distinct from cognitive transmission as it necessarily involves attention to specific social mores, rather than universal processes, and the concept is necessarily bound up with the reproduction of social stratification. Bourdieu (1984) sees the development of *habitus* as an essentially unconscious ascribing of social conditions on individuals, whereas other social scientists, such as Mahmood (2012 [2001]) in her work on Islam, insist on a pedagogical dimension. A pedagogical process seems to fit more closely with what we found about Islamic nurture.

From the first moments of life, a Muslim child is marked as Muslim by having the *adhaan*, and perhaps also *iqamah*, spoken into her ear. This happened in almost all the families in our study. The child will probably be given a name which marks her as Muslim. As she grows up she will probably be expected to identify first and foremost as Muslim, before any national or ethnic identification. It is likely she will grow up in a home where religion is made material (Orsi, 2004) to some degree or other, for example with few or no images of people displayed but instead verses from the Qur'an and images of famous mosques up on the walls.

In many family homes there will be frequent repetition of ritual and religious teachings. As other researchers working on Muslim *habitus* have noted (Winchester, 2008 Oestergaard, 2009), there is interaction between the repetition of embodied ritual and the development of moral deportment. Each reinforces the other. If a great deal of children's time and space features other Muslims, because of parents' own social networks and their control of children's, as well as attendance at supplementary education classes and mosques, then socialization into a religious *habitus* is quite likely to be successful.

None of this means that religious socialization is inevitable. There is room for agency. But just as growing up in a middle class home means you are likely to develop middle class tastes, this micro-level socialization through social interaction, embodied learning and material religion is likely to be absorbed by children and may well remain till adulthood. Some things are almost impossible to shake off. For example, Mr Islam, who had the least conventional belief and practice of all our Muslim parents, told us that despite his scientific learning which had clearly led him to question some aspects of the religion he grew up with, he could never envisage being able to eat pork. To regard pork as *haram* was deeply ingrained in his *habitus*.

Minority defence

Both of the above perspectives would shed light on religious nurture in any context. Although consideration of a particular religious *habitus* has to be context specific, the theory can be universalized.

So these above perspectives are, for example, relevant in the UK for Christianity, which has historically been the dominant religion of the country, albeit in more recent times there has been some rapid secularization. The above theories can also be applied to Islam in Muslim-majority countries. However, there needs to be serious consideration of how being in a social minority in the UK (or other Western countries) might affect the transmission of Islam.

The first thing to note is that the secondary analysis of HOCS presented in Chapter 2 shows that other non-Christian and non-Muslim religious groups also had much higher transmission of religion than Christians. Since most people in these other religious groups are from minority ethnic backgrounds, we can hypothesize that minority status may be important. This might be because minorities have a stronger need than the majority population to work hard to preserve their cultural heritage because it feels under pressure from the dominant culture in the country. This defence of cultural heritage might be reinforced by socializing with others who share the same language and cultural background. Also it may be that minority populations experience social and economic hardship associated with migration, including experience of discrimination. Religion can be a comfort in the face of hardship and also identification with a marginalized culture might become stronger as a reaction to discrimination.

To first consider the issue of preserving distinctiveness: there have only been hints at this in our data at various points in the book and it has not tended to be consciously articulated by parents. This would not mean the theory was invalid, however. It could still be pertinent, but just not reflected on by parents. It is difficult for a study like ours to confirm or deny such a theory. One parent did consciously reflect on this concept, however. The words of Mrs Shahzad here summarize neatly the idea that a religious minority has to work harder to maintain its culture than it would if in a majority:

'So it's natural that the (*Christian*) children are not going to dream of "oh yeah let me just go the church" when they've never been taught in the house and whereas I think as Muslims we're going more and more towards our religion rather than going away from it. I think it's become more important especially in the Western world even more so. I think we're more focused on it than people are in Pakistan. There's more people wearing hijab here than they do in Pakistan. And I think we have this pressure—we think, "oh well we don't want them to stray, they live in this community and they're going to follow their English friends or whatever". So we spend more time, we're under more pressure to teach them that and I think if you do a survey between countries we'd probably be more successful than the people in Pakistan.' (Interview with Mrs Shahzad)

The next idea mentioned above was the reinforcement of religious identity and practice through social networks which are dominated by the same minority culture. There is ample evidence for this in our data. Chapter 6 described parents' preferences for Muslim (and usually same-ethnicity) social networks for their children, including wider family members and bonding social capital much more in evidence than bridging. Field's (2011) summary of opinion polling shows that a significant minority of young Muslim adults espouse 'apartism' and think integration into British society had gone too far. This ideological stance is not the opinion of the Muslims majority, however (see Phillips, 2006), and for most people it is more likely that the company of other Muslims and especially those from the same ethnic and linguistic background is just more comfortable and more familiar, as well as providing a guarantee (in theory) of a suitable moral framework for children.

Time spent with people from the same ethnic background is not straightforwardly a choice for Muslims. Employment patterns in Cardiff are certainly racialized, and this may also be true for the housing market. Chapter 5 noted that, in practice, attendance at most mosques is dominated by a single ethnic group. This in turn can reinforce the identification of religion with ethnicity, a phenomenon we saw in data from some of the children—a conflation of ethnic origin and religious identity which, whilst not being about minority *defence* as such, certainly is a feature of being in a social minority. This conflation is particularly to be found in childhood, as amongst adults there is now a dominant discourse of separating ethnic culture from pure Islam; something the children in our study were generally not aware of.

Finally there is the issue of religion being strengthened as a response to hardship and discrimination. Hypothetically this might ring true and it might also mark Muslims out somewhat from other ethno-religious minorities in the UK. Firstly this is because the Muslim population is especially deprived, and indeed more so than Hindus and Sikhs (Mercia Group, 2006). Secondly, a Muslim identity has become highly politicized, since the Rushdie Affair to an extent and then even more so since 9/11. Voas and Fleischmann (2012) note that some scholars have speculated about this process, i.e. Islam being strengthened as a reaction to discrimination, but evidence is currently lacking. On the basis of our qualitative study we would suggest there is indeed *some* evidence for this phenomenon but it is not overwhelming. There was some talk of needing to defend the reputation of Islam. There were some glimmers of resistance identity. There were also some examples of hostility experienced since 9/11 but in fact there were fewer of these examples than might have been expected. Parents were asked what it was like being in a minority in Cardiff and the vast majority were very positive about their experience of living in the city as Muslims. Several made positive comparisons with living in a Muslim country.

Religious organizations

The final theoretical perspective that we argue is necessary to aid understanding of religious nurture in Muslim families is the role of religious organizations. Almost all parents with children old enough arranged for them to attend some kind of formal learning, usually to read the Qur'an and sometimes too to learn Islamic Studies. These classes are of central importance to religious nurture. There is a combined influence of mosques which organize classes, well-known local teachers who take small groups in their own homes or the homes of their students and the

Islamic media such as TV channels and websites which are increasingly available to parents for religious nurture.

It is worth re-stating that we are not dealing here with large bureaucracies and complex hierarchies. There are no UK-wide organizations which have any particular influence on religious nurture. Field (2011: 163) notes that opinion polls confirm 'the fragmentation and relative irrelevance to grass-roots Muslims' of British Islam's national leadership. Rather there are mosques and other Islamic institutions set up by local social networks, but building on wider traditions of epistemological authority. Despite the recent tendency to deculturation described by Roy (2004), there was evidence of continuing respect for historical threads of Islamic authority, in the form of local scholars and respected local teachers and also sometimes in the form of nationally or internationally recognized *shaykhs*.

Supplementary schools are strongly connected to other Muslim organizations so are part of a nexus of Islamic institutions. They facilitate participation in a Muslim community, so children who attend Islamic education classes not only learn about the Qur'an and the foundations of Islam, but they are also socialized to be members of a faith community; one which in most cases is made of people from the same ethnic background. Religious organizations therefore have an important role to play in the development of Muslim *habitus* and the reinforcing of minority identity.

There are tentative comparisons to be made with the roles of religious organizations in other faiths; tentative because this has not been a comparative qualitative study. Data from the HOCS Young People's Survey (YPS) in Table 2.5 (Chapter 2) suggest attendance at 'out-of-school clubs' in religious organizations is more prevalent amongst 11–15 year old Muslims than in other religious groups. It is not too clear whether, in making this survey response, Muslim children are referring to supplementary religious education classes. The data might underestimate the attendance at such classes if respondents did not regard them as 'out-of-school clubs'. The same methodological limitations apply to the other faith groups, however. It is therefore reasonably valid to compare religious groups and the differences between them should be taken seriously.

One difference between religions is that whereas Islam is in phase of global resurgence (Sutton and Vertigans, 2005), Christianity is experiencing decline, at least in the UK (Crockett and Voas, 2006). Although we lack comparative data, it is likely that regimes of religious teaching in most churches are relatively 'light touch' compared to those organized by mosques and Muslim families. Certainly there has been a historical move away from disciplinarian teaching in the Catholic Church, for example (see Orsi, 2004, on the US). The material on the religious nurture of Hindu and Sikh children in Nesbitt's (2004) book, although referring occasionally to supplementary education, does not give the impression of classes taking places several times a week as is the case for close to half of the Muslim families in our study.

One theory of organizations which has been applied to religion is that of resource dependency (see Scheitle and Dougherty, 2008). This might suggest that the non-negotiable truth claim of Islam (there is one God and Muhammad is his Messenger) makes individuals more dependent on the religious organization than would be the case in those belief systems without a taken-for-granted core of universally accepted truths. This might suggest that the tendency towards theological and textual conservatism that we have noted in the book, wherein the Qur'an and *hadith* are literally applicable in the 21st Century, rather than being historically contextualized, might reinforce people's affiliations to Islamic organizations.

To reconsider the five concepts of religion outlined by Woodhead (2011), therefore, whilst our book has predominantly leaned towards 'religion as practice', other concepts need to be applied if the religious nurture of Muslim children is to be properly understood. So 'religion as belief' and perhaps especially the subcategory of 'religious as discourse' helps us understand how a conservative reading of religious texts might cement religious affiliation (the point made immediately above) and parents' dichotomizing of religion and culture. Understanding the effects on religious nurture of being in a ethno-religious minority requires attention to 'religion as identity' and 'religion as relationship'. An emphasis on 'religion as power' is also necessary for understanding minority effects as well as understanding the role of religious authority and religious organizations.

Individualization and Agency

In Chapter 1 we raised the question of whether or not there is evidence of individualization in British Islam. Our conclusion would be that there is some evidence in our qualitative research of parents' reflexivity and life-planning. Parents did tend to reflect critically on their own religious upbringing and often saw themselves as making their own decisions about their children, in relation to formal learning, birth rituals and so on. Individualized faith choices tended to mean embracing a fairly conservative decentralized religiosity, as Roy (2004) describes.

Criticism of ethnic cultures was also used to further gender equality, up to a point, with Islam (unlike ethnic culture) seen as treating men and women as equal, though different. There was a limit to this critical thinking about gender, however, in so far as gender inequalities specified in religious texts were not seen to be open to question.

Despite there being evidence of parents' reflexivity, we would argue that to emphasize individualization in Islam is to focus on a religious phenomenon of relatively marginal significance. Much more striking, at least when we consider Islamic nurture, is the commonality of belief and conformity to collective obligations. We are of course not claiming that all Muslims are the same. There is considerable diversity of practice, though not really of the fundamentals of belief. Our point is that we see what Guest (2009: 663) terms a 'soft individualism' of parents on the whole choosing conformity.

Children's agency in Islamic nurture seems to be fairly limited. Many children in middle childhood, regardless of religion or ethnicity, have their routines set largely by parents and their freedom to roam is often very limited. The YPS data in Chapter 2 (Table 2.7) show that Muslims are more likely than children from other religious groups to say they do not attend more clubs because they are not allowed to or because they are too busy. This might indicate Muslim parents are especially likely to control children's routines, something we saw illustrated in qualitative data in Chapter 6.

Agency is not altogether removed of course. We saw examples of children resisting Qur'an classes in small ways, for example through very frequent trips to the toilet. We heard about children resisting Christian worship in school by mouthing words but not sounding them. These examples show children exercising agency but they also illustrate how limited the opportunities for agency are in middle childhood if time and space are controlled by adults and institutions. To use the distinction made by Woodhead (2012) in discussing everyday religion, it could be said that children in middle childhood are able to be tactical, but not strategic about their faith. It could be expected that very different findings would emerge from research with older children, who tend to have more freedom of independent movement in communities. Children's agency in religious nurture is nicely described in this next excerpt from Orsi's writing on Catholic children. He is discussing children's religiosity and he acknowledges the discipline and unconscious socialization that children are subject to but also the necessity of them responding positively to this regime in order to become religious.

Some of this was conscious, but much was also there by discipline, inference, in feelings produced in them by the stories adults told them and in which children were implicated. Bodily apprehensions are not always conscious, but they are real. Catholic reality took hold of children's bodies, whether they knew it or not, and their bodies bore the realness of this world, at the same time that children took hold of the world given them by their teachers and parents. (Orsi, 2004: 107)

In ending the book, we now turn to practical, rather than academic implications of the study. Although the research was funded as a purely academic research project, there was dialogue throughout the process, with Muslim organizations and with providers of public services, especially in health, social care and education. We therefore conclude with some tentative suggestions about what the Muslim childhood we describe might mean for each of these groups of stakeholders.

Practical Implications of Our Study

For Muslim communities

The following ideas emerged from our discussion with Muslim organizations in Cardiff. This is simply a short list of some issues which Muslim communities might find it useful to reflect on. The first set of issues is to do with what might be seen as 'good practice' in Islamic nurture. We did not set out to pass judgement on families and this book is not being written from a faith position. However, taking the range of research data into account, there seems to be a degree of consensus from parents themselves about some aspects of what makes for successful Islamic nurture. So these suggestions are theirs more than ours.

The first point is that most parents agreed the meanings of Islamic practices should be explained to children from a young age. Not all parents managed to do this, but there was a general view that the best approach was to explain the purpose of rituals and the reasons that certain kinds of behaviour are encouraged and others discouraged. Explaining *why* is more likely to be effective than simply telling children *what* to do. Equally, explaining why is more likely to be effective than simply invoking the afterlife, in telling them that some things lead to Hellfire and others to Paradise. The second point to do with good practice relates to formal education. There was a range of different pedagogies in evidence, from traditional rote-learning of the Qur'an through to the highly participative re-enactment of the Hajj. There is no doubt room for several different approaches. Some rote-learning may be appropriate for memorization. However, some more interactive education is also necessary. We saw examples of modern teaching methods such as small group learning. We also saw some examples of charismatic individual teachers. Not all children in the study experienced these more engaging methods of learning, however. Children clearly valued classes that engaged them more than those which did not. And the testimonies of parents when talking about their own upbringing were evidence of the necessity, again, for *meanings* to be explained in formal supplementary education, in addition to learning the sound of the Arabic words of the Qur'an which will no doubt continue to be required.

The second set of issues is broadly to do with equality and diversity. Many interviewees were critical of mosques which were exclusively male. Given the importance of mothers in religious nurture, mosques could potentially support this vital role more pro-actively by becoming more accessible to women. And providing the option for girls to participate in mosques in the teenage years is another issue needing attention. Mosques could also reflect on the strength that can be derived from the multiculturalism inherent in Islam, especially for British Muslims from smaller ethnic groups. We heard some criticism of most mosques being dominated by particular ethnic groups. Not all interviewees emphasized the need for multi-ethnic mosques, as some seemed to value the opportunity to mix with those who speak the same community language, for example, but the current picture at least in this city, is of provision being fairly unbalanced, with few mosques which are genuinely ethnically mixed. Finally, Muslims organizations could potentially think about realistic ways of supporting the greater involvement of fathers in religious nurture, given the challenges of some men's working hours. The Fatherhood Institute (2010), a UK Think Tank, has done some useful work on this issue along with the An-Nisa Society.

For public services

This last subsection considers some general implications from the study which are relevant to health, social care and education staff. One general implication seems to be the need to appreciate the monotheistic world view of Islam and the importance of religious obedience. A very generalized and individualized concept of 'spirituality' is often used in connection with health and social care. Whilst this is potentially useful in working with a range of different interpretations of meaning and purpose in diverse populations, it seems to be inadequate in capturing the significance of formal religion for many people, including most Muslims (Gilliat-Ray, 2003). However, although we emphasize collective practice and maintenance of traditions, we are by no means suggesting that 'Muslims' are a homogenous group. In addition to core skills of cultural competence, front-line staff in health care, social care and education would benefit from some core basic knowledge of Islam and also from education about Muslim diversity, recognizing that there is not just one 'Muslim community' but a diverse collection of communities, ethnic backgrounds, schools of thought and individual religious histories. The Dave Eggers (2009) novel *Zeitoun* contains a well-expressed summary of Muslim diversity. He is referring in this passage to the character Kathy who converted to Islam.

> She'd assumed that Muslims were a monolithic group, and that all Muslims were made of the same devout and unbending stock. But she learned that there were Shiite and Sunni interpretations of the Qur'an, and within any mosque there were the same variations in faith and commitment as there were in any church. There were Muslims who treated their faith lightly, and those who knew every word of the Qur'an and its companion guide to behavior, the *hadith*. There were Muslims who knew almost nothing about their religion, who worshiped a few times a year, and those who obeyed the strictest interpretation of their faith. There were Muslim women who wore T-shirts and jeans and Muslim women who covered themselves head to toe. There were Muslim men who modeled their lives on the life of the Prophet, and those who strayed and fell short. There were passive Muslims, uncertain Muslims, borderline agnostic Muslims, devout Muslims, and Muslims who twisted the words of the Qur'an to suit their temporary desire and agendas. It was all very familiar, intrinsic to any faith. (Eggers, 2009, p. 72)

In our study we described considerable consensus between parents that formal supplementary education was a central part of Islamic nurture. There was diversity and difference between classes, with some being arranged privately in the home and others taking place in mosques. There were three main kinds of classes: learning the Qur'an in the original Arabic; Islamic Studies; and spoken Arabic language with some Islamic Studies. However, the fact that all but one of the families in our study with children old enough sent them to one or more of these classes speaks to their continuing importance. Service providers need to be conscious of the significance of this tradition when working with Muslim children. Schools need to appreciate the amount of out-of-school learning Muslim children are involved in. There is little point in regarding supplementary education as a problem, since it is unlikely to fade away and it has to be worked with. One positive approach would be to value the transferable skills involved in religious learning. In general terms, dialogue and collaboration between state schools and Muslim organizations would be helpful. It may be that supplementary education can be combined with mainstream schooling in some way, as is being tried in some areas. This might, for example, involve homework clubs after school which include some religious education.

We have created six digital stories on the theme of 'learning to be a Muslim', for use in schools and in the training of teachers and other professionals who work with Muslim children. These were made by the children themselves with the assistance of Storyworks at the University of Glamorgan. These are freely available online at <http://vimeo.com/channels/learningtobeamuslim>. The content reflects the children's experiences of religious nurture and strongly echoes themes from this book, although not all the children who have made digital stories were research participants. The stories give a sense of diversity, as some children focus more on formal learning than others and some are more focused on specific aspects of Islamic conduct, such as wearing hijab.

Given that the inter-generational transmission of Islam is relatively strong and Muslim families are likely to have a clear monotheistic world view, public services might need to explore the potential for some services being provided from an Islamic perspective. This is not a straightforward issue because not all Muslims will agree on what constitutes an Islamic perspective. A Salafi perspective might look quite different from a Sufi one, for example. However, there are now several examples in some British cities of Islamic social welfare organizations being established and these have found a way to negotiate a variety of traditions and schools of thought. These religious third sector social welfare organizations are likely to be part of the picture in future and their development would seem quite appropriate in responding to the religious needs of British Muslims. One specific family-related example of mainstream services from an Islamic perspective is parenting education. Several interventions have been found in randomized controlled trials to be very effective in improving attachment and parents' management of children but most interventions have seen little cultural adaptation. To combine behaviour management techniques or the strengthening of attachment with messages about parenting from the Qur'an and *hadith* would seem to have great potential for supporting Muslim families. Examples of programmes attempting to do this in the UK are Approachable Parenting (2013) and Family Links (2012).

References

Abbas, T. (2010). Muslim-on-Muslim social research: knowledge, power and religio-cultural identities. *Social Epistemology* 24(2): 123–36.

Abercrombie, N. (2004). *Sociology: A Short Introduction*. Cambridge: Polity.

Ahmed, F. (2012). Tarbiyah for shakhsiyah (educating for identity): seeking out culturally coherent pedagogy for Muslim children in Britain. *Compare: A Journal of Comparative and International Education*: 42(5): 725–49.

Ali, S. H. (2009). *Islam and Education: Conflict and Conformity in Pakistan's Madrassahs*. Oxford: Oxford University Press.

Amer, F. (1997). *Islamic supplementary education in Britain—a critique*. PhD, Birmingham: University of Birmingham.

Ammerman, N. (ed.) (2007). *Everyday Religion: Observing Modern Religious Lives*. New York: Oxford University Press.

Ammerman, N. (2009). Congregations: local, social and religious. In P. B. Clarke (ed.) *The Oxford Handbook of the Sociology of Religion*. Oxford: Oxford University Press, pp. 562–80.

Ansari, H. (2004). *The 'Infidel' Within: Muslims in Britain, 1800 to the Present*. London: Hurst.

Anthias, F. (2002). Where do I belong? Narrating collective identity and translocational positionality. *Ethnicities* 2(4): 491–514.

Anwar, M. (1979). *The Myth of Return*. London: Heinemann Educational Books.

Approachable Parenting (2013). 5 Pillars of Parenting. <http://www.approachableparenting.com>

Association of Muslim Social Scientists/FAIR (2004). *Muslims on Education: A Position Paper*. Richmond: Association of Muslim Social Scientists.

Bagnall, G., Longhurst, B., and Savage, M. (2003). Children, belonging and social capital: the PTA and middle class narratives of social involvement in the northwest of England. *Sociological Research Online* 8(4): <http://www.socresonline.org.uk/8/4/bagnall.html>

Bak, M. and van Bromssen, K. (2010). Interrogating childhood and diaspora through the voices of children in Sweden. *Childhood* 17(1): 113–28.

Barnes, M. and Morris, K. (2007). Networks, connectedness and resilience: learning from the Children's Fund in context. *Social Policy and Society* 6(2): 193–7.

Barrett, J. (2007). Cognitive science of religion: What is it and why is it? *Religion Compass* 1(6): 768–86.

Barrett, J. (2011). Cognitive science of religion: looking back, looking forward. *Journal for the Scientific Study of Religion* 50(2): 229–39.

Barrett, M. (2005). Children's understanding of, and feelings about, countries and national groups. In M. Barrett and E. Buchanan-Barrow (eds) *Children's Understanding of Society*. Hove: Psychology Press.

Barthes, F. (1993). *Balinese Worlds*. Chicago: Chicago University Press.

Barton, S. (1986). *The Bengali Muslims of Bradford: a Study of their Observance of Islam with Special Reference to the Function of the Mosque and the Work of the Imam*. Leeds: Community Religions Project, University of Leeds.

Bauman, Z. (2004a). *Identity*. Cambridge: Polity.

Bauman, Z. (2004b). *Wasted Lives: Modernity and its Outcasts*. Cambridge: Polity.

Beaujouan, É. and Ní Bhrolcháin, M. (2011). Cohabitation and marriage in Britain since the 1970s. *Population Trends* 145: 35–59.

Becher, H. (2008). *Family Practices in South Asian Muslim Families: Parenting in a Multi-Faith Britain*. Basingstoke: Palgrave.

Beck, U. and Beck-Gernsheim, E. (2001). *Individualization*. London: Sage.

Bengtson, V. L., Copen, C. E., Putney, N., and Silverstein, M. (2009). A longitudinal study of the intergenerational transmission of religion. *International Sociology* 24(3): 325–45.

Berger, P. (1967). *The Sacred Canopy: Elements of a Sociological Theory of Religion*. New York: Anchor Books.

Berger, P. (1999). The desecularization of the world: a global overview. In P. Berger (ed.) *The Desecularization of the World: Resurgent Religion and World Politics*. Washington, DC: Ethics and Public Policy Center.

Berliner, D. and Sarró, R. (eds) (2007a). *Learning Religion: Anthropological Approaches*. New York: Berghahn.

Berliner, D. and Sarró, R. (2007b). On learning religion. An introduction. In D. Berliner and R. Sarró (eds) *Learning Religion: Anthropological Approaches*, New York: Berghahn.

Bierens, H., Hughes, N., Hek, R., and Spicer, N. (2007). Preventing social exclusion of refugee and asylum-seeking children: building new networks. *Social Policy and Society* 6(2): 219–29.

Birt, J. and Lewis, P. (2010). Producing Islamic knowledge: transmission and dissemination in Western Europe. In Allievi, S. and Bruinessen, M. V. (eds) *Producing Islamic Knowledge in Western Europe*. London: Routledge, pp. 91–120.

Birt, Y. (2008). Takeaway lives. *Emel*, February issue, p. 18.

Bolognani, M. (2007). Islam, ethnography and politics: methodological issues in researching amongst West Yorkshire Pakistanis in 2005. *International Journal of Social Research Methodology* 10(4): 279–93.

Bond, R. (2006). Belonging and becoming: national identity and exclusion. *Sociology* 40(4): 609–26.

Borland, M., Laybourn, A., Hill, M., and Brown, J. (1998). *Middle Childhood: The Perspectives of Children and Parents*. London: Jessica Kingsley.

Bourdieu, P. (1984). *Distinction. A Social Critique of the Judgement of Taste*. New York: Routledge.

Boyatzis, C. J., Dollahite, D. C., and Marks, L. D. (2006). The family as a context for religious and spiritual development in children and youth. In E. Roehlkepartain, P. Ebstyne King, L. Wagener, and P. L. Benson (eds) *The Handbook of Spiritual Development in Childhood and Adolescence*. London: Sage, pp. 297–309.

Boyle, H. (2004). *Quranic Schools: Agents of Preservation and Change*. London: Routledge Falmer.

Boyer, P. (1994). *The Naturalness of Religious Ideas. A Cognitive Theory of Religion*. Berkeley: University of California Press.

Boyer, P. (2000). Functional origins of religious concepts: ontological and strategic selection in evolved minds. *Journal of the Royal Anthropological Institute* 6: 195–214.

Breen, D. (2009). Reflections on the positionality of the white, male non-Muslim researcher in Muslim primary schools: the realities of researching Muslim women. Presentation at the 'Researching Muslims in Britain' conference, Cardiff, April 15.

Brice, K. (2010). *A Minority Within a Minority: A Report on Converts to Islam in the United Kingdom*. London: Faith Matters.

Brubaker, R. and Cooper, F. (2000). Beyond 'identity'. *Theory and Society* 29: 1–47.

Bruce, S. (1996). *Religion in the Modern World: From Cathedrals to Cults*. Oxford: Oxford University Press.

Bruce, S. (2002). *God is Dead: Secularization in the West*. Oxford: Blackwell.

Bunt, G. (1998). Decision-making concerns in British Islamic environments. *Islam and Christian-Muslim Relations* 9(1): 103–13.

Cadge, W. and Ecklund, E. H. (2007). Immigration and religion. *Annual Review of Sociology* 33: 359–79.

Cadge, W., Levitt, P., and Smilde, D. (2011). De-centering and re-centering: rethinking concepts and methods in the sociological study of religion. *Journal for the Scientific Study of Religion* 50(3):437–49.

Cantle, T. (2001). *Community Cohesion: A Report of the Independent Review Team*. London: Home Office.

Castells, M. (1997). *The Power of Identity,* Oxford: Blackwell.

Cesari, J. (2004). Islam in the West: modernity and globalization revisited. In B. Schaebler and L. Stenberg (eds) *Globalization and the Muslim World: Culture, Religion, and Modernity.* New York: Syracuse University Press, pp. 80–92.

Chambers, P. (2006). Secularisation, Wales and Islam. *Journal of Contemporary Religion* 21(3): 325–340.

Charsley, K. (2006). Risk and ritual: the protection of British Pakistani women in transnational marriage. *Journal of Ethnic and Migration Studies* 32(7): 1169–87.

Charsley, K. (2007). Risk, trust, gender and transnational cousin marriage among British Pakistanis. *Ethnic and Racial Studies* 30(6): 1117–31.

Cherti, M. and Bradley, L. (2011). *Inside Madrassas*. London: Institute for Public Policy Research.

Clarke, A. (2004). The Mosaic approach and research with young children In V. Lewis, M. Kellett, and C. Robinson (eds) *The Reality of Research with Children and Young People*. London: Sage.

Clayton, J. (2011). Living the multicultural city: acceptance, belonging and young identities in the city of Leicester, England. *Ethnic and Racial Studies* 35 (9): 1673–93.

Coffey, A. (1999). *The Ethnographic Self.* London: Sage.

Cohen, J. (1960). A coefficient of agreement for nominal scales. *Educational and Psychological Measurement* 20: 37.

Cohen, R. (1995). Fuzzy frontiers of identity: The British case. *Social Identities* 1(1): 35–62.

Coles, M. (2008). *Every Muslim Child Matters.* Stoke-on-Trent: Trentham Books.

Condor, S. (2000). Pride and prejudice: identity management in English people's talk about 'this country'. *Discourse and Society* 11(2): 175–205.

Connor, P. (2010). Contexts of immigrant receptivity and immigrant religious outcomes: the case of Muslims in Western Europe. *Ethnic and Racial Studies* 33(3): 376–403.

Crockett, A. and Voas, D. (2006). Generations of decline: religious change in 20th century Britain. *Journal for the Scientific Study of Religion* 45(4): 567–84.

Dahya, B. (1973). Pakistanis in Britain: transients or settlers? *Race* 14(3): 241–77.

Dahya, B. (1974). The nature of Pakistani ethnicity in industrial cities in Britain. In A. Cohen (ed.) *Urban Ethnicity.* London: Tavistock, pp. 77–118.

Davie, G. (1994). *Religion in Britain Since 1945: Believing Without Belonging.* Oxford: Blackwell.

Davie, G. (2007). *The Sociology of Religion.* London: Sage.

Dawkins, R. (2006). *The God Delusion.* New York: Bantam Books.

Demerath, N. J. III (2007). Secularization and sacralisation deconstructed and reconstructed. In J. A. Beckford and N. J. Demerath III (eds) *The Sage Handbook of the Sociology of Religion.* London: Sage, pp. 56–80.

Dinham, A. Furbey, R., and Lowndes, V. (eds) (2009). *Faith in the Public Realm: Controversies, Policies and Practices.* Bristol: Policy Press.

Eggers, D. (2009). *Zeitoun.* London: Hamish Hamilton.

Eickelman, D. E. and Piscatori, J. (2004). *Muslim Politics* second edition. Princeton: Princeton University Press.

Esposito, J. and Mogahed, D. (2007). *Who Speaks for Islam? What a Billion Muslims Really Think.* New York: Gallup Press.

Evans, N. (1985). Regulating the reserve army: Arabs, Blacks and the local state in Cardiff, 1919–1945. *Immigrants and Minorities* 4(2): 68–115.

Family Links (2012). Information on the Nurturing Programme's 'Islamic values' parenting programme. <http://www.familylinks.org.uk/training/nurturing-programme-islamic-values.html>

Fatherhood Institute (2010). Research Summary: Muslim Fathers. <http://www.fatherhoodinstitute.org/2010/fatherhood-institute-research-summary-muslim-fathers/>

Field, C. D. (2011). Young British Muslims since 9/11: a composite attitudinal profile. *Religion, State and Society* 39(2/3): 159–75.

Finch, J. (2007). Displaying families. *Sociology* 41(1): 65–81.

Finch, J. (2008). Naming names: kinship, individuality and personal names. *Sociology* 42(4): 709–25.

Foucault, M. (1977). *Discipline and Punish: The Birth of the Prison.* London: Penguin.

Fowler, J. (1981). *Stages of Faith: The Psychology of Human Development.* NY: Harper and Row.

Gellner, E. (1981). *Muslim Society.* Cambridge: Cambridge University Press.

Gent, B. (2005). Intercultural learning: education and Islam—a case study. In: R. Jackson and U. McKenna (eds) *Intercultural Education and Religious Plurality.* Oslo: Oslo Coalition on Freedom of Religion or Belief, pp. 43–53.

Gent, B. (2006). The educational experience of British Muslims: some life-story images, *Muslim Education Quarterly* 23(3–4): 33–42.

Gent, B. (2006a). The educational experience of British Muslims: some life-story images, *Muslim Education Quarterly* 23(3–4): 33–42.

Gent, B. (2006b). *Muslim supplementary classes and the wider learning community.* Ed.D, Coventry: University of Warwick

Gent, B. (2011). The world of the British hifz class student: observations, findings and implications for education and further research. *British Journal of Religious Education* 33(1): 3–15.

Gent, B. (2011a). 'But you can't retire as a hafiz': Fieldwork within a British Hifz class. *Muslim Education Quarterly* 24(1–2): 55–63.

Gent, B. (2011b). The world of the British *hifz* class student: observations, findings and implications for education and further research. *British Journal of Religious Education* 33(1): 3–15.

Gibbon, J. (2008). God is great, God is good: teaching God concepts in Turkish Islamic sermons. *Poetics* 36: 389–403.

Giddens, A. (1991). *Modernity and Self-Identity: Self and Society in the Late Modern Age.* Cambridge: Polity Press.

Giddens, A. (1992). *The Transformation of Intimacy: Sexuality, Love and Eroticism in Modern Societies.* Cambridge: Polity.

Giddens, A. (2002). *Runaway World.* Exeter: Profile Books.

Gilliat-Ray, S. (2000). The sociology of religious specialists. In P. Baltes and N. Smelser (eds) *International Encyclopaedia of the Social and Behavioural Sciences.* Surrey: Elsevier Science 19: 13132–6.

Gilliat-Ray, S. (2003). Nursing, professionalism and spirituality. *Journal of Contemporary Religion* 18(3): 335–49.

Gilliat-Ray, S. (2005). Closed worlds: (not) accessing Deobandi dar ul-uloom in Britain. *Fieldwork in Religion* 1(1): 7–33.

Gilliat-Ray, S. (2006). Educating the *Ulema*: centres of Islamic religious training in Britain. *Islam and Christian–Muslim Relations* 17(1): 55–76.

Gilliat-Ray, S. (2010). Body-works and fieldwork: research with British Muslim chaplains. *Culture and Religion* 11(4): 413–32.

Gilliat-Ray, S. (2010). *Muslims in Britain: An Introduction.* Cambridge: Cambridge University Press.

References

Gilliat-Ray, S. (2011). Being there: the experience of shadowing a British Muslim hospital chaplain. *Qualitative Research* 11(5): 469–86.

Gilliat-Ray, S. and Mellor J. (2010). *Bilad al-Welsh* (Land of the Welsh): Muslims in Cardiff, south Wales: past, present and future. *The Muslim World* 100(4): 452–75.

Goffman, E. (1990 [1959]). *The Presentation of Self in Everyday Life*. London: Penguin.

Greenlaw, L. (2007). *The Importance of Music to Girls*. London: Faber and Faber.

Guest, M. (2009). The reproduction and transmission of religion. In P. B. Clarke (ed.) *The Oxford Handbook of the Sociology of Religion*. Oxford: Oxford University Press.

Hafez, S. (2003). *Safe Children, Sound Learning: Guidance for Madressahs*. Huddersfield: Kirklees Metropolitan Council.

Haider, G. (1996). Muslim space and the practice of architecture. In B. D. Metcalf (ed.) *Making Muslim Space in North America and Europe*. Berkeley: University of California Press, pp. 31–45.

Hall, R (2004). Inside out: some notes on carrying out feminist research in cross-cultural interviews with South Asian women immigration applicants. *International Journal of Social Research Methodology* 7: 2.

Halstead, J. M. (2004). 'An Islamic Concept of Education'. *Comparative Education* 40(4): 517–29.

Halstead, M. (2005). Muslims in the UK and education. In Choudhury, T. (ed.) *Muslims in the UK: Policies for Engaged Citizens*. Budapest: Open Society Institute, pp. 101–92.

Hammad, I. M. (2012). Factors that cause stress for Islamic Studies teachers in the UK. *European Journal of Social Sciences* 30(4): 597–611.

Hayes, B. C. and Pittelkow, Y. (1993). Religious belief, transmission, and the family: an Australian study. *Journal of Marriage and Family* 55: 755–66.

Heelas, P. and Woodhead, L., with Seel, B., Szerszynski, B., and Tusting, K. (2005). *The Spiritual Revolution. Why Religion is Giving Way to Spirituality*. Oxford: Blackwell.

Heffner, R. and Zaman, M. Q. (2007a). Introduction. In: R. Heffner and M. Q. Zaman (eds) *Schooling Islam: The Culture and Politics of Modern Muslim Education*. Princeton/Oxford: Princeton University Press, pp. 1–39.

Heffner, R. and Zaman, M. Q. (eds) (2007b). *Schooling Islam: The Culture and Politics of Modern Muslim Education*. Princeton/Oxford: Princeton University Press.

Hemming, P. (2011). Educating for religious citizenship: multiculturalism and national identity in an English multi-faith primary school. *Transactions of the Institute of British Geographers* 36: 441–54.

Hemming, P. J. and Madge, N. (2011). Researching children, youth and religion: identity, complexity and agency. *Childhood* 19(1): 38–51.

Herberg, W. (1955). *Protestant, Catholic, Jew: An Essay in American Religious Sociology*. Garden City, NJ: Doubleday.

Hervieu-Léger, D. (1998). The transmission and formation of socioreligious identities in modernity. *International Sociology* 13(2): 213–28.

Hervieu-Léger, D. (2000). *Religion as a Chain of Memory*. New Brunswick: Rutgers University Press.

Hewer, C. (2001). Schools for Muslims. *Oxford Review of Education* 27(4): 515–27.

Hewitt, R. (1996). *Routes of Racism*. Trentham Books: Stoke on Trent.

Hill, M. (1989). The role of social networks in the care of young children. *Children and Society* 3(3): 195–211.

Hill, M. (1997). Research review: participatory research with children. *Child and Family Social Work* 2: 171–83.

Hoge, D. R., Petrillo, G. H., and Smith, E. I. (1982). Transmission of religious and social values from parents to teenage children. *Journal of Marriage and Family* 44(3): 569–80.

Holland, J., Reynolds, T., and Weller, S. (2007). Transitions, networks and communities: the significance of social capital in the lives of children and young people. *Journal of Youth Studies* 10(1): 97–116.

Holland, S. and O'Neill, S. (2006). 'We had to be there to make sure it was what we wanted': Enabling children's participation in family decision-making through the family group conference. *Childhood* 13(1): 91–111.

Hopkins, P. (2007). 'Blue squares', 'proper Muslims' and transnational networks: Narratives of national and religious identities amongst young Muslim men living in Scotland. *Ethnicities* 7: 61.

Hurdley, R. (2006). Dismantling mantelpieces: narrating identities and materializing culture in the home. *Sociology* 40(4): 717–33.

Husain, A. (2004). Islamic education: why is there a need for it? *Journal of Beliefs and Values* 25(3): 317–23.

Hussain, S. (2008). *Muslims on the Map: A National Survey of Social Trends in Britain*. London: I. B. Tauris.

Institute of Community Cohesion (2008). *Understanding and Appreciating Muslim Diversity: Towards Better Engagement and Participation*. Coventry: iCoCo.

Jackson, R. and Nesbitt, E. (1993). *Hindu Children in Britain*. Stoke on Trent: Trentham.

Jacobson, J. (1998). *Islam in Transition: Religion and Identity amongst British Pakistani Youth*. London: Routledge.

James, A., Jenks, C., and Prout, A. (1998). *Theorising Childhood*. Cambridge: Polity.

James, A. and Prout, A. (1997). *Constructing and Reconstructing Childhood: Contemporary Issues in the Sociological Study of Childhood*. London: Routledge.

Jamieson, L. (1998). *Intimacy*. Cambridge: Polity.

Jenkins, R. (2002). *Pierre Bourdieu*. London: Routledge.

Kalra, V. (2000). *From Textile Mills to Taxi Ranks: Experiences of Migration, Labour and Social Change*. Aldershot: Ashgate.

Kemp, C. (1996). Islamic cultures: health care beliefs and practices, *American Journal of Health Behaviour* 20(3): 83–9.

King, J. (1997). Tablighi Jamaat and the Deobandi mosques in Britain. In S. Vertovec and C. Peach (eds) *Islam in Europe: the Politics of Religion and Community*. Basingstoke: Macmillan Press, pp. 129–46.

Leonard, M. (2004). Bonding and bridging social capital: reflections from Belfast. *Sociology* 38(5): 927–44.

Leonard, M. (2005). Children, childhood and social capital: exploring the links. *Sociology* 39(4): 605–22.

Lewis, P. (2007). *Young, British, and Muslim.* London: Continuum.

MacInnes, J. (2004). The sociology of identity: social science or social comment? *British Journal of Sociology* 55(4): 531–43.

Mahmood, S. (2012 [2001]). Rehearsed spontaneity and the conventionality of ritual: disciplines of salat. In J. Kreinath (ed.) *The Anthropology of Islam Reader.* Abingdon: Routledge, pp. 121–41.

Mandaville, P. (2001). *Transnational Muslim Politics: Reimagining the Umma.* London: Routledge.

Martin, D. (2005). *On Secularization: Towards a Revised General Theory.* Aldershot: Ashgate.

Martinez, P. (2009). Muslim homeschooling. In Y. Y. Haddad, F. Senzai and J. I. Smith (eds) *Educating the Muslims of America.* New York: Oxford University Press.

Mateos, P., Longley, P. A., and O'Sullivan, D. (2011). Ethnicity and population structure in personal naming networks. *PLoS ONE* 6(9): e22943. DOI: 10.1371/journal.pone.0022943.

Mazumdar, S. and Mazumdar, S. (2005). The articulation of religion in domestic space: rituals in the immigrant Muslim home. In: P. Stewart and A. Strathern (eds) *Contesting Rituals: Islam and Practices of Identity-Making.* Durham, North Carolina: Carolina Academic Press, pp. 125–45.

McGuire, M. (2008). *Lived Religion: Faith and Practice in Everyday Life.* Oxford: Oxford University Press.

McIntosh, I., Sim, D., and Robertson, D. (2004). 'We hate the English, but not you because you're our pal': Identification of the 'English' in Scotland. *Sociology* 38(1): 43–59.

McLoughlin, S. (2000). Researching Muslim minorities: some reflections on fieldwork in Britain. *Journal of Semitic Studies Supplements, Oxford University Press* 12: 175–94.

Meer, N. (2007). Muslim Schools in Britain: challenging mobilisations or logical developments? *Asia Pacific Journal of Education* 27(1): 55–71.

Meer, N. (2009). Identity articulations, mobilization, and autonomy in the movement for Muslim schools in Britain. *Race Ethnicity and Education* 12(3): 379–99.

Mellor, P. and Shilling, C. (2010). Body pedagogics and the religious *habitus*: a new direction for the sociological study of religion. *Religion* 40: 27–38.

Mercia Group (2006). *Review of the Evidence Base on Faith Communities.* London: Office of the Deputy Prime Minister.

Merry, M. (2007). *Culture, Identity and Islamic Schooling: a Philosophical Approach.* London: Macmillan.

Metcalf, B. (ed.) (1996). *Making Muslim Space in North America and Europe.* Berkeley: University of California Press.

Mills, S. (2009). Citizenship and faith: Muslim scout groups. In R. Phillips (ed.) *Muslim Spaces of Hope: Geographies of Possibility in Britain and the West.* London: Zed Books, pp. 85–103.

Mirza, K. (1989). *The Silent Cry: Second Generation Bradford Women Speak.* Birmingham: CSIC.

Modood, T. (2010). *Still Not Easy Being British: Struggles for a Multicultural Citizenship.* Stoke-on-Trent: Trentham Books.

Modood, T., Beishon, S., and Virdee, S. (1994). *Changing Ethnic Identities.* London: Policy Studies Institute.

Modood, T., Berthoud, R., Lakey, J., Nazroco, J., Smith, P., Virdee, S., and Beishon, S. (1997). *Ethnic Minorities in Britain: Diversity and Disadvantage.* The Fourth National Survey of Ethnic Minorities in Britain. London: Policy Studies Institute.

Mogra, I. (2004). Makatib education in Britain: a review of trends and some suggestions for policy. *Muslim Education Quarterly* 21(4): 19–27.

Mogra, I. (2005). Moving forward with Makatib: the role of reformative sanctions. *Muslim Education Quarterly* 22(3 and 4): 52–64.

Mogra, I. (2010). Teachers and teaching: a contemporary Muslim understanding. *Religious Education* 105(3): 317–29.

Mogra, I. (2011). On Being a Muslim Teacher in England. *American Journal of Islamic Social Sciences* 28(2): 34–62.

Mohammad, R. (2005). Negotiating spaces of the home, the education system, and the labour market: The case of young, working-class, British Pakistani Muslim women. In G.-W. Falah and C. Nagel (eds) *Geographies of Muslim Women: Gender, Religion and Space.* New York: The Guildford Press, pp. 178–200.

Mondal, A. (2008). *Young British Muslim Voices.* Oxford: Greenwood World Publishing.

Morgan, D. (1996). *Family Connections: An Introduction to Family Studies,* Cambridge: Polity.

Morgan, D. (2011a). Locating 'family practices'. *Sociological Research Online* 16(4): 14. <http://www.socresonline.org.uk/16/4/14.html>

Morgan, D. (2011b). *Rethinking Family Practices.* Basingstoke: Palgrave Macmillan.

Morrow, V. (1999). Conceptualising social capital in relation to the well-being of children and young people: a critical review. *Sociological Review* 47(4): 744–65.

Mukadam, M. and Scott-Baumann, A. (2010). The training and development of Muslim Faith leaders: Current practice and future possibilities. London: Communities and Local Government.

Murata, S. (1992). *The Tao of Islam: A Sourcebook on Gender Relationships in Islamic Thought.* New York: State University of New York Press.

Nesbitt, E (1999). Researching 8 to 13 year-olds' perspectives on their experience of religion. In A. Lewis and G. Lindsay (eds) *Researching Children's Perspectives.* Buckingham: Open University Press.

Nesbitt, E. (2004). *Intercultural Education: Ethnographic and Religious Approaches.* Brighton: Sussex Academic Press.

Nesbitt, E. and Arweck, E. (2010). Issues arising from an ethnographic investigation of the religious identity formation of young people in mixed-faith families. *Fieldwork in Religion* 5(1): 8–31.

Nielsen, J. (1981). Muslim education at home and abroad. *British Journal of Religious Education* 3(3): 94–9.

O'Beirne, M. (2004). *Religion in England and Wales: Findings from the 2001 Home Office Citizenship Survey.* Home Office Research Study 274. London: Home Office Research, Development and Statistics Directorate.

O'Brien, M., Rustin, M., Jones, D., and Sloan, D. (2000). Children's independent spatial mobility in the urban public realm. *Childhood* 7(3): 257–77.

Oakley, A. (1981). Interviewing women: a contradiction in terms. In H. Roberts (ed.) *Doing Feminist Research.* London: Routledge and Kegan Paul.

Oestergaard, K. (2009). The process of becoming Muslim: ritualization and embodiment. *Journal of Ritual Studies* 23(1): 1–14.

Office for National Statistics (ONS) (2005). *The National Statistics Socio-Economic Classification User Manual.* Basingstoke: Palgrave Macmillan.

Office for National Statistics (ONS) (2006). *Focus on Ethnicity and Religion,* 2006 edition. Basingstoke: Palgrave Macmillan.

Ollwig, K. F. and Gulløv, E. (2003). Towards an anthropology of children and place. In K. F. Ollwig and E. Gulløv (eds) *Children's Places: Cross-Cultural Perspectives.* London: Routledge, pp. 1–20.

Omar, A. (2009). *Fiqh* of charity in the UK: Methodological issues in researching amongst Muslims in Wiltshire. Presentation at the 'Researching Muslims in Britain' conference, Cardiff, April 15.

Orsi, R. (2004). *Between Heaven and Earth. The Religious Worlds People Make and the Scholars who Study Them.* Princeton: Princeton University Press.

Østberg, S. (2006). Islamic nurture and identity management: The life world of Muslim children and young people in Norway. In R. Jackson and A. McGrady (eds) *The International Handbook of the Religious, Moral and Spiritual Dimensions in Education.* Berlin: Springer.

Parker-Jenkins, M. (1995). *Children of Islam. A Teacher's Guide to Meeting the Needs of Muslim Pupils.* Stoke on Trent: Trentham Books.

Peach, C. (2006). Muslims in the 2001 Census of England and Wales: gender and economic disadvantage. *Ethnic and Racial Studies* 29(4): 629–55.

Peter, F. (2006). Individualization and religious authority in Western European Islam. *Islam and Christian-Muslim Relations* 17(1): 105–18.

Phillips, D. (2006). Parallel lives? Challenging discourses of British Muslim self-segregation. *Environment and Planning D: Society and Space* 24(1): 25–40.

Phillips, D. (2009). Creating home spaces: young British Muslim women's identity and conceptualisations of home. in Hopkins, P. and Gale, R. (eds) *Muslims in Britain: Race, Place and Identities.* Edinburgh: Edinburgh University Press, pp. 23–36.

Phillipson, C., Ahmed, N., and Latimer, J. (2003). *Women in Transition: A Study of the Experiences of Bangladeshi Women Living in Tower Hamlets.* Bristol: The Policy Press.

Pinker, S. (2003). *The Blank Slate. The Modern Denial of Human Nature*. London: Penguin.

Pinquart, M. and Silbereisen, R. K. (2004). Transmission of values from adolescents to their parents: the role of value content and authoritative parenting. *Adolescence* 39(153): 83–100.

Pluss, C. (2009). Migration and the globalization of religion. In P. B. Clark (ed.) *The Oxford Handbook of the Sociology of Religion*. Oxford: Oxford University Press, pp. 491–506.

Prout, A. (2005). *The Future of Childhood*. Abingdon: Routledge.

Putnam, R.D. (2000). *Bowling Alone*. New York: Simon and Schuster.

Qureshi, K., Charsley, K., and Shaw, A. (2012). Marital instability amongst British Pakistanis: transnationality, conjugalities and Islam. *Ethnic and Racial Studies*: online advance access. DOI: 10.1080/01419870.2012.720691.

Revell, L. (2010). Religious education, conflict and diversity: an exploration of young children's perceptions of Islam, *Educational Studies* 36(2): 207–15.

Roberts, B. (1995). Welsh identity in a former mining valley: social images and imagined communities. *Contemporary Wales* 7: 77–95.

Roehlkepartain, E., Ebstyne King, P., Wagener, L., and Benson, P. L. (eds) (2006a). *The Handbook of Spiritual Development in Childhood and Adolescence*. London: Sage.

Roehlkepartain, E., Ebstyne King, P., Wagener, L., and Benson, P. L (2006b). Spiritual development in childhood and adolescence: Moving to the scientific mainstream. In E. Roehlkepartain, P. Ebstyne King, L. Wagener, and P.L. Benson (eds) (2006). *The Handbook of Spiritual Development in Childhood and Adolescence*. London: Sage, pp. 1–15.

Rosowsky, A. (2012). Faith, phonics and identity: reading in faith complementary schools. *Literacy*: on-line 'early view' in advance of print. DOI: 10.1111/j.1741-4369.2012.00669.x.

Roy, O. (2004). *Globalized Islam*. New York: Columbia University Press.

Saifullah-Khan, V. (1976). Pakistanis in Britain: perceptions of a population. *New Community* 5(3): 222–9.

Sanghera, G. and Thapar-Bjorkert, S. (2008). Methodological dilemmas: gatekeepers and positionality in Bradford. *Ethnic and Racial Studies* 31(3): 543–62.

Scheitle, C. P. and Dougherty, K. D. (2008). The sociology of religious organizations. *Sociology Compass* 2/3: 981–99.

Schwartz, K. D., Bukowski, W. M., and Aoki, W. T. (2006). Mentors, friends, and gurus: peer and nonparent influences on spiritual development. in E. Roehlkepartain, P. Ebstyne King, L. Wagener, and P. L. Benson (eds) *The Handbook of Spiritual Development in Childhood and Adolescence*. London: Sage, pp. 310–23.

Scourfield, J. and Davies, A. (2005). Children's accounts of Wales as racialised and inclusive. *Ethnicities* 5(1): 83–107.

Scourfield, J., Dicks, B. Drakeford, M., and Davies, A. (2006). *Children, Place and Identity: Nation and Locality in Middle Childhood*. London: Routledge.

Scourfield, J., Evans, J., Shah, W., and Beynon, H. (2005). The negotiation of minority ethnic identities in virtually all-white communities: research with children and their families in the South Wales Valleys. *Children and Society* 19: 211–24.

Seddon, M. S. (2010). Constructing identities of 'difference' and 'resistance': the politics of being Muslim and British. *Social Semiotics* 20(5): 557–71.

Shankland, D. (2004). Modes of religiosity and the legacy of Ernest Gellner. In H. Whitehouse and J. Laidlaw (eds) *Ritual and Memory: Toward a Comparative Anthropology of Religion*. Walnut Creek, CA: Alta Mira.

Shaw, A. (2000). Kinship and Continuity: Pakistani Families in Britain. London: Routledge.

Sherif, J. (2011). A Census chronicle—reflections on the campaign for a religion question in the 2001 Census for England and Wales. *Journal of Beliefs and Values* 32(1): 1–18.

Sherwood, M. (1988). Racism and resistance: Cardiff in the 1930s and 1940s. *Llafur: Journal of the Society for the Study of Welsh Labour History* 5(4): 51–71.

Shirani, F., Henwood, K., and Coltart, C. (2012). Meeting the challenges of intensive parenting culture: gender, risk management and the moral parent. *Sociology* 46(1): 25–40.

Smart, C. (2007). *Personal Life*. Cambridge: Polity.

Smart, C., Neale, B., and Wade, A. (2001). *The Changing Experience of Childhood: Families and Divorce*. Cambridge: Polity.

Smith, C. (2005). *Soul Searching: The Religious and Spiritual Lives of American Teenagers*. Oxford: Oxford University Press.

Smith, D. (1999). *Wales: A Question for History*. Bridgend: Seren.

Song. M. (2003). *Choosing Ethnic Identity*. Cambridge: Polity.

Spalek, B. (2005). A critical reflection on researching Black Muslim women's lives post-September 11th. *International Journal Social Research Methodology* 8(5): 405–18.

Strathern, A. (1996). *Body Thoughts*. Ann Arbour: University of Michigan Press.

Sutton, P. W. and Vertigans, S. (2005). *Resurgent Islam: A Sociological Approach*. Cambridge: Polity.

Tackey, N. D., Casebourne, J., Aston, J., Ritchie, H., Sinclair, A., Tyers, C. Hurstfield, J., Willison, R., and Page, R. (2006). *Barriers to Employment for Pakistanis and Bangladeshis in Britain*. Leeds: Department for Work and Pensions Research Report No. 360.

Thomas, N., and O'Kane, C. (1999). Children's participation in reviews and planning meetings when they are 'looked after' in middle childhood. *Child and Family Social Work* 4(3): 221–30.

Tinker, C. (2006). Islamophobia, social cohesion and autonomy: challenging the arguments against state funded Muslim schools in Britain. *Muslim Education Quarterly* 23(1 and 2): 4–19.

Tinker, C. (2009). Rights, social cohesion and identity: arguments for and against state-funded Muslim schools in Britain, *Race, Ethnicity and Education* 12(4): 539–53.

Tinker, C. and Smart, A. (2012). Constructions of collective Muslim identity by advocates of Muslim schools in Britain. *Ethnic and Racial Studies* 34(4): 643–63.

Tohidi, N. and Bayes, J. H. (2001). Women redefining modernity and religion in the globalized context. In J. H. Bayes and N. Tohidi (eds) *Globalization, Gender and Religion*. New York: Palgrave Macmillan.

Van Gennep, A. ([1909] 1960). *The Rites of Passage*. London: Routledge and Kegan Paul.

Voas, D. (2003). Intermarriage and the demography of secularisation. *British Journal of Sociology* 54(1): 83–108.

Voas, D. and Bruce, S. (2004). The 2001 census and Christian identification in Britain, *Journal of Contemporary Religion* 19(1): 23–8.

Voas, D. and Crockett, A. (2005). Religion in Britain: neither believing nor belonging. *Sociology* 39, 11–28.

Voas, D. and Fleischmann, F. (2012). Islam moves West: religious change in the first and second generations. *Annual Review of Sociology* 38: 525–45.

Waddy, C. (1990). *The Muslim Mind*. London: Grosvenor Books.

Welsh Assembly Government (2008). *Welsh Index of Multiple Deprivation Summary Report*. <http://wales.gov.uk/docs/statistics/2010/100712wimd08summaryen.pdf>

Wenger, E. (1998). *Communities of Practice: Learning, Meaning and Identity*. Cambridge: Cambridge University Press.

Werbner, P. (1990). *The Migration Process*. Oxford: Berg.

Whitehouse, H. (2002). Modes of religiosity: towards a cognitive explanation of the sociopolitical dynamics of religion. *Method and Theory in the Study of Religion* 14: 293–315.

Whitehouse, H. (2004). *Modes of Religiosity: A Cognitive Theory of Religious Transmission*. Walnut Creek, CA: Alta Mira.

Whitty, G. (2001). Education, social class and social exclusion. *Journal of Education Policy* 16(4): 287–95.

Williams, M. (2000). Interpretivism and generalisation. *Sociology* 34(2): 209–24.

Wilson, B. and Smallwood, S. (2008). The proportion of marriages ending in divorce. *Population Trends* 131: 28–36.

Winchester, D. (2008). Embodying the faith: religious practice and the making of a Muslim moral *habitus*. *Social Forces* 86(4): 1753–80.

Woodhead, L. (2010). Epilogue. In S. Collins-Mayo and B. Dandelion (eds) *Religion and Youth*. Aldershot: Ashgate, pp. 239–41.

Woodhead, L. (2011). Five concepts of religion. *International Review of Sociology* 21(1): 121–43.

Woodhead, L. (2012). Tactical and strategic religion. Keynote address at the conference 'Sacred Practices of Everyday Life', University of Edinburgh, May 11th. <http://www.religionandsociety.org.uk/events/programme_events/show/linda_woodead_s_plenary_at_sacred_practices_of_everyday_life>

Yee, W. C. and Andrews, J. (2006). Professional researcher or 'good guest'? Ethical dilemmas involved in researching children and families in the home setting. *Education Review* 58(4): 397–413.

Zebiri, K. (2008). *British Muslim Converts: Choosing Alternative Lives*. Oxford: Oneworld.

Index

Index

Index

Index